THE AGE OF THE WORLD: MOSES TO DARWIN

THE
AGE
OF THE
WORLD

MOSES TO DARWIN

FRANCIS C. HABER

THE JOHNS HOPKINS PRESS
BALTIMORE, 1959

Manufactured in the U.S.A. by the William Byrd Press, Richmond, Va.

Distributed in Great Britain by Oxford University Press, London

Library of Congress Catalog Card Number 59-14893

This book has been brought to publication with the assistance of a grant from The Ford Foundation

TO

MY WIFE RUTH

AND

SON ROBERT

PREFACE

This work is intended as a study in the history of ideas, and, although a specific theme is pursued, I hope that its total effect will be to shed some light on "historicism," which has been described by Friedrich Meinecke, in his classic *Die Entstehung des Historismus* (1936), as "the greatest spiritual revolution Western thought has undergone." Although Meinecke's claim has been contested, and the validity of the underlying assumptions of historicism seriously questioned, much of our thinking is still shaped within the framework of historicism.

The meaning of the term "historicism" varies slightly in the hands of different writers, but in the main it represents a view of history wherein it is held that individual events are unique, time is irreversible, and the whole is permeated with a process of change and development. In a recent anthology touching on this subject, Hans Meyerhoff, as editor, remarks: "Process and individuality, change, the transiency of time and the concreteness of historical facts have remained the cornerstones of historicism." (*The Philosophy of History in Our Time* [Doubleday Anchor Books, 1959], p. 11.) Again, in criticizing it, Geoffrey Barraclough has said of historicism: "It substituted the concepts of development and individuality for belief in the stability of human nature and in reason." (*Ibid.*, p. 29.)

As history grew into a specialized discipline in the last century, its subject matter was narrowed to human history alone. The historical aspects in the natural sciences, such as the history of an organism or the history of the physical earth, are now no longer

vii

considered proper to history, and R. G. Collingwood, in his *The Idea of History* (1946), has made a convincing justification for the separation of human history and the history in natural science. In the process, however, historians have appropriated historicism as a phenomenon peculiar to human history or historiography, but historically, historicism was an outlook on the totality of nature, the whole of creation. It was symptomatic of a major shift in cosmology which graduated as easily into theories of evolution in science as into theories of development in civilization. Around 1800, for instance, historicism was making its way with as much vigor in geology and paleontology as it was in human history, and how could it be otherwise when human history and cosmogony had been so thoroughly welded together in theology through the account of creation in Genesis? If historicism is seen in a broad way as the shift to a view about the nature of things in which a time process is leading to continuous change and development, the claim made for it by Meinecke may be less of an exaggeration than is supposed by those who have applied it to interpretations of human history alone.

Although I hope that this study will shed light on historicism, I have confined myself to the task of sketching only one theme in it, which has, I believe, enough autonomy for an independent treatment. Many closely related materials and subjects have, as a result, had to be silently passed over.

No bibliography has been included, because the general background against which this study has been set covers so much ground that it would be pretentious on my part to offer one. The subject itself, on the other hand, has been largely neglected in the history of ideas. Charles Coulston Gillispie was cognizant of it in his excellent work, *Genesis and Geology* (Cambridge: Harvard University Press, 1951), and after reading my doctoral dissertation, and making a number of helpful suggestions for revision for which I extend my thanks, he kindly called my attention to a penetrating excursion into the subject by Heinrich Meyer, *The*

Age of the World, a chapter in the history of the Enlightenment (multigraphed at Muhlenberg College, Allentown, Pa., 1951). Since my text was written, another work has been published which covers some of the same areas as this study and recognizes the importance of "The Time Voyagers," *Darwin's Century, Evolution and the Men who Discovered it* (Garden City: Doubleday, 1958), by Loren Eiseley.

The present study is an extension of my doctoral dissertation, *Revolution in the Concept of Historical Time: a study in the relationship between Biblical chronology and the rise of modern science* (Baltimore: The Johns Hopkins University, 1957). Through the generosity of the American Philosophical Society, I was given a grant from the Penrose Fund in the summer of 1958 for further research and revision.

My obligations are extensive, but I would like to single out Professors Sidney Painter and Bentley Glass for sponsoring this study as a doctoral dissertation and for their many kindnesses during its progress and subsequently. I also wish to thank Professors Richard H. Shryock, Frederic C. Lane, Ludwig Edelstein, William Foxwell Albright, Don Cameron Allen, Owsei Temkin, James H. Oliver, Charles A. Barker, and C. Vann Woodward, all of Johns Hopkins; Professor Robert P. Sharkey of South Carolina, and Professor Clifton K. Yearley, Jr., my colleague at the University of Florida, for reading the manuscript either in whole or in part during its various stages of development and for other help and encouragement.

The staffs of many libraries have assisted me, especially those of The Johns Hopkins University, the Peabody Institute Library of Baltimore, Yale University, and the Library of Congress. I owe special thanks to Lloyd A. Brown, former librarian of the Peabody Institute Library, for his interest and kindly offices, and to the present librarian, Frank Jones, for continuing to give me sanctuary in the magnificent collections of the Peabody.

I wish to extend my appreciation to The Johns Hopkins Press

for allowing me to use in the present work portions of my two chapters in *Forerunners of Darwin, 1745-1859*, edited by Bentley Glass, Owsei Temkin, and William L. Straus, Jr., which they published in the spring of 1959. To the Graduate School of the University of Florida, I am also deeply indebted for a splendid typing of the final manuscript.

Gainesville, Florida   *Francis C. Haber*
July 15, 1959

CONTENTS

I
INTRODUCTION

THE TIME REVOLUTION

A controversy, long in the making, flared up in the early nineteenth century between theology and science over the age of the world. A vast scale of time was needed in historical branches of science, but in front of them "stood the thorny barrier with its comminatory notice-board—'No Thoroughfare. By order. Moses.' "[1]

The ostensible issue at stake was the Biblical date of creation, not an exact date such as the 3700 B.C. of Rabbinical chronology based on the Hebrew text, or the 5199 B.C. of the Roman Catholic Church based on the Clementine edition of the Vulgate, or the 4004 B.C. of Archbishop Ussher in the margins of the King James Authorized Version, but the approximate date of about six thousand years which was supported in common by all the versions. The actual date of creation had itself been a subject of controversy since the Patristic period, and although particular dates had been favored and taught as the gospel truth, none of the major religious groups were willing to set up one particular date of creation as infallibly true. However, there was consensus amongst those who accepted the doctrine of the plenary inspiration of

[1] Thomas Henry Huxley, *Science and Christian Tradition* (New York, 1896), p. viii.

I

Scripture that all the data needed for chronology in prehistory was contained in Genesis. Against this closed system of Mosaic history and chronology in orthodox Christian thought many trends and forces were coming to bear by the early nineteenth century, but none proved more dynamic and irresistible than those in astronomy where the solar system was being measured in millions of years, and in geology where evidence was accumulating that the antiquity of the earth, too, was in the scale of millions instead of thousands of years. As these developments caught the attention of the public, there was a tremendous outcry of heresy from the orthodox. Periodic compromises made between orthodoxy and geology prevented an open warfare, but the controversy burned like a ragged brushfire for several decades. In recalling it, Asa Gray (1810-1888) wrote in 1880:

> Among the questions which disquieted pious souls in my younger days, but which have ceased to disquiet any of us, are those respecting the age and gradual development of the earth and of the solar system, which came in with geology and modern astronomy. I remember the time when it was a mooted question whether geology and orthodox Christianity were compatible. . . .[2]

That many of the orthodox were willing to stake Christianity itself on the truth of the Biblical age of the world suggests, however, that they felt that the question involved more than merely the date of creation. There was in fact a whole world outlook at stake.

In the Christian view then dominant, sacred history was supposed to embrace a plan of salvation and a record of the steps along the road to redemption. Nature was regarded as only a setting for this movement towards grace. According to Genesis, nature had been brought into existence in completed form. The earth, plant and animal species, and man were created instantly,

[2] Asa Gray, *Natural Science and Religion, Two Lectures Delivered to the Theological School of Yale College* (New York, 1880), p. 6.

though successively, by divine fiat, and subsequent major changes in nature, such as the disruption of the earth by the Flood of Noah, were wrought by the same supernatural agency. All this seemed credible when it was believed that the world had been in existence only six thousand years and would probably expire in but a few thousand more. Such a view had survived from the Patristic period and was strengthened by the Reformation as the religionists tried to restore the cosmogony of Genesis to the place which the system of Aristotle had taken in the medieval Cosmos.[8]

While the scientific revolution dealt severely with the medieval-Aristotelian Cosmos, in many respects it was only a half-way revolution which left sacred history intact. When viewed from the perspective of concepts of space and time, it was a spatial revolution, and the attack on Aristotle had no importance for sacred history. The endless cycles of Aristotle's cosmos were consistently opposed by the Church, even though the rest of his system was embroidered into Christian cosmology. There were attempts during the scientific revolution to eternalize the world, but on the whole the "new mechanical philosophy" was confined to a spatial reconstruction of the universe, both in the arrangement of its parts and in the nature of its composition.

There are many equally valid perspectives by which the scientific revolution of the sixteenth and seventeenth centuries may be viewed. Professor Alexandre Koyré, in his *From the Closed World to the Infinite Universe*, mentions a number of them, but he expresses his own conviction that the main line of development was the destruction of the medieval-Aristotelian Cosmos and the infinitization of the universe:

> This scientific and philosophical revolution—it is indeed impossible to separate the philosophical from the purely scientific aspects of this process: they are interdependent and closely

[8] See J. K. S. Reid, *The Authority of Scripture, A Study of the Reformation and Post-Reformation Understanding of the Bible* (New York: Harper & Bros. [1957]) for a recent discussion of this subject.

linked together—can be described roughly as bringing forth the destruction of the Cosmos, that is, the disappearance, from philosophically and scientifically valid concepts, of the conception of the world as a finite, closed, and hierarchically ordered whole (a whole in which the hierarchy of value determined the hierarchy and structure of being, rising from the dark, heavy and imperfect earth to the higher and higher perfection of the stars and heavenly spheres), and its replacement by an indefinite and even infinite universe which is bound together by the identity of its fundamental components and laws, and in which all these components are placed on the same level of being.[4]

While what Professor Koyré describes is very much more than a spatial revolution, that is certainly one aspect of it. The earth was displaced from the center of the universe. Its surrounding crystalline spheres, in which the planets were rotated by angelic beings, were dissolved. The finite, outer sphere of fixed stars was opened up, and the successive spatial links between man the microcosm and the macrocosm were ruptured. The distinction between sublunar matter and celestial substance was eliminated. Matter was stripped of all qualities except those of a spatial nature: form, extension, and impenetrability. Inert, space-occupying corpuscles, at rest or in motion, constituted the physical universe. A measurable, quantitative universe displaced the medieval qualitative Cosmos.

The basic tools in the reconstruction of the universe were mathematics, geometry, and instruments of measurement, and the new model bore the marks of its tools. The universe was geometricized—geometrical magnitudes occupy space—and became a three-dimensional machine comprised of a concatenation of parts moving in harmony as a functioning whole. Like a completed machine, it could be viewed by the Master Craftsman "all at once." The lapse of time marked, but did not alter, the movement of its parts.

[4] Alexandre Koyré, *From the Closed World to the Infinite Universe* (Baltimore: The Johns Hopkins Press, 1957), p. 2.

Time was not absent in the philosophy of the scientific revolution. The machine most admired was the clock, and the world-machine was usually portrayed as a huge clock. Indeed, without accurate time-keeping the measurement of motion could not have been carried out with sufficient precision for the formulation of natural laws, either for accelerating bodies or for the movement of the planets. Galileo's mathematical analysis of motion opened a new consideration of the nature of time as well as of space, but space was the first to be explored philosophically. Professor E. A. Burtt has observed:

> Descartes, bold metaphysician that he was, had an answer ready as regards space—he seized upon it as the very substance of the material universe, crowding into the immaterial world of thought whatever could not be fully treated geometrically. . . . It took somewhat longer, however, for a philosophy of time to develop. . . . When men gradually attempted, however, to make more precise the notions and interrelations of force, acceleration, momentum, velocity, etc., it was natural that they found themselves compelled to an exact statement of what they meant by time. As they grew more confident on this point, time came gradually to seem as natural and self-justifying a continuum as space, quite as independent of human perception and knowledge, and to be metaphysically disposed of on the same principles.[5]

The work of Newton established the idea that space had an absolute existence, independent of matter and motion, and filled the universe. The same attributes were given to time by transferring the idea of a geometrical, spatial continuum to it. Both Newton's absolute time and absolute space appear to have been propounded, not without some metaphysical contradictions, to account for the omnipresence of the Creator in His creation.[6] These metaphysical concepts were more successful in glossing over

[5] Edwin Arthur Burtt, *The Metaphysical Foundations of Modern Physical Science*, 2nd ed. (Garden City, N. Y.: Doubleday & Co., 1954). pp. 160-1.

[6] See *ibid.*, p. 259.

difficulties than in explaining them. Newton's conception of time did not challenge the traditional Christian view of time, and Newton himself passed many of his later years working on Biblical chronology.[7]

One of the most striking effects on theology from the destruction of the medieval-Aristotelian Cosmos was the displacement of man from the center of the spatial universe. If there was a "plurality of worlds," possibly inhabited by other creatures, it became less credible that man had been the center of creation and that the existence of other solar systems depended upon the salvation of the creatures on one tiny planet in the universe. It was a shock to anthropocentric Christian teleology, but refuge was found in the belief that man was the center of the temporal universe. The medieval-Christian time scale remained intact as long as Mosaic history, literally interpreted, went unbreached. Seventeenth-century science was concerned with the operation of the world as it is, not as it was, and it was only when the scientific movement entered a new phase that the medieval temporal universe came under serious attack.

A fruitful line of scientific exploration reached its apex in the magnificent work of Newton, and the brilliant confirmatory work of his eighteenth-century successors was largely anticlimactic. There was a widespread feeling in the middle of the eighteenth century that the Newtonian phase of science was drawing to its completion. Diderot, for instance, wrote:

> I dare almost assert that in less than a century we shall not have three great geometers left in Europe. This science will very soon come to a standstill where Bernoullis, Eulers, Maupertuis, Clairauts, Fontaines, d'Alemberts, and LaGranges will have left it. They will have erected the columns of Hercules. We shall not go beyond that point.[8]

[7] Isaac Newton, *The Chronology of Ancient Kingdoms Amended* (London, 1728).
[8] Denis Diderot, *On the Interpretation of Nature* (1754), quoted in

Diderot was wrong, of course, in his prediction of a standstill. He was right, however, when on the basis of the above conclusions, he advocated a new approach to the study of nature for fresh scientific advances. This new approach, had already been set in motion through the work of Leibniz, Maupertuis, Buffon, and others, in natural history. Considerable pioneering progress had been made in natural history in the early scientific revolution, but during the eighteenth century it was rapidly expanded. There was a shift of interest from dead matter to living matter, from the mathematical analysis of nature to descriptive and comparative methods, and from mechanical patterns of movement to genetic ones. At the same time, there was a widespread growth in the secularization of life and an accelerating interest in the historical aspects of life and civilization. A sense of historical time and process began to contest the view of nature as a timeless machine, while the age experienced an increased sense of progress in civilization which was incompatible with the religious view of a great conflagration looming around the corner to separate the righteous from the sinners. Some *philosophes* who were emancipated from the authority of revelation speculated freely about the lapse of time in an embryo-like universe which contained within itself the principles of growth.

By the end of the eighteenth century, literary criticism, historical studies, philosophy, and rationalism were conspiring with scientific speculation about biological and geological development and theories of cosmic evolution to change the intellectual climate towards a feeling for development in history, but in the conservative reaction following the French Revolution the orthodox view was strongly reasserted in Western thought, and with it the most literal acceptation of the Mosaic history of creation. Geology, however, growing at too rapid a pace to be held back

---

Ernst Cassirer, *The Philosophy of the Enlightenment*, tr. F. C. A. Koelln and J. P. Pettegrove (Beacon Paperback edition, 1955), p. 74.

by the no-thoroughfare sign of Moses, brought the issue into the open. The orthodox rightly suspected that if geological ages were admitted, the literal interpretation of Genesis and all the doctrine based upon it would be endangered. Many questions besides chronology would be raised. If Moses were proved to be wrong on cosmogony and history, would he be reliable on anything? What of the doctrine that man had been created in God's image? If the earth and its productions had been existing for millions of years, were they then created for man? And what of the providential course of salvationist history from the fall to redemption in a time scale of untold ages? Mosaic history and cosmogony had kept man in the center of all creation as surely in the years following the scientific revolution as had the Aristotelian Cosmos prior to it. This outlook was the stake which the orthodox were defending, and they were afraid to venture away from the safety of the literal text and its primitive cosmology. Their fears proved as ungrounded as far as Christianity was concerned as those of the Anti-Copernicans, but this they did not know.

The battle over the scale of time commenced the empirical work of displacing that temporal part of the medieval Cosmos which had been virtually unscathed by the scientific revolution of the seventeenth century, and it opened the new phase of the scientific movement concerned with concepts of time, an important prelude to the theory of evolution put forward by Darwin and to the struggle which ensued.

However, the great revolution in concepts of time was undoubtedly in the twentieth century. Sweeping through early twentieth-century thought like a tidal wave, time saturated physics, cosmology, philosophy, psychology, literature, and art, to such an extent that the world outlook of Western man was thoroughly transformed to include a fourth dimension. A new specialized vocabulary arose to express the various objective and subjective aspects in which the time relationship was extended: relativity, space-time, mathematical time, cosmic time, mental time, duration (*durée*), stream of consciousness, the river of time, time-process, and time sense, to mention only a few. Gertrude Stein has exemplified the time revolution in all its complexity:

> There must be *time*. . . . This is the thing that is at present the most troubling and if there is the time that is at present the most troublesome the time-sense that is at present the most troubling is the thing that makes the present the most troubling.[9]

A stormy critic of the time revolution, Wyndham Lewis, wrote in his *Time and Western Man* (1927) that he was going to undertake "a comprehensive study of the 'time'-notions which have now, in one form or another, gained an undisputed ascendancy in the intellectual world." He was bent on defeating what he termed the "time-cult" and the "Time-mind," whose main characteristic "has been a hostility to what it calls the 'spatializing' process of a mind *not* a Time-mind. It is this 'spatializing' capacity and instinct that it everywhere assails. In its place it would put the Time-view, the flux. It asks us to see everything *sub specie temporis*."[10] Beneath his witty, flamboyant attacks on the time philosophy there is much good sense and keen insight. In spite of Lewis's exaggeration, he saw that his age had proceeded far in the direction of temporalizing the world—as far, indeed, as the seventeenth century had gone in spatializing it. Continued progress in all aspects of science led up to the time revolution in the twentieth century, but the organic and genetic views of evolution certainly played a vital part in establishing the fourth dimension in our cosmology. I have no intention of tracing either the history of the time revolution or evolution in the late nineteenth century, I merely point out the space and time poles, two phases in the growth of modern science, to orientate the controversy over the age of the world. Again let me fall back on Wyndham Lewis's attack on the time philosophy:

[9] Quoted in Wyndham Lewis, *Time and Western Man,* 1st ed., 1927 (Beacon Paperback edition, 1957), p. 57.
[10] *Ibid.,* p. xv.

Everywhere the *snobbery of scale* is employed to drive home
these doctrines. All recorded human history is *merely a ripple*
on the immense ocean of being, etc., we are assured. And feeling very, very small indeed, after that, in the ensuing discour-
agement almost *any* "truth" can be put across. This browbeat-
ing by means of *scale*, the immensity of light-years, of
geological epochs, of massed constellations and universes—that
associated with ecstatic cosmic raptures—all the sickly flattery
of the *élan vital* type of optimism—is how, on the emotional,
propagandist side, the thing is done.[11]

Such a grandiose scale of time is a relatively recent outlook,
and merely one hundred years before Wyndham Lewis wrote
the above lines in 1927, an inverse *snobbery of scale* was being
employed to browbeat those who wanted to unveil the immense
ocean of being. That snobbery was provided by the Judaeo-
Christian conception of history. When the six-thousand-year
scale of time was broken, there was room for a time process in
nature to be realized—a time process which could help explain
the deposition of fossil remains by natural means, the evolution
of species, the evolution of man, the development of languages
long before the Biblical date of creation, archaeological remains
of cultures at the height of their civilization when the world was
supposed to be uncreated, the primitive remains of prehistoric
man, the passage of light which had left its source ages before
light was supposed to have been created, and the evolution of the
universe itself several billions of years ago. The Biblical time
barrier did little to promote the sciences, but it did much to in-
vert and obscure the rudimentary principles of the historical
branches of science. In a larger view, however, Christianity may
have been the seed-bed out of which sprouted modern notions
of time.

[11] *Ibid.*, p. 177.

ETERNALISM AND PATRISTIC TIME

The significance of opening up the Biblical time scale during the controversy over the age of the world did not rest merely in the enlargement of the scale, for the doctrine of eternalism immediately carried it to the maximum, and eternalism had been known and resisted by Christians from the time of the early church. It was the enlargement of a particular kind of time concept which was important—a potential created by Christianity itself, namely, the idea of a universal history moving along a unique, linear time course in which there was directional progress. For Christians that progress was the progress of salvation, but, as S. G. F. Brandon has pointed out, the concept was susceptible of being secularized, and, after Darwin, of being given scientific justification in the modern doctrine of progress.[12] It was a concept of time which involved historical process rather than that time in endless repetition which seems to have been the norm of pre-Christian thought.

In his study of archaic attitudes towards time, *The Myth of the Eternal Return*, Mircea Eliade has concluded that interest in the "irreversible" and the "new" in history is a recent discovery in the life of man, and that archaic humanity defended itself to the utmost against all the novelty and irreversibility which history entails.[13] Archaic societies revolt against concrete, historical time, and try to return periodically to a lost paradise of mythical time at the beginning of things, to the "Great Time." They find meaning in archetypes which they relive through symbols, myths, rituals, and ceremonies. Profane history is chaos, from which they

[12] S. G. F. Brandon, *Time and Mankind, An Historical and Philosophical Study of Mankind's Attitude to the Phenomena of Change* (London: Hutchinson, [1951]), p. 179ff.

[13] Mircea Eliade, *The Myth of the Eternal Return*, 1st ed., Paris, 1949, tr. Willard R. Trask (New York: Pantheon Books, Bollingen Series XLVI, 1954), p. ix. This work contains an excellent bibliography on ideas of time and history from the cultural and philosophical point of reference.

try to escape by a reactualization of the mythical moment of pure creation, as in New Year rites. They seek a regeneration, a cyclical recurrence or eternal return, of creation upon all planes—cosmic, biological, historical, human.

> Everything begins over again at its commencement every instant. The past is but a prefiguration of the future. No event is irreversible and no transformation is final. In a certain sense, it is even possible to say that nothing new happens in the world, for everything is but the repetition of the same primordial archetypes; this repetition, by actualizing the mythical moment when the archetypal gesture was revealed, constantly maintains the world in the same auroral instant of the beginnings. Time but makes possible the appearance and existence of things. It has no final influence upon their existence, since it is itself constantly regenerated.[14]

Although there is an element of symbolic regeneration in Christianity, it is not the determining characteristic of the Christian view of time. It did dominate the Greco-Oriental world in which the early Christians lived, and one of the revolutionary aspects of primitive Christianity appears to have been its breaking away from the non-historical myth of eternal return. The Greeks, of course, had passed beyond the merely mythical aspects in their concept of eternal regeneration to a highly intellectualized philosophical interpretation of reality and natural process through archetypes. Yet the same attitude towards the cyclical nature of time remained. The Greek view has been admirably summarized by Henri-Charles Peuch:

> For the Greeks, indeed, the passage of time is cyclical and not rectilinear. Dominated by an ideal in intelligibility which finds authentic and full being only in that which is in itself and remains identical with itself, in the eternal and immutable, the Greeks regarded movement and change as inferior degrees of reality, in which, at best, identity can be apprehended in the form of permanence and perpetuity, hence of recurrence. The

[14] *Ibid.*, pp. 89-90.

circular movement which assures the survival of the same
things by repeating them, by bringing about their continuous
return, is the perfect and most immediate expression (hence
that which is closest to the divine) of the absolute immobility
at the summit of the hierarchy. According to the famous Platonic definition, the time which is determined and measured
by the revolution of the celestial spheres is the mobile image
of immobile eternity which it imitates by moving in a circle.
Consequently both the entire cosmic process and the time of
our world of generation and decay develop in a circle or according to an indefinite succession of cycles, in the course of
which the same reality is made, unmade, and remade, in con-
formity with an immutable law and determinate alternations.
The same sum of being is preserved; nothing is created and
nothing lost . . . ; moreover, certain thinkers of dying antiquity
—Pythagoreans, Stoics, Platonists—went so far as to maintain
that within each of these cycles of time, of these *aiones*, these
aeva, the same situations recur that have already occurred in
the preceding cycles and will occur in subsequent cycles—and
so *ad infinitum*. No event is unique, nothing is enacted but once
(for example the condemnation of Socrates); every event has
been enacted, is enacted, and will be enacted perpetually; the
same individuals have appeared, appear, and will appear at
every turn of the circle. Cosmic time is repetition and *anaku-
klosis*, eternal return.[15]

In some of the early systems, the cosmic cycle was elaborated
in various combinations of years. The Indian complete cycle, or
Mahayuga, lasted 12,000 years in a sequence of creation-destruc-
tion-creation. Each of the years in the Mahayuga was a divine
year, lasting 360 of our regular years, so that a single cosmic cycle
spanned 4,320,000 years. A thousand of these cycles constituted
a Kalpa; one Kalpa was a day in the life of Brahma, another
Kalpa, a night in his life, and a hundred, the span of his life. The
Buddhists had a similar cosmic cycle. Other systems of cosmic

[15] Henri-Charles Peuch, "Gnosis and Time," [1951] in *Man and Time*,
Papers from the Eranos Yearbooks (New York: Pantheon Books, Bollingen
Series XXX, 3, 1957), pp. 40-1. Also quoted in part in Eliade, *op. cit.*, p. 89,
n. 59.

cycles appeared amongst the Chaldean, Babylonian, and Iranian peoples in the pre-Christian period.[16] A system that became popular in Greece and Rome was the Great Year, which included a Great Winter when the cosmos underwent inundation and a Great Summer when it dried up and finally passed through a fiery conflagration. Although there were expressions of the Great Year by the Greeks at an earlier period, Berossus, the Babylonian, was apparently responsible for popularizing it amongst the Greeks and Romans. His special influence may have been in associating the Great Year with the astronomical phenomenon of precession in Hellenic thought. Plato referred to a "Complete Year" when all the eight orbits of the heavenly bodies finished their revolutions together, and the "Platonic Year," also called the *magnus annus*, passed into medieval thought as a period of 36,000 years.[17] Hipparchus, in the second century before Christ, had determined the rate of precession with considerable accuracy,[18] close to the present estimate of about 26,000 years, and astronomy undoubtedly confirmed belief in the Platonic Year.

The Christian view of worldly time rejected the circle dominated by astral fatality for the straight line, finite at its two extremities. The events between the Creation and the Last Judgment were unique and would never be repeated. The direction of this finite time course was irreversible and had intrinsic meaning which took cognizance of the "new" in history. If this contrast between the classical and Christian view of time is valid, the first decisive step in the twentieth-century time revolution was taken by pious Christians almost two thousand years earlier.

The first Christians apparently had little interest in history, because they thought that the Parousia was imminent, possibly in their own lifetime. But, as this hope faded, they became conscious

[16] See Eliade, *op. cit.*

[17] Thomas Heath, *Aristarchus of Samos, the Ancient Copernicus* (Oxford; Clarendon Press, 1913), pp. 171-2, suggests how this concept was worked out.

[18] *Ibid.*, p. 101.

of the fact that the Church could lay claim to the whole corpus of Hebrew history, that they were the spiritual heirs to the most venerable of traditions, and that they could claim the Church was no novel phenomenon thrown up from the religious under-world.[19] The apologists, many of them trained in Greek philoso-phy, were concerned with making Christianity intellectually re-spectable to their prospective converts, and one of the serious charges made against the Christians was their novelty. Their cult was regarded as a current fad. Almost all of the early Church Fathers attempted to meet this charge, and most of them fell back on the history of the Old Testament to prove that Christianity was the oldest of religions. At the same time, they amplified the Christian view of linear and unique time, also of supreme impor-tance in the Christian position that the Incarnation was a unique event—Christ died but once for our sins, once and for all (I Peter 3: 18).

Peuch has listed three essentials in the development within Christianity of the idea of an organic, oriented time and a the-ology of history: (1) the adoption of Mosaic history, (2) escha-tology, and (3) the idea that progressive realization of universal redemption is to be effected with the aid of education—history becomes *Heilsgeschichte*, and not only for mankind as a whole, but for each unique individual; that is, there is a kind of cumula-tive progress. Of the first, Peuch has written:

First of all, Christianity, a new religion and in the eyes of the pagans a *superstitio nova*, had to provide itself with a past and furnish proofs of its authenticity. This it could do only by attaching itself to Judaism, by situating itself—as a true Israel—at the end of the long preceding development of Jewish his-tory. By adopting this history it was able to claim a lineage going back to the very origin of the world as recorded in Genesis. The advantage was twofold: Christianity was thus en-abled to represent itself as the oldest, most pristine of religions, having its sources and seeds in an age far predating the most

[19] See Brandon, *op. cit.*, p. 181.

ancient events narrated in the profane annals of the classical, Babylonian, or Egyptian civilizations. And indeed, taking as its basis the Bible and a comparative chronology, Christian historiography, born of apologetic requirements, was soon employed in demonstrating the legitimacy of such a pretension. Moreover, the sacred literature of Israel provided the Christian apologists with the testimony they required in order to prove that the coming of Jesus had been foreshadowed, foreseen, and prophesied in the past. Thus although the early Christians were sorely tempted for a time to break with Judaism and affirm the entire novelty, the absolute originality, of the Gospel, the Church finally annexed the Hebrew books to its corpus of canonical scriptures, set the New Testament after the Old, and established a line between its own history and that of ancient Israel which prepared the way for Christianity and prefigured it. In this way it succeeded in creating an organic, continuous bond between the present and the past.[20]

The appeal to Old Testament history to establish the greater antiquity of Christianity over the heathens was well under way with Justin Martyr (110-165), who maintained that Plato was obligated to Moses for his conception of God. Heathen mythology, he claimed, was a set of lies perpetuated by evil men who knew from the prophets that they were doomed, but who hoped to deceive the people as to their coming fate. Egyptian and Greek history came after the time of Moses, Justin said, and Plato as much as confessed it in the *Timaeus* when he related the incident of the Egyptian priest telling Solon that the Greeks were but children.[21] Tatian the Assyrian (110-172) carried the claims for Moses even further and stated that Berossus, the Babylonian priest-historian, had known of the events announced by the prophets and the only reliable part of his history of the Chaldeans was based upon it.[22]

As the defense was intensified, it led to historical research, and

[20] Peuch, *op. cit.*, pp. 50-1.

[21] *Justin's Hortatory Address to the Greeks* in *The Ante-Nicene Fathers*, (New York, 1893-6), I, 272ff.

[22] *Address of Tatian to the Greeks* in *ibid.*, II, 65ff.

Theophilus of Antioch (115-181) probably deserves credit for being the founder of scholarship traditions in Christian chronology. Like the other apologists he attacked the claims of heathen history and turned to the investigation of Biblical chronology, not "to furnish mere matter of much talk, but to throw light upon the number of years from the foundation of the world, and to condemn the empty labour and trifling of these authors [heathens], because there have neither been 20,000 times 10,000 years from the flood to the present time, as Plato said, affirming that there had been so many years; nor yet 15 times 10,375 years, as we have already mentioned Apollonius the Egyptian gave out; nor is the world uncreated, nor is there a spontaneous production of all things, as Pythagoras and the rest dreamed. . . ."[23]

To establish the Christian view of time, Theophilus apparently pored over many extant profane histories and source materials. He proceeded to work out the chronology of the world's history in terms of actual elapsed years. The creation of the world had taken place 5,698 years ago (5529 B.C.), he concluded, but he did not pretend to have ascertained the exact date. As he threw back his results at the heathens, he remarked, "I think I have now, according to my ability, accurately discoursed both of the godlessness of your practises, and of the whole number of the epochs of history. For if even a chronological error has been committed by us, of, e.g., 50 or 100, or even 200 years, yet [it is] not of thousands and tens of thousands, as Plato and Apollonius and other mendacious authors have hitherto written."

Apologetic requirements began to push the Fathers into history to confirm their view of history, and the program outlined by Tertullian (145-220) leaves little to be desired in comparative method:

> The other prophets also [in addition to Moses], though of later date, are, even the most recent of them, as far back as the first of your philosophers, and legislators, and historians. It is

[23] *Theophilus to Autolycus*, Book II, Ch. 26, in *ibid.*, II, 119.

not so much the difficulty of the subject, as its vastness, that
stands in the way of a statement of the grounds on which these
statements rest; the matter is not so arduous as it would be tedious. It would require the anxious study of many books, and
the fingers' busy reckoning. The histories of the most ancient
nations, such as the Egyptians, the Chaldeans, the Phoenicians,
would need to be ransacked; the men of these various nations
who have information to give, would have to be called in as
witnesses. Manetho the Egyptian, and Berosus the Chaldean,
and Hieromus the Phoenician king of Tyre; their successors
too, Ptolemy the Mendesian, and Demetrius Phalereus, and
King Juba, and Apion, and Thallus, and their critic the Jew
Josephus, the native vindicator of the ancient history of his
people, who either authenticates or refutes the others. Also the
Greek censors' lists must be compared, and the dates of events
ascertained, that the chronological connections may be opened
up, and thus the reckonings of the various annals be made to
give forth light. We must go abroad into the histories and literature of all nations. And, in fact, we have already brought the
proof in part before you, in giving those hints as to how it is
to be effected. But it seems better to delay the full discussion of
this, lest in our haste we do not sufficiently carry it out, or lest
in its thorough handling we make too lengthened a digression.[24]

This scientific approach to historical chronology was to a large
degree carried out by Julius Africanus (200-245). He aimed at
producing a universal chronicle which would synchronize all the
leading events in the history of the important nations, and thus
furnish a solid base upon which Christian Apologists could build.
He, too, was motivated by the desire to check the "boastful notions" of the Egyptians about their antiquity, as well as the
"follies of the Chaldeans" with their forty-eight myriads.[25] The
chronology of Africanus was to have a lasting influence in Christianity, especially through Eusebius of Caesarea (260-340) who
utilized it in his *Chronicle* and *Church History*. Lactantius and
Clement of Alexandria also accepted the chronology of Afri-

[24] *Apology*, Ch. 19, in *ibid.*, III, p. 33.
[25] *Five Books of Chronology* [extant fragments], in *ibid.*, VI, 130ff.

canus. Until the end of the Middle Ages the only significant changes which were to be made in Christian historical chronology were modifications of the time of creation as a result of textual variations of the Old Testament[26] and a belief in the coming of a millenium.

The early Christians used the Greek Septuagint, and their claims that in it the messiahship of Jesus was prophesied aroused the Jews to contest the claim and the Septuagint rapidly lost favor among the Jews. The Pentateuch had been transmitted orally in the Temple, but when Jerusalem fell in A.D. 70, and with it the central safeguard for the authenticity of their tradition, they set about purifying the text of their holy writings. Rabbinical scholars undertook extensive research and study and achieved a relatively standardized text in the second century, although the process of correction and notation continued for centuries. The Hebrew text had a shorter chronology than the Septuagint and Christians accused the Jews of falsifying the text to invalidate the claim of Jesus to the messiahship, but the meticulousness of the Jewish scholarship was recognized among some Christians. Jerome was influenced by it in establishing the text of the Vulgate, and Augustine regarded both the Septuagint and Hebrew text as authentic. He attributed their differences to scribal errors in the transmission of the Septuagint and he insisted that there was a concord between all the texts in spirit, though the words might vary slightly.

Eschatology also had an important influence on the Christian time scale. The apocalyptic writers not only accepted Genesis as an account of the beginning of the world, but they also regarded the days of creation as a prophecy of the ages of the world. It was widely believed that as the world was created in six periods,

[26] Recent works on the history of Biblical texts are Bleddyn J. Roberts, *The Old Testament Text and Versions: the Hebrew Text in Transmission and the History of Ancient Versions* (Cardiff: University of Wales Press, 1951), and the more popular, H. G. G. Herklots, *How Our Bible Came To Us, Its Texts And Versions* (New York: Oxford University Press, 1957).

it would last for six periods, or ages. An age was associated with
one thousand years on the basis of statements such as in Psalm 90,
"For a thousand years in thy sight are but as yesterday when it is
past, as a watch in the night," and II Peter 3: 8, "But, beloved,
be not ignorant of this one thing, that one day *is* with the Lord
as a thousand years, and a thousand years as one day." The *Divine
Institutes* of Lactantius illustrates how this belief was tied in with
chronology:

> Plato and many others of the philosophers, since they were
> ignorant of the origin of all things, and of that primal period
> at which the world was made, said that many thousands of ages
> had passed since this beautiful arrangement of the world was
> completed; and in this they perhaps followed the Chaldeans,
> who, as Cicero has related in his first book respecting divina-
> tion, foolishly say that they possess comprised in their me-
> morials four hundred and seventy thousand years; in which
> matter, because they thought that they could not be convicted,
> they believed that they were at liberty to speak falsely. But we,
> whom the Holy Scriptures instruct to the knowledge of the
> truth, know the beginning and the end of the world. . . .
> Therefore let the philosophers, who enumerate thousands of
> ages from the beginning of the world, know that the six thou-
> sandth year is not yet completed, and that when this number
> is completed the consummation must take place, and the con-
> dition of human affairs be remodelled for the better, the proof
> of which must first be related, that the matter itself may be
> plain. God completed the world and this admirable work of
> nature in the space of six days, as is contained in the secrets of
> Holy Scripture, and consecrated the seventh day, on which He
> had rested from His works. . . .
> Therefore, since all the works of God were completed in six
> days, the world must continue in its present state through six
> ages, that is, six thousand years. For the great day of God is
> limited by a circle of a thousand years, as the prophet shows,
> who says, "In Thy sight, O Lord, a thousand years are as one
> day."[27]

[27] *Divine Institutes,* Book vii, Ch. 14, in *Ante-Nicene Fathers,* vii, p. 211.

Many of the Church Fathers believed in the Millenium, or, as it was also called, the Great Sabbatism: St. Barnabas, St. Irenaeus, St. Cyprian, St. Jerome, St. Augustine, and St. Hilary, among others. In its extreme form this chiliasm was closely tied to the non-historical concepts of periodic regeneration. The destruction of the world by a conflagration, in which the good would escape unharmed, was an essential part of eschatological optimism, as Eliade has pointed out:

> Strange as it may seem, the myth was consoling. In fact, fire renews the world; through it will come the restoration of "a new world, free from old age, death, decomposition and corruption, living eternally, increasing eternally, when the dead shall rise, when immortality shall come to the living, when the world shall be perfectly renewed" (Yašt, XIX, 14, 89). This, then, is an *apokatastasis* from which the good have nothing to fear. The final catastrophe will put an end to history, hence will restore man to eternity and beatitude.[28]

Although there were variant time periods associated with this archaic concept of periodic regeneration, the Hebrew tradition limited the duration of the world to seven millenia, and this was largely adhered to in Christian chiliastic thought. The first five millenia of Biblical chronology marked the time already elapsed. A sixth age would mark the return of the Messiah, and in a seventh, the godly would be restored to eternal life. This chiliasm of the Christians, also present in Judaic and Iranian philosophy, differed from the current Greek, Roman, and Oriental systems of periodic regeneration in that the duration of the cosmos was limited to a specific number of millenia, after which history would cease. However, as Eliade observed, "there still survive certain traces of the ancient doctrine of the periodic regeneration of history. In other words, history can be abolished, and consequently renewed, a number of times, before the final *eschaton* is realized. Indeed, the Christian liturgical year is based upon a

[28] Eliade, *op. cit.*, p. 124.

periodic and real repetition of the Nativity, Passion, death, and
Resurrection of Jesus, with all that this mystical drama implies
for a Christian; that is, personal and cosmic regeneration through
reactualization *in concreto* of the birth, death, and resurrection of
the Saviour."[29]

Chiliastic thought strongly reinforced the belief in a time span
of a few thousand years, while Biblical chronology in turn endowed the millenia with concrete reality and significance. There
was a blending of abstract eschatology and historical actuality in
the minds of the early Christians which remained in the Western
tradition. Christ was a central fact in the eschatological history,
and his birth came to be a central date in the organization of all
history.[30] The work of arranging profane history in exact chronological equivalence with sacred history carried Christians even
further into historical scholarship. In addition, the apologists took
great pains to discredit heathen history step by step to show its
degeneracy. This path was not unmarked by criticism. St. Jerome
defended himself for using heathen authors in his writings, and
after listing a number of the leading Christian writers who had
also done this, he wrote, "All these writers so frequently inter-
weave in their books the doctrines and maxims of the philosophers that you might easily be at a loss which to admire most,
their secular erudition or their knowledge of the scriptures."[31]
This historical approach provided a germinal idea about the
nature of history, a familiar precedent for subsequent generations,

[29] *Ibid.*, p. 130. See also G. Van der Leeuw, "Primordial Time and Final
Time" [1949], in *Man and Time, op. cit.*, pp. 324-50; Karl Löwith, *Mean-
ing in History* (Chicago: University of Chicago Press, 1949); and Roland
H. Bainton, "Patristic Christianity," and Erich Dinkler, "Earliest Christi-
anity," in *The Idea of History in the Ancient Near East*, ed. Robert C.
Dentan (New Haven: Yale University Press, 1955).

[30] See Gilles Quispel, "Time and History in Patristic Christianity," [1951],
in *Man and Time, op. cit.*, pp. 85-107.

[31] *Letter to Magnus and Orator of Rome*, in Philip Schaff, ed., *Select
Library of Nicene and Post-Nicene Fathers* (Buffalo & New York, 1886-90),
VI, 151.

and a sense of continuity and progression, or development in history, which was of great significance in the scholarly tradition of the West. The appeal to history enhanced the position of Biblical history, the more so since it was based on the best historical evidence known at the time. Professor Albright has said of the Old Testament history which covers the historical period:

> There can be no doubt that archaeology has confirmed the substantial historicity of Old Testament tradition. Divergences from basic historical fact may nearly all be explained as due to the nature of oral tradition, to the vicissitudes of written transmission, and to honest, but erroneous combinations on the part of Israelite and Jewish scholars.[32]

Until the nineteenth century when Egyptian hieroglyphics, Babylonian cuneiform, and other early records were deciphered, the Old Testament presented the earliest record of consecutive events. The apologists made this discovery and discounted as fabulous the traditions of earlier civilizations. It was altogether reasonable that they should accept Mosaic history and cosmogony when so much of the Old Testament proved reliable, and even in the eighteenth century rationalists who attacked Mosaic revelation often accepted Mosaic history for the lack of a better substitute. The best historical scholarship of the sixteenth century had only confirmed the main outlines of the work of the apologists.

St. Augustine, who is often pictured as standing midway between the antique man of classical culture and the Christian man of the new Gospel, represents a turning point in the history of the two worlds. He sums up much of the Patristic thought on time and history and projects it forward with his own modifications as a main line of Christian doctrine. Much has been written about his conceptions of time and duration. However, since the

---

[32] William Foxwell Albright, *Archaeology and the Religion of Israel* (Baltimore: The Johns Hopkins Press, 1942), p. 176.

meaning of time need not concern us here, on this subject it is sufficient to note that he declared that the world was created as told in Genesis and that there was no time before the world was created. The world was not created *in* time, but time was created with the world and would expire with it.

The City of God, compendium that it is, contains a considerable amount of historical detail as a result of St. Augustine's attempt at historically justifying Christianity against the imputation that the calamities which had fallen on Rome could be pinned on Christianity. "For there are some others amongst them [vile persons] that are learned, and love that very history that makes these things plain to their understanding: but because they love to set the blind and erroneous vulgar at enmity and dissension with us Christians, they dissemble and conceal this understanding of theirs. . . ." (II: Ch. 3.) St. Augustine therefore resolved "to cast up a reckoning of the sundry mischiefs that this city of Rome hath suffered since she was first founded." He also gave a detailed exposition of Old Testament history in connection with the city of God, and in so doing he attacked "that history that says the world has continued many thousand years," those that advocate eternalism, and "those that hold not the eternity of the world, but either a dissolution and generation of innumerable worlds, or of this one at the expiration of certain years." Refuted, too, were those philosophers who "believed that this world had no other dissolution, but a renewing of it continually at certain revolutions of time, wherein the nature of things was repaired, and so passed on a continual rotation of ages past and coming; whether this fell out in the continuance of one world, or the world arising and falling gave this succession and date of things by its own renovation." (XII, Ch. 13.) His answer was that by Scripture's authority man's creation had been made "as recently as within this six thousand years. If the brevity of the time be offensive, and the years since man was made seem so few, let them consider that nothing that has a limit is continual: and that all the definite spaces of the ages being compared to interminable eternity are as a very little, nay as just nothing."

History was utilized by St. Augustine as instruction in the perils that besought the Christian pilgrim in the earthly city and in the succession of judgments already made by God along the path of salvation. The latter had meaning in the continuous redemption which took place in time and it tended to emphasize the concrete in history, but, at the same time, death offered an escape from history. And the Last Judgment was thought to be imminent, so history became all the more tolerable since time was limited and short. The individual was regenerated at death, and the cosmos would be regenerated with the "consummation of time." Nevertheless, St. Augustine had placed the conception of a unique, concrete, course of time in the mainstream of Christian eschatology. If, in the eighteenth century, the time scale of Biblical chronology became an onerous barrier to scientific progress, it had served an heroic role during the Patristic period in establishing the archetype of progress itself which science so readily borrowed. However, the influence of cosmic cycles remained in the Western tradition and was manifested in the Middle Ages after the introduction of Arabic and ancient learning. Eternalism was revived under the influence of Aristotle and the Arabic Aristotelians, and interest in astronomy encouraged belief in the *magnus annus*, or Great Year. Pierre Duhem in his review of medieval thought about the Great Year has pointed out that it was characterized by the idea that the Great Year had a duration of 36,000 years, that this period marked the completion of the revolution of the sphere of fixed stars, that at the end of the period the planets would reach the same position they had at its beginning, that the world was subject to periodic generation and corruption, and that these periods were equal to the Great Year.[33]

[33] Pierre Duhem, *Le système du monde, histoire des doctrines cosmologiques de Platon à Copernic* (Paris: Libraire scientifique Hermann et cie, 1954-56), II, 223. On the Great Year, see also I, 65-85, 275-96, II, 214-23,

Duhem also traces the origin of this concept, particularly noting the influence of Plato.

The Augustinian position was reaffirmed, however, by St. Thomas Aquinas in his *Summa Theologica.* Although few held Aristotle in greater esteem than St. Thomas, on the subject of creation there was no ground for compromise with Genesis, and he reiterated, "In the beginning God created heaven and earth." Nothing but God could be eternal, he maintained. The world exists because God willed it to exist, and God created time and the world together. And "the articles of faith cannot be proved demonstratively, because faith is of things *that appear not.* But that God is the Creator of the world: hence that the world began, is an article of faith."[34]

Writing of the two fundamental conceptions of time and history, cyclical and linear, Eliade points out how much cycles and periodicities penetrated the eschatological outlook of the Middle Ages at the expense of the linear concept.

> In the Middle Ages, the germs of this theory [linear progress of history] can be recognized in the writings of Albertus Magnus and St. Thomas; but it is with the *Eternal Gospel* of Joachim of Floris that it appears in all its coherence, as an integral element of a magnificent eschatology of history, the most significant contribution to Christianity in this field since St. Augustine's. . . .
>
> But, as we said, the tendency which gains increasing adherence is that of an immanentization of the cyclical theory. Side by side with voluminous astrological treatises, the considerations of scientific astronomy assert themselves. So it is that in the theories of Tycho Brahe, Kepler, Cardano, Giordano Bruno, or Campanella, the cyclical ideology survives beside the

---

447-54, v, 133-7, 223-6. Also in Lynn Thorndike, *A History of Magic and Experimental Science* (New York: Columbia University Press, 1923-58), II, 203, 370, 418, 439.

[34] *Summa Theologica,* tr. Fathers of the English Dominican Province (London, 1937), Part I, Q. 46, Art. 2. See also *Summa contra Gentiles,* Chaps. xv-xxi.

new conception of linear progress professed, for example, by a Francis Bacon or a Pascal. From the seventeenth century on, linearism and the progressivistic conception of history assert themselves more and more, inaugurating faith in an infinite progress, a faith already proclaimed by Leibniz, predominant in the century of "enlightenment," and popularized in the nineteenth century by the triumph of the ideas of the evolutionists.[35]

I would suggest that the Reformation restored the Augustinian position on time to dominance, after it had been seriously weakened in the medieval-Aristotelian Cosmos. And, as in the case of St. Augustine, the concrete, albeit literal, scholarly preoccupation with sacred history emphasized the uniqueness of time, even though the Biblical time span of about six thousand years, upon which it was so strongly based, eventually proved to be a barrier instead of a support to the progressivistic conception of history, and especially when it was transposed to the history of nature. In the destruction of the medieval-Aristotelian Cosmos, Marjorie Nicolson and others have emphasized the importance to sixteenth-century thought of "breaking the circle" by the astronomers in the scientific revolution.[36] The circle was a key concept of the Aristotelian cosmology, and had been interwoven into the whole qualitative hierarchy of values. However, the scientific revolution left the cosmic cycle virtually untouched, and the displacement of this survival of qualititative and eschatological circularity from medieval-classical thought owed something to the work of the reformers, who could say with Augustine on the philosophers of cycles and periodicity:

> The next verse I think fits them best: "The wicked walk in a circuit"; not because their life (as they think) is to run circularly, but because their false doctrine runs round in a circular maze. (XII, Ch. 13.)

[35] Eliade, *op. cit.*, p. 145.
[36] Marjorie Hope Nicolson, *The Breaking of the Circle: Studies in the Effects of the New Science upon Seventeenth Century Poetry* (Evanston, 1950).

CHRISTIAN RATIONALISM

The marriage of rationalism and mysticism in Christianity was reflected in the work of St. Augustine, and although his view of time and history was a reversal of cyclical eternalism, it had been shaped on the Hellenic die. Antique rationalism had provided the hammer and the forge for shaping his mystical doctrines, and while the mystical interest in the chiliastic abolition of history through redemption was the aspect of his view which seems to have predominated in the early Middle Ages, the appeal to reason, to doctrine, to texts, and to precedent, which his work reflected, was kept alive so that the scholar retained his place beside the priest.

With the revival of Aristotle in the Middle Ages, the scholars proceeded to raise that magnificent work of art, the cathedral of cathedrals, the medieval-Aristotelian Cosmos. The scholastic craftsmen trimmed and fitted the massive system of Aristotle onto the floor plan of the cross, graced the structure with lofty arches of Platonism, and decorated the whole with scriptural and salvationist motives. Like many of the medieval cathedrals, the Cosmos took shape slowly and was never completely finished, although its ideal archetype was manifest by 1300 in Dante's *Divine Comedy*.

The medieval Cosmos embraced an astronomical system, a physics, and a cosmology. It was a rational construct, but above all, it was spiritually uplifting and aesthetically satisfying to an age concerned with salvation.

The spheres in the heavens, in which angelic guides turned the celestial bodies, were stepping stones to the throne of God, and despite the fact that man was born in misery, had to toil and suffer for the sin of Adam, and was doomed to death, he could console himself with the belief that the whole beautiful construct of the heavens was pinpointed around his existence. What then did this round of earthly existence matter in the prospect of eternal bliss? The gross, corruptible nature in which man must briefly dwell was beneath contempt. One's eyes should be lifted upward towards the main goal, the flight through the spheres into the Empyrean to inhabit the pure, perfect, and eternal regions with the divine spirits. Such was the theological outlook.

The Cosmos was a kind of intellectual institution which characterizes medieval thought, but as in the case of other institutional structures of medieval society, it was permeated with activity. The scholastic craftsmen had not only been busy constructing the Cosmos, they had also been learning to use the tools of rationalism and had been slowly reshaping their inherited materials to fit their own experiences and predilections, which included a desire to master nature as well as to understand it. Professor A. C. Crombie has emphasized the practical leanings of the scholars, evident as early as the twelfth century, and how they increasingly turned the rational and critical tools borrowed from Hellenic logic and geometrical demonstration towards the verification of principles through experiment and mathematical measurement in the world of phenomena.

Thus the experimental and mathematical methods were a growth, developing within the medieval system of scientific thought, which was to destroy from within and eventually to burst out from Aristotelian cosmology and physics. Though resistance to the destruction of the old system became strong among certain of the late scholastics, and especially among those whose humanism had given them too great a devotion to ancient texts and those by whom the old system had been too closely linked with theological doctrines, it was the growth of these 13th- and 14th-century experimental and mathematical methods that brought about the movement which by the 17th century had become so striking as to be called the Scientific Revolution.[37]

Modern historians of science have shown considerable interest

[37] A. C. Crombie, "From Rationalism to Experimentalism," in Philip P. Wiener and Aaron Noland, eds., *Roots of Scientific Thought: A Cultural Perspective* (New York: Basic Books, 1957), p. 135.

in the role of the Middle Ages in forging the conceptual framework for the Scientific Revolution in the sixteenth and seventeenth centuries. Without entering into a discussion of the overall history of this subject, or its historiography, I should like to touch upon one aspect which appears to have had some importance in the relations of theology and science over the history of nature. A. N. Whitehead, among others, has stressed the importance of the general idea of order in nature, which was present in Hellenic thought and which was intensified in medieval thought. "The Middle Ages formed one long training of the intellect of Western Europe in the sense of order."[38] The concept of moral order and the order of nature had been enshrined in Stoic philosophy and Roman law, for instance, and "the habit of definite exact thought was implanted in the European mind by the long dominance of scholastic logic and scholastic divinity. The habit remained after the philosophy had been repudiated, the priceless habit of looking for an exact point and of sticking to it when found."[39] The medieval insistence on the rationality of God had fortified the Greek and Roman concepts of order with the idea that every detail in nature was supervised and ordered, and every detailed occurrence could be correlated with its antecedents in a perfectly definite manner to exemplify general principles. The idea, associated with William of Ockham, that simplicity should be sought behind multiplicity, was an expression of the trend, and it also discouraged the use of *ad hoc* hypotheses in explaining nature.

The Greeks, especially the Alexandrian school, had utilized the empirical method in their science, but in the new social and intellectual conditions of medieval society, the degree of importance which came to be attached to the brute facts themselves had a revolutionary import. Under a well-integrated philosophical sys-

[38] Alfred North Whitehead, *Science and the Modern World: Lowell Lectures,* 1925 (New York: Pelican Mentor Books, 1948), p. 12.
[39] *Ibid.,* p. 13.

tem such as the medieval-Aristotelian Cosmos, the dominant theological tendency was to dismiss, ignore, or rationalize away those facts which conflicted with the system. However, the growth of the empirical attitude towards nature among the scholars, and medieval society in general, led to the recognition of discordance between facts and rational principles. The *ad hoc* hypotheses used to explain the discordance tended to become logically unconvincing and led eventually to the process of revamping the principles to include the discordances. This practice had the effect of making the region of aberrant data a moving frontier of knowledge. The existence of such a frontier does not, of course, explain the dynamic forces directed towards it, but it was, nevertheless, a significant factor in focussing attention in certain directions in the development of modern thought and science.

The discordance of the observed behavior of a projectile with the Aristotelian theory of motion focussed attention on this problem for centuries before it was resolved by Galileo, who rejected Aristotelian physics in the process. The attempt of Copernicus to simplify the multiplicity of *ad hoc* epicycles and eccentrics in astronomy moved him to substitute a heliocentric theory for the geocentric system of Ptolemy. The telescopic observation of spots on the sun and mountains on the moon rendered the Aristotelian distinction between a corruptible sublunar material and a perfect, immutable, celestial substance untenable. Examples of this process could be multiplied without end, and it appears as an all too-obvious concomitant of the scientific method, too-obvious because it is so well established in our frame of thinking. But imagine the revolution in value systems when a few data from the despised material world could topple such a Cosmos! The rejection of sense data as deceptive had been consistently taught in Christianity, and when Cremonini refused to look through Galileo's telescope, it might very well have been because he thought that whatever he saw with his eyes was irrelevant to the truths upheld by the Church about the Cosmos. The priest and the scholar had been moving in different directions while serving God.

The influence of Aristotle and Averroes had encouraged eternalistic thinking among some of the medieval Scholastics and there were advocates of the cyclic Great Year philosophy. Speculation about the omnipotence of God forced some, like Nicolas Cusanus, to reject a finite universe, and as this strain of thought passed to Giordano Bruno, it was elaborated into a cosmology of an infinite and eternal universe with a plurality of worlds. These threats to the Augustinian view of time were checked by the Church, rather dramatically in the case of Bruno, though this was not the only reason why he was burned at the stake. More serious was the course of humanist scholarship in the Renaissance, which not only continued to recover more of the texts of the ancients, but their worldly spirit as well, and this, combined with the growth of secularism and naturalism from other directions during the Renaissance, threatened to displace the whole supernaturalist base of the Christian outlook.

The medieval-Aristotelian Cosmos began to fall apart during the Renaissance, but its theological orientation was heroically salvaged by the reformers who, in the tradition of St. Augustine, were both mystics and scholars. They placed a strong emphasis on the textual foundation of Christianity, and the literal approach to the interpretation of Scripture by which they tried to establish the authority of dogma helped to restore the Augustinian view of time and history in all its pristine vigor. The words of Scripture were brought into the area of concrete, nominalistic facts, and, thanks to the printing presses and the distribution of Bibles, they could be dealt with as familiarly by Mr. Everyman as the brute facts of nature. This trend was not confined to the Protestant sects alone.

In the Council of Trent, the Roman Catholic Church had condemned the doctrine of the supremacy of the Bible, but, in the zeal of a counter-reformation, did not hesitate to condemn the

Copernicans for being in opposition to Scripture. When the Congregation of the Index took action against Galileo, it decreed, "the doctrine of the double motion of the earth about its axis and about the sun is false, and entirely contrary to the Holy Scripture." The Roman Catholic Church abandoned much of the medieval scholastic metaphorical and symbolic interpretation of Scripture in favor of the plain meaning, even though it reserved the right of authoritative interpretation and did not encourage the distribution of Bibles.

The scholarly world proceeded to compare natural data with the Scriptural accounts of animals, plants, and history, much as they were wont to do in the case of classical texts, while Holy Writ was itself subjected to more and more historical criticism. The work of Julius Caesar Scaliger (1484-1558) was typical of the trend, and his son Joseph Justus Scaliger (1540-1609) brought it to high technical achievement. The latter's *De emendatione temporum* (1583) revolutionized chronology. He showed that ancient history was not confined to that of the Greeks and Romans, but should include Persian, Babylonian, Egyptian, and the secular Jewish history. He gathered extant fragments of ancient history, succeeded in reconstructing the lost *Chronicle* of Eusebius (printed in his *Thesaurus temporum* [1606]), and studied the ancient systems of time keeping. He was thus able to compile for the first time in the modern period a sound—though sometimes erroneous—universal chronology of profane history, as distinguished from the uncritical and somewhat mythological sacred history of traditional Christianity.

The method of comparing historical data, ancient authorities, and the rapidly accumulating natural knowledge against Mosaic history and cosmogony quickly multiplied the area of discordant facts in the world of sixteenth-century scholarship. Professor Don Allen has shown how the literalist scholars were led into difficulties over the interpretation of the Flood of Noah.

We have followed the progress of this once dubious human gift of reason as it marched through a section of the Pentateuch in the company of the literal interpreters. We have seen how it first wormed its way into the legend of Noah in the form of innocent answers to the impious questions of pagans; then we watched it grow and burgeon to such conceited stature that it began to ask questions itself, which it attempted to answer. But answering questions is something like committing murder or telling lies; it merely begets more questions and answers. So we have noticed that the first truly important question about the Noah story was concerned with the adequacy of the Ark's size, and we shall observe that almost at the moment that the question was answered in what seemed a sure and scientific way, seafarers and zoologists arrived bearing large burdens of strange birds and unknown animals that had to be enrolled on the Ark's list of passengers. We have also been spectators while the rational exegetes attempted to iron out the chronological difficulties of the great watery event, and we have been as dismayed by their flounderings among a variety of calendars and conflicting dates as they were themselves. Finally, we have read the fluttering attempts of the commentators to assemble enough gallons of water to flood the whole earth, and we have not been surprised to see them retract the size of their maps, first to the inhabited world and then to Palestine itself. Such a process of attempted rationalization and subsequent consternation occurred when the literal commentators attempted to expound other sections of the Bible. When to this intellectual defeat was added the uncertainties arising from canonical and textual studies, the reputation of the Bible as an inspired book was seriously threatened.[40]

The rational exegetes, despite the threatening direction of their questioning, generally stopped short of doubting the accuracy of the Mosaic history, however, and turned instead upon one another's interpretations. Genesis would continue to exert a dominant influence over biological and geological thought for two

[40] Don Cameron Allen, *The Legend of Noah, Renaissance Rationalism in Art, Science, and Letters* (Urbana, Ill.: University of Illinois Press, 1948), p. 90.

centuries and be the source of a succession of well-meant, but fallacious, *ad hoc* hypotheses designed to protect theological doctrines. It provided a priori principles for the historical sciences on how the world came into being, and it left no room in history for the process of change, either in species, or geology. Although a shift in mental attitudes precedes and conditions an intellectual revolution, it is manifested in particulars, and against this Mosaic framework, observations in natural history continued to pile up discordant data until, in the nineteenth century, the Mosaic system was burst as decisively as the Aristotelian Cosmos had been in the seventeenth century. For both revolutions, however, the Christian heritage had placed in the minds of the scientists some of the basic attitudes and intellectual tools which made the revolutions possible.

In view of this Christian matrix, it seems to be somewhat inaccurate to say that as science developed it waged a warfare with theology. Conflict and compromise marked the path of theology itself long before modern science was an issue, and the so-called warfare may be regarded as an internal schism within the Christian composite of thought of far less intensity than that of the Reformation. On the other hand, whenever theology maintained doctrines contrary to scientific evidence, there was conflict, not harmony, even though it was not always recognized by pious scientists and though harmonious relations in general may have prevailed between theology and science.

II
HISTORICISM AND THE SCIENTIFIC REVOLUTION

Although the man of the Middle Ages had his mind filled with historical lore, he was scarcely aware of historical change. He may have realized that the dramas of Biblical history, upon which he was nurtured, had taken place a long time ago, but he did not suspect that those olden times were much different from his own. Biblical characters and scenes, as medieval paintings show, were envisaged in terms of his own life and society. The past ran along with the present and was a part of everyday living. The only changes in history of interest to him were miracles and supernatural manifestations, and these were no respecters of the finality of events and times. But if an awareness of historical process was largely undeveloped in the Middle Ages, there was a movement towards it which began to be manifest in the Renaissance.

The medieval clerk was busy making records and preserving them, while the scholar was engaged in recovering and interpreting the records of antiquity. Records, the yardstick for measuring changes in history, were thus becoming available for a long and fairly continuous stretch of human activity and the flowering of humanist scholarship in the Renaissance not only brought to light the thought and knowledge of the ancients, it also stimulated interest in the remnants of ancient civilization—another kind of record. The medieval Christian had been an inveterate relic gatherer, and the neo-classical Christian proved to be no less avid in collecting artifacts of antiquity. As pride of family, locality, and country blossomed, the study of medieval antiquities was also pursued. Out of such varied interests the seeds of anthropology, archeology, and philology began to sprout.

Natural records indicating that the earth and life upon it had undergone alterations in the past were also found. The most important of these records were fossils, although a knowledge of the extent to which they could serve as records had to await the development of geology and paleontology in the nineteenth century, when they provided the content and chronology of prehistory. But they had a significant place in Western thought for the part they played in first stimulating man to realize that nature had undergone a series of changes in the course of time.

The earth has the appearance of stability and indestructibility, despite the occurrence of earthquakes, volcanoes, floods, and small changes here and there, and it is natural to think of it as permanent in its principal features. How then can masses of marine shells found in the earth and the mountains, sometimes in deposits hundreds of feet deep, be explained? This question had stirred man's curiosity from time immemorial. It appeared in antiquity and the Middle Ages. It was inherited by the men of the Renaissance and became one of the most provocative enigmas of the seventeenth and eighteenth centuries. Systems of cosmogony had to take fossils into account, and interest in the enigma was a strong motivating force in the exploration of the earth's surface by naturalists. Georges Cuvier, who did so much to demonstrate that the fossil beds were archives of a prehistoric world, wrote in 1811, that it was to these fossil remains alone that we owe even the commencement of a theory of the earth, and that without them we should perhaps never have suspected that successive epochs and series of different operations had existed in the formation of the globe.[1] As the early modern naturalists took up the problem

[1] Georges Cuvier, *Essay on the Theory of the Earth*, 4th ed. (Edinburgh, 1822), p. 54.

of the fossils, these natural memorials of earth history provided another source of data with a direct bearing on traditional views of history and thereby contributed to the rise of historicism in the seventeenth century.

THE FOSSIL ENIGMA

Xenophanes of Colophon (c. 570-c. 480 B. C.) appears to have been the first person to recognize fossil remains as witnesses of geological change. He was of the opinion that the world had once been a mixture of earth and sea, and that in this mud life was generated. In the process of time the moisture was disengaged from the earth, but things originally generated in the mud could now be found embedded in the earth. Shells in the midst of the earth and in mountains and the prints of marine plants and animals in quarry stone were given as proofs.[2] His cosmology was apparently some form of the periodic regeneration and destruction philosophy.

Xanthus of Lydia also drew attention to shells in the lands of Armenia, Phrygia, and Lydia, and concluded that these places had once been the bed of the sea.[3] He further suggested that the land and sea areas must be constantly undergoing a change of positions. Herodotus noted fossil shells in the hills of Egypt and deduced that those lands were once submerged.[4] Eratosthenes, in the third century before Christ, trying to explain the changes taking place on the earth's surface, observed "that this question in particular has presented a problem: how does it come about that large quantities of mussel-shells, oyster-shells, scallop-shells and also

[2] Hermann Diels, *Fragmente der Vorsokratiker* (Berlin, 1906), I⁵, 122, or John Burnet, *Early Greek Philosophy*, 4th ed. (London, 1930), pp. 123-4.
[3] *The Geography of Strabo*, Intro., Bk. I, Ch. III, par. 4.
[4] Herodotus, *History*, II, 10.

salt-marshes are found in the interior at a distance of two or three thousand stadia from the sea."[5]

Even at this early period the two opposing outlooks on geologic process, catastrophism and uniformitarianism, or actualism, became manifest. Some Greek philosophers who believed in a created world may have had in mind one phase of the Great Year instead of a unique time course with an absolute beginning and ending. In any case, those who were called creationists maintained that the level of the sea was diminishing, as evidenced by marine fossils in the mountains, and they used this as a proof that the world had been created and was now degenerating towards its extinction through a conflagration.[6] In this particular kind of creationism, as well as in the periodic regeneration in the Great Year philosophy, catastrophism marked the pattern of events.

Aristotle directed the arguments of his *Meteorologica* against the creationists.[7] The recurring cycle underlay his cosmogony,[8] but cataclysms in it were restrained to occasional intensified natural events, such as the heavy rainfall during the Deucalion Flood, which he considered to be a local phenomenon.[9] The even tenor, gradualism, and continuity of geological change in Aristotle's system suggest modern uniformitarianism. Springs shift their location and affect the moisture in an area, marshy land dries sufficiently for the support of agriculture, then it becomes too dry and people move to more luxuriant regions, erosion carries off the dry land, sediments build up into offshore banks, behind which lakes are created, and these in turn become marshes, tillable land, and desert. Little by little all the lands and seas alternate their positions on the earth's surface, not once, but again and again. "The whole vital process of the earth takes place so gradu-

[5] Strabo, *loc. cit.*
[6] See Pierre Duhem, *Études sur Léonard de Vinci* . . . (Paris, 1906-9), II, 286ff. on the *Liber de Mundo* of Philo, or pseudo-Philo.
[7] *Meteorologica*, Bk. II, Ch. I, par. I.
[8] E. g., *ibid.*, Bk. I, Ch. XIV, p. 352a.
[9] *Ibid.*

ally and in periods of time which are so immense compared with
the length of our life, that these changes are not observed, and
before their course can be recorded from beginning to end whole
nations perish and are destroyed."[10]

The *Meteorologica* was an almost ever-present source for ideas
on the nature of change in cosmogony whenever such problems
came under consideration in Western thought, and it undoubtedly
had an influence on the formulation of uniformitarian views in
modern geology. But the eternalism in Aristotle's cosmogony
made it unacceptable to the generality of Christians. Aristotle
wrote:

> It is therefore clear that as time is infinite and the universe
> eternal that neither Tanais nor Nile always flowed but the place
> whence they flow was once dry: for their action has an end
> whereas time has none. And the same may be said with truth
> about other rivers. But if rivers come into being and perish
> and if the same parts of the earth are not always moist, the sea
> also must necessarily change correspondingly. And if in places
> the sea recedes while in others it encroaches, then evidently
> the same parts of the earth as a whole are not always sea, nor
> always mainland, but in the process of time all change.[11]

Aristotle's cosmogony was helpful in giving an enlarged view
of dynamical geology, but the catastrophists criticized his conception of process, holding that if the natural place of water was
above earth, and the upraised parts of the land were eroded
throughout eternity, at some point all the land must be transported to its natural place below the water. How then, could the
proportion of exposed land area to sea area remain constant, as
Aristotle maintained? But Theophrastus and other Aristotelians
countered these criticisms by insisting that lands emerged constantly through the action of fiery gases enclosed within the
earth.[12] Strabo even ingeniously deduced that the land of vast

[10] *Ibid.*, p. 351a (E. W. Webster tr., Oxford ed.).
[11] *Ibid.*, p. 353a (H. D. P. Lee tr., Loeb Classical Library).
[12] See Duhem, *Études*, II, 286ff.

regions was slowly uplifted by the pressure of hot gases below it which could not find a vent for escape.[13] With the addition of the principle of igneous forces and the uplift of land masses to the effects of erosion in the geologic process, the Greeks were able to reach a general view of cosmogony which contained some of the leading principles of modern geology.

Important as the uniformitarianism in Aristotle's picture of changes on the earth's surface was to the development of geological science, its value was offset by other aspects of his cosmogony. The agencies of change—rain, wind, floods, earthquakes, volcanoes, evaporation, condensation—were themselves caused by variations in the action of the sun as it moved closer or farther away from the earth along the path of the ecliptic. There was a measure of truth in such a conception, but the cyclical course of the sun, as he imagined it, was one of endless repetition and so was the flux in its wake. Furthermore, the sun and other celestial bodies exerted a direct action on the elements, as well as an indirect one through meteorological agencies. By means of celestial influences fossil bodies could be generated in the earth. This removed with one stroke the argument of the creationists of a diminution of the seas as evidenced by fossil remains, but it also put the organic origin of fossils in doubt and thereby lessened their importance in Aristotelian thought as an indication of geological change.

In antiquity the term fossil meant anything dug from the ground, and the distinction between organic fossils and minerals was not clearly made until the modern period. Aristotle must have been familiar with fossil remains, but the only probable reference to them in his writings occurs in *De Respiratione*, where he remarks that a great many fishes live in the earth motionless and are found when excavations are made.[14] He apparently be-

[13] Geography, *Intro.*, Bk. I, Ch. III, par. 5.
[14] See Frank Dawson Adams, *The Birth and Development of the Geological Sciences* (Baltimore, 1938), p. 12.

lieved that most organic fossils were akin to minerals and were
generated in the earth out of exhalations under celestial influences:
"For there are, we maintain, two exhalations, one vaporous and
one smoky; and there are two corresponding kinds of body produced within the earth, 'fossiles' and metals."[15] Such at least was
the development of thought on fossils among Aristotelians in the
Middle Ages and Renaissance. It was also expressed by Aristotle's
successor at the Lyceum, Theophrastus, who maintained that fossil ivory and large stone-like bones had been spontaneously generated in the earth. However, Theophrastus also voiced the opinion that fish might have grown in the earth from spawn left by
fish moving in underground passages connected with the sea.
This theory could have stemmed from observing goby-like walking fish in the mud flats of the Black Sea,[16] and a similar observation may have been the basis of Aristotle's remark in *De Respiratione*.

Fossils continued to attract attention, even at the Lyceum. They
were often casually collected as curiosities. Large bones were
regarded as remnants of giants who lived in the heroic age, and
marine fossils were thought to be witnesses of a diminution of the
sea, or relics of the Deucalion Flood.[17] No attempt will be made
here to assay the many reasons behind the failure of the ancients
to develop a science of geology, but certainly one reason was that
fossils, outside of presenting the enigma of changes on the earth's
surface, were not systematically investigated. Such an investigation of the fossils would have soon disposed of the idea that they
were spontaneously generated, but here again, the belief in
archetypes in nature probably would have led the naturalists to

---

[15] *Meteorologica*, Bk. III, Ch. VI, par. 2.

[16] See Pliny, *Natural History*, Bk. IX, Ch. 83, and Bk. XXXVI, Ch. 29.

[17] See Ernst von Lasaulx, "Die Geologie der Griechen und Römer. Ein
Beitrag zur Philosophie der Geschichte," *Abhandlungen der Philosophisch-
Philologischen Classe der Königlich Bayerischen Akademie der Wissensch-
aften*, Bd. XXVII, Abth. 3 [München,] 1852, for examples, especially pp.
522-30.

dismiss extinct species as aberrations from the norm. Such an attitude certainly lay behind the philosophy on fossils of a later period, immortalized in the designation of fossils as "sports of nature." Lacking a knowledge of the order of successive changes in the history of the earth furnished by the fossil record, the character of the geological process was left timeless in the thought of the ancients.

With the advent of Christianity, celestial determination passed out of favor, at least in human destiny,[18] but the belief that fossils were created in the earth by a plastic or mineralizing force under celestial influences survived and passed over into the medieval period. The fossil question had been raised by Arabic philosophers, and Avicenna revived the theory of an organic origin of fossils. His ideas were subsequently put in circulation by Albertus Magnus and by Vincent of Beauvais. Avicenna thought that vegetable and animal bodies could be converted into stone, either by a *vis lapidificativa* to be found in stony places, or by the drying up of mud in which they were enclosed. His views on a mineralizing virtue were probably derived from Aristotle, and his cosmogony was unquestionably influenced by *Meteorologica*, since his account of geological changes was appended to his translation of this work of Aristotle.[19] Subsequently another theory of the organic origin of fossils was stated by Ristoro d'Arezzo in *La Composizione del Mondo* (1282),[20] but this time it was in terms of Mosaic history. D'Arezzo reasserted the belief, first expressed by Tertullian,[21] that marine animals had been left in the mountains by the Noachian Deluge.

The flood theory of fossil origins became increasingly popular in Italy in the late Middle Ages and Renaissance, but along with it flourished the alternative theories that fossils were abortive at-

[18] Marshall Clagett, *Greek Science in Antiquity* (New York, 1955), p. 139, on St. Augustine.

[19] See Duhem, *Études*, II, 302-19, and Adams, *op. cit.*, pp. 19, 82-3, 333-5.

[20] See Duhem, *Études*, II, 302-19, and Adams, *op. cit.*, pp. 335-41.

[21] *De Pallio*. See Lasaulx, "Geologie," pp. 529, 538.

tempts of astral forces to generate in the earth imitations of the productions of nature on its surface, or that fossils were organic remains petrified by the mysterious "mineralizing virtue." These views also continued as the main explanations of fossil origins well into the eighteenth century; but before passing the Renaissance, a few exceptions are worthy of notice, although their ultimate influence is debatable.

The writings of Leonardo da Vinci present a remarkable illustration of the scientific potential of medieval Aristotelian cosmogony when infused with the modern spirit of observation. Leonardo asked himself, "Why the bones of great fishes and oysters and corals and various other shells and sea-snail are found on the high tops of mountains that border on the sea, in the same way in which they are found in the depths of the sea?"[22] Turning to nature for an answer, Leonardo saw detail with the eye of an artist and looked at the operations of natural forces with the understanding of an engineer. From some lofty elevation he scanned the surrounding countryside and saw how the topography bore the appearance of having been sculptured by running waters. He studied how the waters in flood-swollen rivers carried their burden of mud and debris from the land to the sea. "When the floods of the rivers which were turbid with fine mud deposited this upon the creatures which dwelt beneath the waters near the ocean borders, these creatures became embedded in this mud, and finding themselves entirely covered under a great weight of mud they were forced to perish for lack of a supply of the creatures on which they were accustomed to feed."[23] The mud displaced the soft parts of these shell animals, and both the mud inside the shells and in the surrounding bed turned to stone in the process of time. Strata were formed in a succession in which "may be counted the winters of the years during which the sea multiplied

[22] *The Notebooks of Leonardo da Vinci*, ed. Edward MacCurdy (New York, 1939), p. 342.
[23] *Ibid.*, p. 311.

the layers of sand and mud brought down by the neighbouring rivers, and spread them over its shores."[24] In such a manner, Leonardo thought the fossil beds seen in the mountains had been formed.

By the study of the living counterparts of the fossils, Leonardo explained why the Deluge could not have deposited the fossils. The arrangement of the fossils in pairs and rows as in living colonies was proof that the deposition had taken place slowly and in quiet waters. The succession of layers itself indicated a long process of time, and ". . . between the various layers of the stone are still to be found the tracks of the worms which crawled about upon them when it was not yet dry."[25] Corals could be found in the fossil beds with worm holes in them, and mixed with the corals in the stone were stocks and families of oysters, as in the undisturbed waters of the seas today. Furthermore, the waters of the Deluge could not have carried the heavy live shell animals on their crest and thus to the tops of the mountains. Nor could the animals have transported themselves. The oysters were fastened to the bottom of the sea, while cockles could not have traveled from the Adriatic to the mountains of Lombardy in forty days, since their rate of travel was only three or four braccia a day.[26]

As to the alternative theory of the generation of fossils in the earth through celestial influences, Leonardo said it was maintained only by a set of ignoramuses,[27] and then he listed the anatomical and morphological evidences that rendered such a theory ridiculous. However, the keen analysis Leonardo gave to the processes of erosion, deposition of fossils, and petrifaction of strata still did not explain the elevation of the fossil beds into the mountains. Here his powers of observation were inadequate. Some theory

[24] *Ibid.*, p. 339.
[25] *Ibid.*, p. 338.
[26] *Ibid.*, p. 331.
[27] *Ibid.*, p. 338.

was needed, and Leonardo fell back on the cosmogony of Albert of Saxony, a fourteenth-century Aristotelian.[28]

In trying to solve the old problem in Aristotelian cosmogony of why the exposed land did not take its natural place beneath water as a result of erosion over the course of an eternity, Albert had postulated that the earth has two centers, one of weight and one of form, which do not coincide. The center of the earth's form, he thought, is at the fixed center of the universe, whereas the center of the earth's weight is set slightly off from the fixed center as a result of the irregularities of the earth's bulk. He also thought that every change of weight on the surface of the earth is transmitted all the way across the fixed center to the opposite side, so that the axis affected by it would be balanced at the fixed center. Thus, as land moves across the surface of the earth by erosion, the adjusting movement of the axes would cause subsidence or elevation at the antipodes while the progressive advance of erosion on the surface of the earth would keep the center of weight slowly rotating around the fixed center. Since water is fluid, its circumference would remain equidistant from the fixed center, but the land surface would be depressed beneath it in one area and elevated above it in another in the progressive rotation of the center of weight. This insured a constant proportion between the exposed land and the seas, at the same time allowing for a continuous alternation of their positions.

Leonardo integrated this system of Albert of Saxony with his own observations of erosion to explain the position of fossils in the mountains, as can be seen in the following notes:

> Because the centre of the natural gravity of the earth ought to be in the centre of the world the earth is always growing lighter in some part, and the part that becomes lighter pushes upwards, and submerges as much of the opposite part as is necessary for it to join the centre of its aforesaid gravity to the centre of the world; and the sphere of the water keeps its sur-

[28] Duhem, *Études*, I, 1-50.

face steadily equidistant from the centre of the world.[29]

[After rephrasing the same thought in another place:] And this may also be the reason why the marine shells and oysters that are seen in the high mountains, which have formerly been beneath the salt waters, are now found at so great a height, together with the stratified rocks, once formed of layers of mud carried by the rivers in the lakes, swamps and seas; and in this process there is nothing contrary to reason.[30]

And now these beds [of the sea] are of so great a height that they have become hills or lofty mountains, and the rivers which wear away the sides of these mountains lay bare the strata of the shells, and so the light surface of the earth is continually raised, and the antipodes draw nearer to the centre of the earth, and the ancient beds of the sea become chains of mountains.[31]

If the earth of the antipodes which sustains the ocean rose up and stood uncovered far out of this sea but being almost flat, how in process of time could mountains valleys and rocks with their different strata be created?

The water which drained away from the land which the sea left, at the time when this earth raised itself up some distance above the sea, still remaining almost flat, commenced to make various channels through the lower parts of this plain, and beginning thus to hollow it out they would make a bed for the other waters round about; and in this way throughout the whole of their course they gained breadth and depth, their waters constantly increasing until all this water was drained away and these hollows became then the beds of torrents which take the floods of the rains. And so they will go on wearing away the sides of these rivers until the intervening banks become precipitous crags; and after the water has thus been drained away these hills commence to dry and to form stone in layers more or less thick according to the depth of the mud which the rivers deposited in the sea in their floods.[32]

How the rivers have all sawn through and divided the members of the great Alps one from another; and this is revealed by the arrangement of the stratified rocks, in which from the

[29] MacCurdy, *Notebooks*, p. 688.
[30] *Ibid.*, p. 356.
[31] *Ibid.*, p. 321.
[32] *Ibid.*, pp. 310-11.

summit of the mountain down to the river one sees the strata on the one side of the river corresponding with those on the other.[33]

Busy with a host of other activities, and with few guides in geology, Leonardo da Vinci pursued the quandary of marine fossils until he had devised an amazingly good system of historical and dynamical geology. His uplift and subsidence of land masses working slowly over long periods of time was hardly more mysterious in its operation than the self-adjusting forces in James Hutton's *Theory of the Earth* (1788), which marks the beginning of modern theories of geological dynamics. Like Hutton, Leonardo was a uniformitarian who appealed directly to nature for an understanding of how geological processes had operated in the past. Leonardo could see that nature had a history, and its record was to be found, not in literary sources, but in the earth itself, or, as he expressed it:

Since things are far more ancient than letters, it is not to be wondered at if in our days there exists no record of how the aforesaid seas extended over so many countries; and if moreover such record ever existed, the wars, the conflagrations, the changes in speech and habits, the deluges of the waters, have destroyed every vestige of the past. But sufficient for us is the testimony of things produced in the salt waters and now found again in the high mountains, sometimes at a distance from the seas.[34]

Although Leonardo failed to see the role of heat in the metamorphosis of strata, geology could have gone far on his principles. Unfortunately, his notes did not appear in print until after Hutton's theory was published. In the meantime, Leonardo's fundamental premises, drawn from Aristotelian cosmogony, were demonstrated as false by the Copernican astronomy, while the Reformation reaffirmed the authority of a literal interpretation

[33] *Ibid.*, p. 338. See also p. 357 on formations.
[34] *Ibid.*, p. 345.

of Genesis, so that the Noachian Deluge was accepted among naturalists as a real and universal catastrophe in natural history.

In the sixteenth century the Flood theory of fossil distribution prevailed among those who recognized the organic origin of the fossil remains, although there were exceptions. Girolamo Fracastoro, a contemporary of Leonardo, after studying the excavations made for building the citadel of San Felice in Verona, asserted that the marine animals whose remains were unearthed had lived and died where they were found and could not have been left by the Flood. Jerome Cardan, who may have had access to the manuscripts of Leonardo, also rejected the idea that one universal flood could have distributed the fossils in the earth. The best reasoning displayed on the nature of fossils in the century after Leonardo was by the self-taught Huguenot potter, Bernard Palissy.[35] From the recognition of the succession of strata containing fossils and an appreciation that each period of deposit involved a considerable lapse of time, Palissy came to the conclusion that it was impossible for the Flood to have put the marine shells inside the stone of the mountains.[36]

There is no evidence that the views of Fracastoro, Cardan, or Palissy on fossils had any appreciable influence on their age. Palissy held lectures at which he displayed his collection of fossils, and the interest he helped to arouse in them as curiosities may have been ultimately more important than his theories about them. The sixteenth century was a period of increased activity in collecting fossils and assembling fossil collections. Alexandri, Sarayna, Agricola, C. Gesner, Moscardo, Fallopio of Padua, Kentmann, Cesalpino, Oliva of Cremona, Mercati, Mattioli, Camden, Im-

[35] Duhem believes that Palissy read a 1556 French edition of Cardan's *De Subtilitate*, and that Cardan had read the manuscripts of Leonardo. See *Études*, I, 234ff.

[36] *Recepte véritable* (La Rochelle, 1563) and *Discours admirables* (Paris, 1580) in *Oeuvres de Bernard Palissy*, ed. Benjamin Fillon (Niort, 1888). An English translation of the *Discours* by Aurèle La Rocque was published by the University of Illinois Press in 1957.

perato, Majoli, Aldrovandi, and Columna, among others, were collecting fossils and writing about them. Gesner's *De Rerum Fossilium* (1565) was the first extensively illustrated work showing fossils; and others soon followed. This activity of collecting, establishing museums, printing illustrations, and focusing attention on fossils in general was a necessary first step in the identification and classification of fossil specimens. The theories that accompanied the activity make amusing reading today, and so too does the classification based on the theories. Nevertheless, collecting took the naturalist into the field, while the display and illustration of collections added to the observational experience of the individual naturalist and his ability to compare specimens. The variety of theories which fossils stimulated was to some extent the result of the conflict which deductions from field data presented to received ideas, classical and Christian, and was an indication of the vigor of the scientific movement. However, as witnesses of tremendous alterations in the earth's surface, the bearing of fossils on cosmogony was the first thing about them to be recognized, aside from their being curiosities, and speculative reasoning to reconcile their existence with philosophical and theologically-based systems of cosmogony flew ahead of empirical knowledge about fossils.

With the beginning of the Reformation, Mosaic history and cosmogony were reinvigorated and had to be taken into consideration in speculations about fossil origins. That fossils were relics of the Deluge became the ruling dogma, but investigations of fossils by naturalists continued unabated and resulted in many questionings of Biblical chronology and history even though most of the researchers were concerned with confirming the Mosaic record. Most important, however, was the advance of geological knowledge, which would establish more reliable evidence with which the naturalist could eventually free himself from Mosaic history. In the advancement of that knowledge, stratigraphy laid the foundation for connecting a sequence of events in geological history, and its principles were first clearly enunciated by Nicolaus Steno in the seventeenth century.

After gaining a reputation in Paris as a physician, Steno went to Florence in 1665 and received an appointment as physician to Grand Duke Ferdinand II. He was also admitted to the brilliant company of scientists at the Accademia del Cimento, and it is probably through this influence that his attention was drawn to the problem of fossils. In 1669, after studying the fossil-rich area around Arezzo in Tuscany, Steno published a *Prodromus* to a *Dissertation concerning a Solid Body enclosed by Process of Nature within a Solid*, a work which displayed keen powers of observation and reasoning. Steno presented a persuasive argument that those bodies which were dug from the earth and which looked like the parts of plants and animals were in fact the parts of plants and animals and were therefore extraneous bodies in the strata enclosing them. His analysis of the processes of petrifaction and the formation of strata enabled him to grasp the basic principles of stratigraphy and to demonstrate that in the formation of the earth's crust, the strata which contained extraneous bodies could not have existed from the beginning of things but must have been laid down in succession, one on top of the other.

On the assumption that each stratum was formed in a fluid medium, Steno pointed out that the fluid had to be bounded below and at its sides (unless it surrounded the earth) by solid material. Although the under and side surfaces would conform to the shape of the enclosing material, because of its fluid origin, the stratum's top surface would be level. If the top surfaces of strata were no longer parallel to the horizon, an alteration of position must clearly have taken place since the solidification, and the mountains of the earth contained the proof that such alterations had occurred. Steno suggested that the strata were uplifted by the pressure of gases in the earth. Erosion or the further action of gases then ate away the under strata in places until there was a collapse of the upper ones, creating a valley, and leaving the edges of strata at the point of fracture exposed in the resulting mountains on either side of the valley, while the rubble of the collapsed parts became the building materials for secondary mountains with a heterogeneous composition.

In a year's time Steno had been able to discover the historical character of geological process, but when he turned to the elaboration of the history, the pattern of Genesis was invoked. Because of the succession of strata, the Flood was ruled out as a means of depositing the fossils, but the last division of his work was devoted to the Universal Flood, to which he gave a large role in disrupting the strata. And the entire investigation was justified by Steno as an attempt to "set forth the agreement of Nature with Scripture by reviewing the chief difficulties which can be urged regarding the different aspects of the earth."[37] Leibniz reports him as saying, "that he congratulated himself with having come to the aid of piety in supporting the faith of the Holy Scriptures and the tradition of the universal deluge on natural proofs."[38]

Although the principle interest in fossils during the latter seventeenth century was in connection with their meaning for cosmogony, the investigation of them as subjects of scientific interest spread throughout the international community of scholars. The scientific societies helped to focus attention on fossils and to encourage a new spirit in their study. Fossils not only were collected ever more diligently, with agents even being hired to collect them in the field,[39] but they also were brought under the experimental methodology. In 1663 we find Robert Hooke slicing and polishing cross-sections of petrified wood and examining them under the microscope. Fossilized substances were subjected

[37] *The Prodromus of Nicolaus Steno's Dissertation* . . . , ed. John Garrett Winter (New York, 1918), p. 263.

[38] Gottfried Wilhelm Leibniz, *Protogée* . . . , ed. Bertrand de Saint-Germain (Paris, 1859), p. 18.

[39] Charles E. Raven, *English Naturalists from Neckham to Ray* (Cambridge, 1947), gives much information on the activity of collecting.

to comparative tests with their living counterparts or similar kinds of materials. One such comparison investigated was the constitution of various kinds of stones, including those produced in the human body, in connection with the question of whether or not stones could grow. Kidney stones, gall stones, heart stones, and every kind of unusual hard growth in the body were excised, measured, weighed, described, and often illustrated.[40] This question was intimately allied to that of the generation of fossils and fossil strata in the earth. The progress of the incipient field of paleontology in the latter part of the seventeenth century can be seen by comparing the attitudes of Robert Hooke about stones in 1663 with his later views. The following is an excerpt from a letter written by him to Robert Boyle about a meeting of the Royal Society:

> There happened an excellent good discourse about petrefaction; upon which occasion several instances were given about the growing of stones: some, that were included in glass viols; others, that lay upon the pasture ground; others, that lay in gravel walks; which was known by putting a stone in at the mouth of a glass viol, through which, after a little time, it would by no means pass. Next, the story of a field's being filled with stones every third year, was confirmed by some instances. And that the stones in gravel walks grows greater, had been often proved by sifting those walks over again, which had formerly passed all through the sieve, and finding abundance of stones too big to pass through the second time. Upon this, mention was made of the production of stones or lapidious concretions in the bodies of animals, and abundance of very strange instances were alledged of the finding of stones in several parts of a man's body, as in the joints of his fingers and toes, and of other parts of his body; and it was generally agreed to by all, that those people, that drink petrifying waters, are extremely subject to the stone. A place was mentioned in *Oxfordshire*, where there is such a water, and the people round about are extremely plagued with that disease. Mr. PELL and some others

[40] R. W. T. Gunther, *The Life and Work of Robert Hooke*, in *Early Science in Oxford*, VI (1930), 131-2.

mentioned to have read somewhere an observation, there were more such concretions taken from one man, than the weight of his whole body amounted to.

Mr. PALMER related a story of a French physician (whose name I have forgot) who landing sick at *Dover*, and taking a glister, voided an incredible number of small and great cockle-shells. The matter of fact was confirmed by very many of the Society, who had either had very good relation of it, or seen some of the shells. Dr. CHARLTON added, that they had lain a good while upon sea, and fed upon nothing but cheese (made of the milk of goats, which fed upon the mountains of *Bononia*, which are very full of such shells) and brandy.[41]

Continued study of fossils convinced Hooke that they could not have grown in the earth, and that the growth of stones in the body was not relevant to the petrifactions. He had observed great quantities of marine animal shells hundreds of fathoms above the level of the sea, hundreds of miles inland, in the depths of the earth, in the midst of stone, and even constituting the stone, species among the shells of a size and character no longer to be found, and the figures of tropical plants in coal. Hooke was brought to the conclusion: "That a great part of the Surface of the Earth hath been since the Creation transformed and made of another Nature; namely, many Parts which have been Sea are now Land, and divers other Parts are now Sea which were once a firm Land; Mountains have been turned into Plains, and Plains into Mountains and the like."[42] The exotic and extinct species provoked him to think that "this very land of England and Portland, did, at a certain time for some ages past, lie within the torrid zone."[43]

Hooke does not seem to have doubted the actual occurrence of the Flood of Noah, but he argued at length against it as the means of placing the fossils in the depths of the earth or of imbedding them in mountains. He thought this was done by earthquakes,

[41] *Ibid.*, pp. 132-3.
[42] *The Posthumous Works of Robert Hooke*, ed. Richard Waller (London, 1705), "Discourse of Earthquakes," p. 290.
[43] *Ibid.*, p. 343.

which could elevate or depress large areas of the earth's surface. The fiery gases accompanying earthquakes would also provide a source of heat for liquefaction, baking, calcining, petrifaction, sublimation, distillation, and other transformations of a chemical nature.

Extinct fossil species further suggested to Hooke the idea of evolution, or perhaps devolution would be more precise, for Hooke was fond of Ovid's *Metamorphosis* and its thesis of degeneration. He thought there was a Golden Age when the earth was soft, flexible, and smooth-skinned like a child, that it had passed through a Silver Age, or maturity, when it dried and hardened, and an Iron Age, when the shell of the earth became petrified, crossed with wrinkles, scars, and furrows, and fell heir to the ailments of earthquakes, floods, and other debilitating disasters of old age. Noting that particular species seemed to thrive better in one climate than another, he wondered if a change of environment would have an influence on species.

We will, for the present, take this supposition to be real and true, that there have been in former times of the world, divers species of creatures, that are now quite lost, and no more of them surviving upon any part of the earth. Again, that there are now divers species of creatures which never exceed at present a certain magnitude, which yet, in former ages of the world, were usually of a much greater and gygantick standard; suppose ten times as big as at present; we will grant also a supposition that several species may really not have been created of the very shapes, they now are of, but that they have changed in great part their shape, as well as dwindled and degenerated into a dwarfish progeny; that this may have been so considerable, as that if we could have seen both together, we should not have judged them of the same species. We will further grant there may have been, by mixture of creatures, produced a sort differing in shape, both from the created forms of the one and other compounders, and from the true created shapes of both of them.

As we see that there are many changings both within and without the Body, and every state produces a new appearance, why then may there not be the same progression of the Species from its first Creation to its final termination?[44]

Hooke's study of fossils had thus brought him to an awareness that there had been great alterations in the earth's surface and "that there have been Species of Creatures in former Ages, of which we can find none at present; and that 'tis not unlikely also but that there may be divers new kinds now, which have not been from the beginning."[45] Hooke also found in such "a trivial thing as a rotten shell" a memorial of nature's history:

> How these shells and other bodies are the medals, urnes, or monuments of nature, whose relievos, impressions, characters, forms, substances, etc. are much more plain and discoverable to any unbiased person, and therefore he has no reason to scruple his assent: nor to desist from making his observations to correct his natural chronology, and to conjecture how, and when, and upon what occasion they came to be placed in those repositories. These are the greatest and most lasting monuments of antiquity, which, in all probability, will far antedate all the most ancient monuments of the world, even the very pyramids, obelisks, mummys, hieroglyphics, and coins, and will afford more information in natural history, than those others put altogether will in civil. Nor will there be wanting *Media* or *Criteria* of chronology, which may give us some account even of the time when, as I shall afterwards mention.[46]

There is no evidence that Hooke actually attempted a chronology of natural history based on fossil evidence, but he clearly saw the possibility of it. Again speaking of the shells as monuments of antiquity, he remarked,

> And tho' it must be granted, that it is very difficult to read them, and to raise a *Chronology* out of them, and to state the intervalls of the times wherein such, or such catastrophes and mutations have happened; yet 'tis not impossible, but that, by

[44] *Ibid.*, p. 435.
[45] *Ibid.*, p. 291.
[46] *Ibid.*, p. 335.

the help of those joined to other means and assistances of information, much may be done even in that part of information also.[47]

The views of Hooke and Steno were available to the public, but neither the intrinsic merit of their views, nor the reputation of the authors, swept paleontology into precipitous progress. Indeed, the distinction of Father of British Paleontology has been assigned by R. W. T. Gunther to Hooke's contemporary Edward Lhwyd,[48] who came to the conclusion that fossils grew in the earth from seeds dispersed by vapors of the sea. Lhwyd was unhappy with this theory, it is true, and adopted it reluctantly in opposition to his good friend, John Ray, who had probably discussed the fossil problem with Steno, and who held out firmly for the organic origin of fossils. Ray, an eminent naturalist and forerunner of Linnaeus in classification, had rejected the principle of spontaneous generation in nature, both on the basis of the researches of Redi, Malpighi, Swammerdam, Lister, and Leeuwenhoek, and on the theological argument that all creation was completed on the sixth day, after which life was passed down from one individual to another.[49] Lhwyd agreed with Ray that spontaneous generation in the earth by plastic forces was impossible, but he kept pressing Ray on the extinction of species and how the masses of animal life represented by fossil remains could have existed and been orderly embalmed in the strata during the short time span of Sacred History. Robert Plot, Martin Lister, William Cole, and other naturalist associates who took up the fossil problem had after extensive studies also doubted the organic origin of fossils. The seed theory of Lhwyd was an attempt to avoid spontaneous generation and still explain the position of exotic species and the quantity of shells in a way which would avoid an exten-

[47] *Ibid.*, p. 411.
[48] R. W. T. Gunther, *Life and Letters of Edward Lhwyd*, in *Early Science in Oxford*, XIV (1945), iii.
[49] Charles E. Raven, *John Ray Naturalist, His Life and Works* (Cambridge, 1942), p. 375.

sion of the time scale of Scripture. Ray, in contrast, toward the
end of his life wavered between rejecting the natural organic
origin of the fossils or the time scale of Scripture.

> Such a diversity as we find of figures in one leaf of Fern and
> so circumscribed in exact similitude to the plants themselves, I
> can hardly think to proceed from any shooting of salts or the
> like. . . . Yet on the other side there follows such a train of con-
> sequences as seem to shock the Scripture-history of the novity
> of the world; at least they overthrow the opinion generally
> received, and not without good reason, among Divines and
> Philosophers that since the first creation there have been no
> species of animals or vegetables lost, no new ones produced.[50]

The celebrated Dr. John Woodward, who went out of his way
to antagonize Ray and Lhwyd, claimed he had resolved the entire
mystery of fossils by a new principle. In his *Essay Towards a
Natural History of the Earth* (1695), he simply dissolved all the
upper crust of the earth in the Deluge and let the fossils settle out
in strata according to their specific gravities. His naivete surprised
Lhywd and Ray, but the *Essay* received much acclaim and was
translated and republished on the Continent. Woodward was
unequivocal about the organic origin of fossils and based some of
his proofs on Steno's *Prodromus.* The inspiration of his system,
and its plausibility, was derived from Newton's "Laws of
Gravity," but the good Doctor wrote that there was a mighty
collection of water in the bowels of the earth, in contradiction to
Newton's conclusion that the center of the earth must be five or
six times as heavy as water.

Another widely acclaimed attempt to explain Mosaic history
on rational principles was that of William Whiston, who succeeded Newton as Lucasian professor of mathematics at Cambridge. He wrote an elaborate account, embracing Newton's principles, of how a passing comet had created the Flood and

[50] R. W. T. Gunther, *Further Correspondence of John Ray* (London:
Ray Society, 1928), p. 259. Also cited in *ibid.,* p. 437.

disrupted the surface of the earth. His *New Theory of the Earth, from its Original to the Consummation of all Things, Wherein the Creation of the World in Six Days, the Universal Deluge, and the General Conflagration, as Laid Down in the Holy Scriptures, are Shown to be Perfectly Agreeable to Reason and Philosophy* (1696) won the praise of John Locke, the philosopher of reason, and of Newton, who was absorbed in trying to unravel the prophecies of Daniel and the apocalypse of St. John.[51]

By the end of the seventeenth century the fossil enigma had been brought into the mainstream of thought about cosmogony. In the humanist tradition, the writings of the ancients, the Church Fathers, and medieval scholars were searched for light on the problem, and the interpretation of observations of natural phenomena was mixed with previous ideas, but, in snowball fashion, the history of ideas on the subject of fossils was continued from writer to writer throughout the seventeenth century. The prejudices were perpetuated, but so too were the accumulating pieces of knowledge and the welter of solutions advanced to solve the fossil enigma. The first step towards such a solution was the unequivocal recognition of the organic origin of fossils, and this was all but achieved, through the study of specimens and their comparison with living counterparts, when the second step became clear, that is, recognizing fossils and fossil strata as the product of time and natural processes. As it became apparent that fossil evidence contradicted the time pattern of Mosaic history, naturalists hesitated, then retreated, before the theologically supported tradition. They turned to a re-examination of the conclusions of their first step, and the issue was carried unresolved over into the eighteenth century. In the meantime, while naturalists

---

[51] For the opinions of Locke and Newton, see *Encyclopaedia Britannica,* 11th ed., article on Whiston. Shortly after the publication of his *Theory,* Whiston embraced Arianism (the influence of Newton?) and was expelled from Cambridge. Newton was at this time working on *Observations upon Prophecies of Daniel, and the Apocalypse of St. John,* published posthumously by Benjamin Smith in 1733.

had been whittling at Mosaic history, there were other developments in seventeenth-century thought which threatened to completely cut Genesis out of cosmology.

CARTESIAN COSMIC EVOLUTION

The seventeenth century has often been called the age of genius, and this characterization was brilliantly exemplified in its contribution to the scientific revolution. It was an age of curiosity, activity, adventure, and bellicosity in which there was a strong impulse to conquer the unknown and reduce the universe to measurement and utility. Men of genius stepped forward to become intellectual, as well as economic, entrepreneurs, and their ability to exploit the natural resources of empirical data, to systematize and formulate it into general principles, and to integrate the principles as they were discovered into an organized and relatively unified world view led to the remodeling of cosmology. Theirs was the work of conquest, colonization, and settlement of a new world outlook, inaugurated by Copernicus and proclaimed by Giordano Bruno.

Through the voice of Albertino in the fifth dialogue of his work *On the Infinite Universe and Worlds* (1584), Bruno exclaims:

> Convince our minds of the infinite universe. Rend in pieces the concave and convex surfaces which would limit and separate so many elements and heavens. Pour ridicule on deferent orbs and on fixed stars. Break and hurl to earth with the resounding whirlwind of lively reasoning those fantasies of the blind and vulgar herd, the adamantine walls of the *primum mobile* and the ultimate sphere. Dissolve the notion that our earth is unique and central to the whole. Remove the ignoble belief in that fifth essence. Give to us knowledge that the composition of our

own star and world is even as that of as many other stars and worlds as we can see.[52]

The intrepid Bruno, fearing no barrier of crystal or glass, spread confident wings to space, soared to the infinite in his cosmological thought, and escaped from the "narrow murky prison" of medieval-Aristotelianism.[53] However, the vulgar herd, so loathed by Bruno, was on the move, reading the Bible, and pronouncing upon theology. It is doubtful if Bruno's voice would have been silenced by mere institutional authority, but he does seem to have taken for granted that he was under the protection of an ancient freedom of thought accorded to scholastics within the Church. In seeking the truth concerning Nature and the excellence of her Author, he wrote, theologians would readily condone the expression of true principles, since they were not being propounded for the ignorant. "This is why theologians no less learned than religious have never opposed the liberty of philosophers, while the true philosophers of civil worth and of good custom have ever fostered religions. For both sides know that faith is required for the rule of the rude populace who must be governed, while demonstration is for the contemplative who know how to govern themselves and others."[54] But the time had passed when a guild of professional thinkers could secretly discourse in writings passed only amongst themselves. The printing presses had taken care of that. Furthermore, heresy had broken out all around the Holy Office, and conspicuously so in the kingdom of Her most Serene Majesty the Queen of England, the heretic upon whom Bruno had bestowed praise in his books. The Church was faced with massive revolts and was not inclined to be tolerant of heresy coming from within the fold. On February 8, 1600, after eight years of trying to induce Bruno to recant, the Church pronounced Bruno a heretic. His martyrdom has served

[52] Dorothea Waley Singer, *Giordano Bruno, His Life and Thought* (New York, 1950), pp. 377-8.
[53] *Ibid.*, pp. 248-9—a paraphrase of sentences in his Introductory Epistle.
[54] *Ibid.*, pp. 264-5.

as a stirring memorial to the spirit of liberty against authority
ever since, no less than 634 publications in which Bruno figures
appeared in the nineteenth century alone.[55]

Still, the fact remains that Bruno was one of the last of the great
medieval scholastics, more akin to Abelard than Galileo. He had
pursued the idea of the omnipotence of God to its ultimate and
disdained the puny, finite, anthropomorphic medieval world view
as inconsistent with the great power of the Creative Spirit. Bruno
found in the atomistic cosmology of Democritus a more suitable
concept of the universe for the expression of his idea of an
Omnipotence which filled all being. He adapted it to his own
cosmology and rejected Aristotelianism and scriptural cosmology.[56] This same trend towards revamping cosmology to make
the universe seem more consistent with an all-powerful God was
also present in the cosmology of Nicolaus of Cusa and Copernicus,
and it reappeared in various forms in the succeeding centuries.

In Bruno, there can also be seen the transition from the tradition
of the nominalist branch of scholasticism to the modern scientific
methodology in the approach to the study of nature. According
to Bruno, the true philosopher must consider with the mind's eye
the foundations, principles, and reasons of a philosophy, after he
has examined the nature, the substance, and the peculiarity of
conflicting philosophies. Each must be weighed against the other
on the scales of the intellect, and their differences compared and
distinguished, before the truth can be found. This is the essence
of the comparative method which has proved to be so useful in
the progress of knowledge. The appeal to the evidence of "regu-
lated sensation" and "true phenomena" ("for these as trustworthy
ambassadors emerge from objects of Nature, rendering themselves present to those who seek them,"[57]) is made a part of his

[55] *Ibid.*, p. 200.
[56] See Angus Armitage, "The Cosmology of Giordano Bruno," *Annals of
Science*, vi (1948), 24-31.
[57] Singer, *op. cit.*, p. 230.

comparative method in the quest for truth, and so too is the critical spirit. For Bruno's ideal philosopher is not dazzled by the fame of authors placed in his hand, as is the case with those who content themselves with becoming expounders and commentators.

> But the others, by whom the received philosophy is clearly understood, have attained a point where they no longer propose to occupy the remainder of their days listening to others; they see by their own light, and with the activity of their mind's eye they penetrate every cranny; and Argus-like, with the eyes of their diverse knowledge they gaze through a thousand doorways on the aforesaid philosophy unveiled. Thus they will be able, on a nearer approach, to distinguish matters of belief accepted as truth on a distant view, by habit and by general consent, from that which truly is and must be accepted as certain, persistent in the very nature and substance of things. Truly, I say, they are ill able to accept our philosophy who have not the good fortune to be dowered with natural wit or are not at least tolerably familiar with diverse branches of knowledge; and especially they must have power of intellectual reflexion, whereby they can distinguish belief by faith from belief based on the evidence of true principles. For often an opinion is accepted as a principle that, if well considered, will be found to lead to an impossible conclusion, contrary to nature.[58]

Because of his mystical tendencies, Bruno was ill-suited for the actual task of overthrowing medieval cosmology. It was left for Galileo to rend in pieces, ridicule, and hurl to earth the crystalline spheres "on which are implanted, impressed, plastered, nailed, knotted, glued, sculptured or painted the stars." Galileo ridiculed the anthropomorphic belief that all creation was directed towards man, using the analogy of the sun shining on a grape to symbolize the relationship of God to man:

> Now if this grape receives all that it is possible for it to receive from the Sun, not suffering the least injury by the Sun's production of a thousand other effects at the same time, well

[58] *Ibid.*, p. 348.

might we accuse that grape of envy or folly if it should think
or wish that the Sun would appropriate all of its rays to its
advantage.[59]

The attack on anthropomorphism was an attack on Scripture
and the whole salvationist philosophy of Christianity, however
broadly phrased. The religionists, reformers as well as Catholics,
were little enough interested in the simplification that the Copernican heliocentric theory gave to the arrangement of epicycles.
Nor were they interested in extending the power of God to include a plurality of worlds. However, they were vitally interested
in the question posed by the new astronomy, "if the earth is not
at the center of the universe, what is man's position in the
hierarchy of creation?" Or, "if man is not the center of the universe, is he the center of God's purpose?"

As it became known, Kepler's theory that the heavenly bodies
moved in ellipses, instead of circles, also proved disturbing to
theologians and philosophers. The doctrine in Aristotelian physics
and cosmology that the perfect motion was circular had been
associated in the Christian mind with divinity itself. The sphericity
of the heavens and their circular motion corresponded to attributes of God—eternity, perfection, immutability, and ethereality.
Kepler's "breaking the circle" violated a widespread feeling about
the nature of Heaven itself, and many regarded it as a tragic
portent of impending doom.[60]

The hostile reaction of religious elements to the "new mechanical philosophy" and the action taken by the Congregation of the
Index against Galileo put a brake on untrammeled flights of speculation about cosmology. This was evident in the work of Descartes, whose system of philosophy was being worked out contemporaneously with Galileo's. Descartes was unquestionably on

---

[59] Galileo Galilei, *Dialogue on the Great World Systems,* ed. Giorgio de
Santillana (Chicago, 1953), p. 378.
[60] See Majorie Hope Nicolson, *The Breaking of the Circle: Studies in the
Effect of the New Science upon Seventeenth Century Poetry* (Evanston, Ill.,
1950).

dangerous ground with the Church when he advocated his corpuscular theory of matter, for his corpuscles or particles, once they had been called into being by the Creator, were at the mercy of mechanistic, if not deterministic forces. In popular medieval thought an anthropomorphic God was immanent and ever-active in the world, and in that branch of scholasticism represented by Nicolaus of Cusa and Giordano Bruno, God was immanent and active in an organically united universe too, but with Descartes God becomes merely the First Cause who created the materials and laws for the formation of the world, while the actual construction of the present world was left to the operation of secondary causes—natural laws. This was an important principle for the emancipation of science from theology, but one not likely to meet with the approval of the Church, so Descartes masked the process of formation behind the façade of Mosaic history and cosmogony.

Descartes wrote the substance of his theory about the formation of the world in *Le Monde, ou Traité de la Lumière,* but he withheld it from publication in 1633 upon learning of the condemnation of Galileo's work.[61] It was published posthumously in 1664, and in the meantime its essence was included in his *Principes de la Philosophie* (1644). Anxious to avoid antagonizing the Church, he unfolded his theory of creation in imaginary space:

> so that this infinity does not embarrass us, let us not try to go to the end; let us go only far enough to lose sight of all the creatures God made five or six thousand years ago, and after we have stopped there in some determined place, let us suppose that God created anew so much material around us that from any direction our imagination may extend it will not see any place that is void.[62]

[61] Descartes to Mersenne, July 22, 1633, in *Oeuvres de Descartes,* ed. Victor Cousin (Paris, 1824-6), VI, 238-9.
[62] *Le Monde,* in *ibid.,* IV, 247. Similar protestations of his belief in Scripture and disavowals that his system is anything more than speculative appear in *Les Principes,* esp. Part III, pars. 1 and 2. The description of the Cartesian system given below was taken from Part IV of *Les Principes.*

The Cartesian particles of matter had only quantitative characteristics. They had form, were impenetrable, and occupied space
in a universe without a void. When first put in motion they began a movement which gave rise to a group of whirlpools (*tourbil-
lons*), and out of these whirlpools the bodies in the solar system
took shape. Through friction, the particles of matter assumed
different shapes, some became extremely fine and constituted the
substance of fire and air, others were worn smooth and rod-shaped
and constituted fluids, while others remained irregular, even
branch-shaped, and these made up earthy matter.

Picking up the evolution of the Cartesian cosmos at the point
where the earth had taken shape, we see it as a core of fiery material surrounded by concentric layers of other kinds of material.
The outer surface was a hard, opaque crust and under it was a
layer of watery substance. The heat of the summer sun dried out
the crust until it was checkered with fissures, while the heat also
expanded the liquid in the next layer until part of it escaped
through the pores of the crust. In the ensuing winter, however,
the fissures were contracted until they blocked the return of the
watery element. The watery layer had also contracted, and the
result was that a vault-like space was left under the crust. Weakened by fissures and with no support under it, the crust collapsed.
Because of the smaller circumference at the base of the waters,
large sections of the crust came to rest at angles and their upraised
edges formed the mountains of the earth, while the water that
was forced out of its place became the seas of the world.

Descartes' theory that the earth passed through successive
stages in its formation, ending with the rupture of the outer crust
and the formation of the present topography of the earth, had a
powerful impact in cosmogony. First of all there was the idea of
evolution in the cosmos as a natural differentiating and combining process. It is the source of a succession of theories of cosmic
evolution. Again, the theory of a uniform series of layers in the
constitution of the earth was a fruitful way of thinking about the

earth's formation. Steno's work in stratigraphy appears to have been directly influenced by it. Descartes had referred to the segments of the earth's outer crust which had been the basis of mountains as a kind of primitive rock, and this idea was borrowed by Steno:

> If all the particles in a stony stratum are seen to be of the same character, and fine, it can in no wise be denied that this stratum was produced at the time of the creation from a fluid which at that time covered all things; and Descartes also accounts for the origin of the earth's strata in this way.[63]

Steno also used the idea of a "broken-crust" on a smaller scale to show how one formation of strata on the earth's surface is undermined and collapses to form rubble out of which secondary strata are composed. As one possible explanation for the way changes in strata might have occurred he suggests:

> The second process is the spontaneous slipping or downfall of the upper strata after they have begun to form cracks, in consequence of the withdrawal of the underlying substance, or foundation. Hence by reason of the diversity of the cavities and cracks the broken strata assume different positions; while some remain parallel to the horizon, others perpendicular to it, many form oblique angles with it, and not a few are twisted into curves because their substance is tenacious. This change can take place either in all the strata overlying a cavity, or in certain lower strata only, the upper strata being left unbroken.[64]

Another Cartesian concept that was important for geology was the fiery origin attributed to the earth. Since it was more easily observed, there was a tendency for the naturalist to regard water as the great causative agent in working geological changes. So it had been with Leonardo da Vinci and Bernard Palissy, and so it would remain under the philosophy of Neptunism, where it was reinforced by Mosaic history. The role of fiery gases had been

[63] *Prodromus, op. cit.*, p. 228.
[64] *Ibid.*, p. 231.

suggested by the ancients, notably Strato, and a fiery hell in the center of the earth was common to Christian thought, but Descartes was the first to give a plausible explanation for the existence of heat in the earth. Leibniz transformed this idea into an igneous theory for cosmogony, as will be shown later.

There was a great outcry against the cosmology of Descartes because of its mechanical determinism, but there was also a rising tide of rationalism, and Descartes was soon at the head of it. His rational system went beyond natural evidence, but it served as an intermediate scaffolding in the process of displacing the medieval Cosmos with a more scientific cosmology. It was also useful to those who wanted to rescue the corpus of Mosaic history from scepticism by making it more reasonable. "How to fit a supernaturalist and poetic scripture into a new world-scheme, how to reconcile Jehovah with the ontologically-certified *Dieu* of Descartes, and the whole miraculous structure of Christianity with the new 'philosophical' principles, this was a major problem confronting the critical intelligence of the age."[65]

The parallels indicated by Descartes between his system of cosmogony and that of Moses were probably an artificial device of the man of genius who had to stoop to the prejudices of his age in order to give a safe conduct to his intellectual construct, but the pragmatic rationalists who were busy with scriptural exegesis took the parallels seriously and tried to use them to vindicate Moses.

Rational exegesis was not absent in the Middle Ages, but the authority of the Church and tradition and the rather free use of allegory to get around difficult passages had kept the text out of undue controversy. However, fresh importance was given to the text when the reformers forced Scripture into the focus of attention by basing dogma upon it. And as the reformers set off to carry Faith forward, Reason, the camel upon which the burden

[65] Basil Willey, *The Seventeenth Century Background*, new ed. (New York, 1953), p. 65.

of faith was borne, began to nudge the reformers out of their spiritual tent.

The Renaissance humanists had done much in establishing the techniques of historical research and textual criticism, and they had, of course, played an important role in the shaping of the Reformation by the restoration of the sources of primitive Christianity. They had made available many new manuscripts of the Bible, as well as those of classical works, and the reformers had a diversity of texts to choose from when they tried to answer simple questions about the "plain meaning" of Scripture. They were faced, first of all, with the task of determining what was the pure text revealed by God, upon which the "plain meaning" could be based.

The Roman Catholic Church had used Jerome's Latin Vulgate, although its need of emendation and correction had long been recognized. Luther claimed that this version contained noncanonical books, and, since he believed that God had spoken in the Hebrew language, he asserted that it could hardly be the pure text. He and Protestants in general favored the Hebrew text at first, but they were not long satisfied with it. The Septuagint and Aramaic texts were also available to choose from, but all the texts, and also manuscripts of each, varied from one another. The problem still remained of establishing the pure text.

Protestant and Catholic scholars turned to the exacting research needed to solve the problem. They studied the original languages of the texts, they pondered questions of authorship and transmission, and they sought light from outside the Bible for an understanding of what was meant within it. A succession of great scholars emerged to grapple with the text of the Bible. Their story has been brilliantly told by Professor Don Allen in his *The Legend of Noah, Renaissance Rationalism in Art, Science, and Letters*, who remarks, "The methods of historical scholarship showed that the Scriptures were filled with many inconsistencies and that they deviated widely from what seemed to be the correct annals of mankind. The new methods of science were at first brought to the defense of Scripture, but it was shortly discovered that the more the Bible was defended by science, the more it had to be defended."[66]

Every detail in Genesis came under scrutiny. To paraphrase Bruno, Genesis was exposed to the activity of the mind's eye penetrating every cranny, and it was unveiled before the eyes of diverse knowledge gazing upon it through a thousand doorways. Great debates arose, first over Biblical chronology, and then over the Noachian Flood, the dispersion of peoples, and confusion of tongues at Babel. The traditions and legends of the ancients were examined in connection with these problems, and also the traditions and legends of the various peoples of the world that the travelers and explorers were meeting. Comparative mythology began to flourish. The tradition of floods was found everywhere, and this seemed to support the Flood of Noah, but the traditions of the ancients and of the Chinese did not bear out Biblical chronology. Doubts began to appear about the universality of the Hebrew chronology. Perhaps the Egyptian, Babylonian, and Chinese claims to a long history were not fantastical. Perhaps Mosaic history was derivative and not the original from which all others were borrowed. Perhaps the Hebrews were only writing the annals of their own nation, hence the Flood was a local affair. Every doubt must be put down, and in doing it, the conservative defenders of orthodoxy frequently became revolutionary innovators. Most of the doubts were well-intended rationalizations at

---

[66] Allen, *The Legend of Noah*, p. 3. An excellent collection of excerpts from sixteenth-, seventeenth-, and eighteenth-century works on the subject of chronology, interspersed with many keen insights by the author, is Heinrich Meyer's *The Age of the World, A Chapter in the History of Enlightenment* (multigraphed at Muhlenberg College, Allentown, Pa., 1951). A scarce, but useful, work on this subject, although written by an exegete, is Otto Zoeckler, *Geschichte der Beziehungen zwischen Theologie und Naturwissenschaft, mit besondrer Rücksicht auf Schöpfungsgeschichte*, 2 v. (Gütersloh, 1877-9). (Copy at Yale University Library.)

their inception, but the sheer flux of questioning and explaining threatened to destroy the reputation of the Bible as a revealed work, and out of the resulting study it was certainly established that all texts were derivative, that there was no "pure" text. The ransacking of history, the comparing of cultures, and the search for relics of the deluge (fossils) broadened the historical and cultural base for textual criticism—leading in the cases of Hobbes, Spinoza, and Simon to the examination of Scripture as an evolved human document—while preoccupation with Biblical questions centered the increments to knowledge and the awareness of changes in the past around the universal chronology of the Biblical exegetes, even as this chronology was itself being subjected to criticism.

Underlying the rational exegesis of Biblical scholars and the geological research of naturalists like Steno, Ray, Lhywd, Plot, Lister, Cole, Woodward, etc., was the desire to bring Revelation into harmony with Nature—to make the Word of God agree with the Works of God—or to find in the works a verification of the Word. One of the most popular of these attempts to explain Mosaic history rationally was Thomas Burnet's *Sacred Theory of the Earth*, first published in Latin in 1681, expanded in English in 1684, and often printed in England and abroad down to the early nineteenth century. Its author, an erudite English divine, had a robust style, a vivid imagination, and an ingenious theory. As long as the Western world remained Biblically oriented, it was a minor classic, known far and wide.

The *Sacred Theory* was based upon II Peter 3, and particularly verse 13: "Nevertheless we, according to his promise, look for new heavens and a new earth, wherein dwelleth righteousness." It is interesting that Burnet should select this verse of St. Peter as a basis for expounding Mosaic history, but he makes his reasons clear. The *Theory* is a work on the coming millenium as well as on the past and is divided into two parts accordingly. The first book concerns the Deluge and the dissolution of the earth, the

second book, the primaeval earth and Paradise. The two last books
are on the fulfillment of prophecy—the burning of the world and
the new heavens and new earth. It is a complete history of the
earth from beginning to end. The prophecy of a millenium in St.
Peter was also used against those who argued that there had been
no changes in nature or in the world from the beginning to this
time—important eschatologically because, otherwise why should
we think there will be any change in the future? In Burnet it is
possible to see the transfer of Christian eschatological thought on
time and process to the natural world. He strongly contested the
view of Mosaic history which held that the earth was unchanged
from its creation, and St. Peter was his authority.

One thing that the Biblical outlook did for the seventeenth-
century man was to orient his thinking towards seeking the origin
of things, and then to trace their subsequent history. Burnet com-
mences his *Theory* thus:

> Since I was first inclin'd to the Contemplation of Nature,
> and took pleasure to trace out the Causes of Effects, and the
> dependence of one thing upon another in the visible Creation,
> I had always, methought, a particular curiosity to look back
> into the Sources and ORIGINAL of Things; and to view in my
> Mind, so far as I was able, the Beginning and Progress of a
> RISING WORLD.
> And after some Essays of this Nature, and, as I thought, not
> unsuccessful, I carried on my enquiries further, to try whether
> this Rising World, when form'd and finish'd, would continue
> always the same; in the same form, structure, and consistency;
> or what changes it would successively undergo, by the con-
> tinued action of the same Causes that first produc'd it. . . .[67]

The revolution in astronomy had begun to push the coverage
of Mosaic history into a narrower circle, and this was clearly
recognized by Burnet, who remarked, "But when we speak of a
Rising World, and the Contemplation of it, we do not mean this

[67] Thomas Burnet, *The Theory of the Earth* [Telluris Theoria Sacra] . . . ,
3rd ed. (London, 1697), Bk. I, p. 1.

of the *Great Universe;* for who can describe the Original of that vast Frame? But we speak of the *Sublunary World,* This Earth and its Dependencies, which rose out of a Chaos about Six Thousand Years ago. . . ."[68] He does not even deny that there might be a plurality of inhabited worlds, and asserts firmly that all Nature was not made for man, but only the sublunary world—the most insignificant of them all, one suitable for an insignificant creature.

In unfolding his theory of the world's progress, Burnet applied a concept of dualism, borrowed from Descartes, to history. Natural Providence governed the progress of the natural world wherein "God made all Things in *Number, Weight* and *Measure,* which are Geometrical and Mechanical Principles."[69] Geometry and mechanics are the true principles of the philosophy of Natural Providence. Running parallel to Natural Providence was Sacred or Divine Providence which was concerned with the rewards and punishments of the Moral World. As God had constantly to intervene in the Cartesian system of mind and body to keep their functioning coordinated, so God kept Natural and Sacred Providence in correspondence:

> Now seeing both in the intellectual and corporeal World there are certain Periods, Fulnesses of Time, and fixt Seasons, either for some great Catastrophe, or some great Instauration; 'tis Providence that makes a due Harmony or Synchronism betwixt these two, and measures out the concurrent Fates of both Worlds, so as Nature may be always a faithful Minister of the divine Pleasure, whether for Rewards or Punishments, according as the State of Mankind may require.[70]

Burnet's task, then, was to make an exegesis on the Book of Nature which would parallel his exegesis on the Books of Scripture. Since the *Theory* was chiefly philosophical, reason was to be the first guide and where that fell short, further light could be

[68] *Ibid.,* p. 2.
[69] *Ibid.,* Bk. ii, p. 216.
[70] *Ibid.,* Bk. ii, p. 221.

gained from the Sacred Writings. By means of these two in-
strumentalities we could determine something about Natural and
Sacred Providence. Literal statements in Scripture, empirical facts
to the seventeenth-century mind, could not be denied or contradicted, but then, neither could the empirical facts of Nature.
When these two sets of facts clashed, there must have been a
misunderstanding of Reason or Scripture.

> Both these are to be lookt upon as of Divine Original, God is
> the author of both; he that made the Scripture made also our
> Faculties, and 'twere a Reflection upon the Divine Veracity for
> the one or the other to be false when rightly us'd. We must
> therefore be careful and tender of opposing these to one an-
> other, because, that is, in effect, to oppose God to himself.[71]

The key to harmony between reason and revelation was the expression "when rightly us'd," and it was, of course, the open door
to fantastic theories. There was one other source of evidence for
Burnet's *Theory*, the classical heritage, also to be "rightly us'd."
"I know no other Guide," wrote Burnet, "but one of these three,
Scripture, Reason, and ancient Tradition; and where the two
former are silent, it seems very reasonable to consult the third."[72]
The truths behind ancient tradition were obscure since they were
written in a primitive stage of civilization when people spoke
through heroic poems, myths and folklore, but with the light of
a clear theory it was possible to distinguish truths from fictions in
the storehouse of tradition.[73]

In bringing the parallel tracks of Sacred and Natural Providence
into harmony, Burnet relegated God to the part of playwright of
a drama. The play took place on a little spot of time lying between
two oceans of eternity, "before the world" and "after the world."
The scenery and props, Nature, were designed to run flawlessly
throughout the drama like a mechanism, because:

[71] *Ibid.*, Bk. I, p. 4.
[72] *Ibid.*, Bk. II, p. 173.
[73] *Ibid.*, Bk. II, p. 180.

We think him a better Artist that makes a Clock that strikes regularly at every Hour from the Springs and Wheels which he puts in the Work, than he that hath so made his Clock that he must put his Finger to it every Hour to make it strike.[74]

The main acts of the drama were Paradise, the Deluge, the Burning of the World, and the New Heavens and New Earth. Scripture was the play, man the actor, good and evil the conflict, and the worship of God the climax towards which the drama was moving.

All I say, betwixt the first Chaos and the last Completion of Time and all Things temporary, this is given to the Disquisitions of Men; On either hand is Eternity, before the World and after, which is without our reach: But that little spot of Ground that lies betwixt those two great Oceans, this we are to cultivate, this we are Masters of, herein we are to exercise our Thoughts, to understand and lay open the Treasures of the Divine Wisdom and Goodness hid in this part of Nature and of Providence.[75]

Viewing the world as a huge mechanism carried with it the danger of interpreting the world as eternal, but Burnet's dualistic approach enabled him to expand the Cartesian historical view of nature and thereby protect Biblical time. Attacking the idea of an eternal world, Burnet wrote:

... only *Aristotle*, whom so great a part of the Christian World have made their Oracle or Idol, hath maintain'd the Eternity of the Earth, and the Eternity of Mankind; that the Earth and the World were from Everlasting, and in that very Form they are in now, with Men and Women and all living Creatures, Trees and Fruit, Metals and Minerals, and whatsoever is of natural Production. We say all these things arose and had their first Existence or Production not six thousand Years ago.[76]

In support of his contention that this was a created world

[74] *Ibid.*, Bk. I, p. 72.
[75] *Ibid.*, Bk. I, p. 4.
[76] *Ibid.*, Bk. I, p. 23.

Burnet advanced proofs from Scripture. Then turning to Reason
he resuscitated the classic argument from geology that the present
surface inequalities would have long since been leveled if the
earth had stood forever. Another proof of the newness of the
earth he found in the progress of civilization; a point which had
already been made many times previously in the century:

> All History, and all Monuments of Antiquity of what kind
> soever, are but of a few thousand of Years date; we have still
> the Memory of the golden Age, of the first state of Nature,
> and how Mortals liv'd then in Innocency and Simplicity. The
> Invention of Arts even those that are necessary or useful to
> Humane Life, hath been within the Knowledge of Men: How
> imperfect was the Geography of the Ancients, how imperfect
> their Navigation? Can we imagine, if there had been Men from
> Everlasting, a Sea as now, and all Materials for Shipping as
> much as we have, that Men could have been so ignorant, both
> of the Land and of the Sea, as 'tis manifest they have been till
> of late Ages? [77]

Along with the progress of the arts and sciences, the growth
of population was an additional proof of the newness of the earth.
If the earth had been from everlasting, it would be so overstocked
with inhabitants by now that it could not contain them. Instead,
we find that the earth is not yet sufficiently inhabited and there is
room for more millions. Both in human achievement and in population there is still nothing completed, indeed their rate of progress
is advancing more rapidly now than in all the former ages put
together, and he asked, "How unlikely is it then that these Ages
were Eternal?" [78]

The main epochs in the history of the earth and its chronology
were drawn from Scripture in Burnet's *Theory*, but the mechanics
were taken from Descartes. During the Chaos all matter was without form or order and its particles were confusedly mingled in a
fluid mass. The first change was a settling out of the heaviest and

[77] *Ibid.*, Bk. i, p. 27.
[78] *Ibid.*, Bk. i, p. 29.

grossest parts into a ball to form the core of the earth. The remainder of the chaotic matter divided into liquid and volatile layers around the core. The liquid layer further separated into oils and water with the oily part rising to the surface of the watery part. The volatile layer consisted mostly of air, but it was filled with terrestrial particles swimming about. These began to settle and fall like snow on the oily liquid, making a "certain slime, or fat, soft and light Earth."[79] The earth gained consistency and became a moist, fertile soil in which vegetation grew luxuriantly.

> In this smooth Earth were the first scenes of the World, and the first Generation of Mankind; it had the Beauty of Youth and blooming Nature, fresh and fruitful, and not a Wrinkle, Scar or Fracture in all its body; no Rocks nor Mountains, no hollow Caves, nor gaping Channels, but even and uniform all over.[80]

It was upon this fruitful soil that Paradise was situated. There was no winter in Paradise, only a perpetual spring, for the earth's axis had no inclination to the sun's. The epoch of Paradise was brought to an end by the sinfulness of man, but the preparation for the fateful day proceeded along natural lines. The sun dried the earth more and more, seaming it with fissures, while the heat from the sun penetrated below into the liquids of the underlying watery layer, or abyss. The rarefaction of the waters created a strong pressure upwards. When the hour of punishment arrived, rain fell heavily. Water ran into the fissures of the earth, softening it, and stopping the escape vents of the vapors below. The vapors struggled more violently to escape, then, "the whole fabrick brake, and the frame of the Earth was torn in pieces, as by an Earthquake; and those great portions or fragments, into which it was divided, fell down into the Abysse, some in one posture, and some in another."[81] Huge chunks of crust falling

[79] *Ibid.*, Bk. I, p. 39.
[80] *Ibid.*, Bk. I, p. 47.
[81] *Ibid.*, Bk. I, p. 50.

into the waters of the abyss hurled waves over even the highest upended parts. So it came to pass that the fountains of the great deep were broken up and the windows of heaven opened in the Burnet version of Genesis.

As the great pieces of concave crust fell into the abyss they trapped air under them, and when the fragments finally settled into a firm position air escaped and was replaced by water. Filling these air pockets allowed the waters to recede, first revealing the tops of newly made mountains, and then high ground. "Thus a new World appear'd, or the Earth put on its new form, and became divided into Sea, and Land; and the Abysse, which from several Ages, even from the beginning of the world, had lain hid in the womb of the Earth, was brought to light and discover'd." [82]

In explaining how the present geography of the world resulted from the break-up of the crust in the Deluge, Burnet suggested that continents were large pieces of crust. [83] These fragments could not descend as fast in the middle as at the extremities because of the air underneath. The edges would come down first, parachute-fashion, and bending the fragment in such a manner decreased the area it would cover on the underlying surface. Spaces would then lie uncovered between the fragments, and these spaces became the channels of the oceans lying between continents. The fact that the crust had a greater circumference than the underlying body was offset by the manner of its collapse. Once the edges of the fragments were firmly fixed, further collapse of the large fragments forced a crumpling effect in the continental crusts and gave rise to mountain ranges. In view of the limited knowledge available to him, Burnet's explanation of the topography of the earth was indeed plausible.

The break-up of the earth's crust redistributed the weight of the earth in Burnet's system, inclined the axis of the earth, and

[82] *Ibid.*, Bk. I, p. 53.
[83] *Ibid.*, Bk. I, p. 90ff.

introduced the seasons. Comparing the earth to an evenly trimmed and ballasted ship sailing about the sun, Burnet remarked,

> So particularly the Earth, which makes one in that Aery Fleet, when it 'scaped so narrowly from being shipwrackt in the great Deluge, was however so broken and disorder'd, that it lost its equal Poise, and thereupon the Center of its Gravity changing, one Pole became more inclin'd towards the Sun, and the other more remov'd from it, and so its right and parallel Situation which it had before to the Axis of the Ecliptick, was chang'd into an oblique; in which skew Posture it hath stood ever since, and is likely so to do for some Ages to come.[84]

The change of seasons had a baleful effect on mankind. The human body, Burnet thought, was like a watch, the stomach and heart being its mainsprings. The seasons introduced stresses and strains on these springs and consequently shortened human life so that postdiluvian men had a far shorter span of life than the Patriarchs. By this means Burnet tried to explain one of the stumbling blocks to a rationalization of Genesis. Some had suggested that the six to nine hundred year ages of the Patriarchs was the result of a different method of computing years, but Burnet would not brook any shortening of sacred chronology. Neither would he tolerate an extension of it. Against those who would have mountains made out of a succession of earthquakes or volcanos, he queried, "how many thousand Ages must be allow'd to them to do their work, more than the Chronology of our Earth will bear?"[85] Burnet stood firm on the validity of the genealogies in Genesis. "The Scripture sets down the precise Age of a series of Antediluvian Patriarchs, and by that measures the time from the beginning of the World to the Deluge; so as all Sacred Chronology stand upon that bottom."[86]

Burnet supposed that after the Deluge a long period of adjust-

[84] *Ibid.*, Bk. ii, p. 134.
[85] *Ibid.*, Bk. i, p. 108.
[86] *Ibid.*, Bk. ii, p. 124.

ment set in as the rubble of crust fragments settled and water
found its way into the air pockets and subterranean cavities still
left. This caused a steady retreat of the sea from age to age.

> We see whole Countries of Land gain'd from it, and by several
> Indications, as ancient Seaports left dry and useless, old Sea-
> marks far within the Land, Pieces of Ships, Anchors, &c. left at
> a great Distance from the present Shores; from these Signs, and
> such like, we may conclude that the Sea reach'd many Places
> formerly that now are dry Land, and at first I believe was gen-
> erally bound in on either Side with a Chain of Mountains.[87]

Looking at the present earth from the moon it would appear as
a vast ruins. Upon closer examination of the ruins they would
resemble a shallow stream into which the arch of a broken bridge
had fallen with parts submerged and other parts out of the water.
"You may see there the Image of all these things in little Continents, and Islands, and Rocks under Water: And in the Parts that
stand above the Water, you see Mountains, and Precipices, and
Plains, and most of the Varieties that we see and admire in the
Parts of the Earth."[88] We were now living in the stage of history
somewhere between the catastrophe which led to this ruins of an
earth and another catastrophe which would restore the earth to
its primitive state of Paradise.

The second half of Burnet's *Theory* was devoted to prophecy
instead of history. He discussed millenial literature at length and
mustered proofs that the earth would be subjected to a tremendous conflagration of fire in the near future. The heavens
would be shut up and no rain would fall. Springs would dry out,
the earth would become parched and dry, and fires in volcanic
mountains would kindle the conflagration. Lakes of pitch, oily
liquors, sulphurous materials, and coal would feed the fires. The
drouth would have reduced the oceans to stagnant pools, but
when the heat and hot oils of the burning earth struck them they

[87] *Ibid.*, Bk. 1, p. 69.
[88] *Ibid.*, Bk. 1, p. 75.

would turn into boiling cauldrons which would further add to the destruction of the earth. The outer layer of the earth would be leveled and liquefied, making the "sea of glass mingled with fire" of the Apocalypse come true.

Burnet pictured a new world forming out of the old one through the settling out of parts into layers, as had happened at creation. Becoming perfectly round again, the earth would assume its former position with its poles parallel to those of the sun, and eternal spring would ensue. The new world would be peopled by the righteous resurrected from the dead and would be ruled over by the Messiah. The little island of time in the oceans of eternity had been traversed and its end reached.

Burnet thought it improbable that the time of the millenium could be determined accurately, but he had no doubt that it would be at the end of a sexmillenial duration of the earth. The problem was to find the point of commencement. The mistake of the Church Fathers who expected the conflagration in their own time, he thought, was the result of their reliance on the Septuagint text rather than the Hebrew. When the terminal period approached he was confident that there would be signs and portents of it.

The millenial aspect of Burnet's *Theory* was in full accord with the interests of the period, even among scientists. It was what Burnet's contemporary, Joseph Glanvill, would have called one of "the usual assumptions of contemporary good sense." It shows how deeply entrenched the concept of Biblical time was in the consciousness of the seventeenth century while the spatial aspects of the universe were being reduced to geometry and mechanics. Had Burnet written only of Sacred Providence, his *Theory* would have taken its place with numerous other theological tracts of the time noted now only for their dull mediocrity. However, his dualistic approach to Providence left Nature quite free of supernaturalism and he specifically warned against using the First Cause (God) when second causes (natural laws) would suffice. He had demonstrated to the satisfaction of theologians that God

had a watchful eye on Nature, but God was sufficiently remote
from ordinary operations to guarantee that the design He had
imposed on natural productions could only be understood on
rational principles.[89] Burnet's debt to Descartes was indirectly
acknowledged in the following statement:

> An eminent Philosopher of this Age, *Monsieur des Cartes*,
> hath made use of the like *Hypothesis* to explain the irregular
> Form of the present Earth; though he never dream'd of the
> Deluge, nor thought that first Orb, built over the Abyss, to
> have been any more than a transient Crust, and not a real
> habitable World that lasted for more than sixteen hundred
> Years, as we suppose it to have been. And though he hath, in
> my Opinion, in the Formation of that first Orb, and upon the
> Dissolution of it, committed some great Oversights, . . . he saw a
> Necessity of such a Thing, and of the Disruption of it, to
> bring the Earth into that Form and Posture wherein we now
> find it.[90]

Burnet's rationalization of Genesis on the Cartesian plan helped
to advance ideas about the manner of creation as a natural process,
from a static decree of God's will to a dynamic differentiation of
a mass of chaotic matter into parts arranged in geometrical patterns through natural laws. Genesis provided the historical sequence for the differentiation, but it served only as an outline in a
detailed history of the earth. The more or less abrupt epochs of
the Mosaic creation gave way to the idea of gradual progression
and geological evolution.

> But when we say the Earth rises from a Fluid Mass, it is not
> to be so crudely understood, as if a rock of Marble, suppose,
> was fluid immediately before it became Marble; no, Things
> had a gradual Progression from one Form to another, and came
> at length to those more permanent Forms they are now settled
> in: Stone was once Earth, and Earth was once Mud, and Mud
> was once fluid. And so other Things may have another kind of
> Progression from Fluidity; but all was once Fluid, at least all

[89] *Ibid.*, Bk. ii, pp. 215-6.
[90] *Ibid.*, Bk. i, p. 77.

the exterior Regions of this Earth. And even those Stones and Rocks of Marble which we speak of, seem to confess they were once soft or liquid, by those Mixtures we find in them of heterogeneous Bodies, and those Spots and Veins disperst thorough [sic] their Substance; for these Things could not happen to them after they were hard and impenetrable, in the Form of Stone or Marble. And if we can soften Rocks and Stones, and run them down into their first Liquors, as these Observations seem to do, we may easily believe that other Bodies also that compose the Earth were once in a fluid Mass, which is that we call a Chaos.[91]

Throughout the *Theory*, Burnet was insistent that Nature, under the guidance of natural Providence was undergoing steady changes, and that it was a pious enterprise to discover them. He suggested that better histories of the early ages be compiled and that natural maps, as distinguished from civil maps, should be drawn up to show the skeleton of the earth in all its parts.[92]

Erasmus Warren, in *Geologia: or a discourse concerning the earth before the deluge* (London, 1690), attacked Burnet because his theory of evolution of the earth would have taken more time than the six days mentioned in Genesis. Burnet had afterthoughts himself, and in his *Archaeologiae Philosophicae* (1692) he treated the Mosaic account of history as an allegory and abandoned the Biblical age of the world as inadequate. The clamour that went up against Burnet forced the king to remove him from his theological office, but the *Sacred Theory* continued to grow in popularity and its picture of geologic evolution around Genesis gave the diluvian interpretation of fossils a tremendous impetus in the eighteenth century, particularly among the many English divines who pursued geology and paleontology as a pastime, thinking that their exploration of the "ruins" of a former world was revealing witnesses in the Works of God of the tragic event described in the Word of God.

[91] *Ibid.*, Bk. II, pp. 221-2.
[92] *Ibid.*, Bk. I, p. 97.

As various writers expounded on cosmology they illustrated their points by analogies drawn from observation and experience. Comparing the earth's surface to a ruined bridge in a stream was undoubtedly drawn from a real observation by Burnet. At other points he fell back on his classical learning to use the doctrine of the Mundane Egg, comparing the yolk to the inner core of the earth, the white to the watery abyss, and the shell to the crust of the earth. And what could be more natural than for an Englishman to liken the earth to a ship sailing in an "Aery Fleet?" From the mining districts of Germany a new set of analogies was introduced into cosmology by Leibniz. Drawing upon his knowledge of metallurgy and the chemical laboratory, he developed a neglected element of geological theory—the concept of a molten earth whose cooling gave rise to the crust on its surface.

Leibniz was commissioned by the Brunswick-Luneburg family to write a history setting forth royal claims. The history occupied his attention off and on for over thirty years, and when he died it extended only from A.D. 768 to 1005. Research for the history furnished him with materials for many studies outside genealogy and carried him from Germany to Italy examining sources. Either in Italy about 1674 or in Saxony after 1674 he met Steno, and their conversations may have aroused the interest of Leibniz in the problems Steno discussed in *Prodromus*. At any rate, Leibniz decided, "in order to show the remotest origin of our state, we must say something about the first configuration of the earth, of the nature of the soil and what it contains."[93] The result was that he commenced his history of a Germanic House with a preamble, *Protogaea* (1691), setting forth the story of Brunswick and Hanover geology from the time of creation. Al-

[93] Gottfried Wilhelm Leibniz, *Protogée ou de la formation et des révolutions du globe*, ed. Bertrand de Saint-Germain (Paris, 1859), p. 1. The appointment of Leibniz as court historian followed a quixotic attempt to institute new mining procedures in Germany. An account of the mining experiment is given in R. W. Mayer, *Leibniz and the Seventeenth-Century Revolution* (Chicago, 1952), p. 108ff.

though the *Protogaea* was not published until 1749, when a Latin edition appeared at Gottingen edited by Louis Scheidt, a two-page resumé appeared in *Acta Eruditorum* for January, 1693, a learned review published at Leipzig.

The review in *Acta Eruditorum* presented the essentials of Leibniz's theory, but few details, and in this form it did not exert much influence. In *Protogaea* itself, Leibniz asserted that the initial fact presented at the origin of things was the separation of light and darkness. Savants had established that vast globes, luminous like fixed stars or the sun, after reaching their last stage of boiling were covered with slag and scum which veiled their light with a hard crust. The formation of the planets and the earth took place in this manner, Leibniz thought, and the divorce of light and darkness described by Moses referred to the veiling of the earth's luminosity by an opaque crust.

While the earth was still incandescent, water was in a vaporized state around it, but when the cooled crust enclosed the heat of the molten mass, the vapors condensed as they came in contact with the outer surface. The waters dissolved chemicals in the crust to form the fixed salts in the seas, and erosive forces reduced the earthy and vitreous outer crust into sands, clays, and other substances of an inorganic nature. Leibniz wrote:

> you will easily understand that glass is in some form the base of the earth, and that it is mostly hidden under the mask of other bodies, its particles having been variously corroded and divided either by the dissolving and movement of the waters, or by repeated sublimations and distillations to the point where the action of the salts, in addition to that of fire, have reduced the hard bodies into a slime fit to nourish plants and animals and has produced volatile bodies.[94]

By glass, Leibniz had in mind the scoria which formed on the surface of metals being fused in the furnaces, rather than our clear window glass or crystal. Sand, however, approached clear glass in

[94] *Protogée*, p. 6.

appearance, and this considerable part of the earth, Leibniz thought, was something that fire could have easily produced if the necessary salts were not lacking when it was formed.

Comparing the cooling of the earth to that of melted metals, Leibniz suggested that the earth's crust was left with enormous bubbles on its surface, some of which hardened into mountains with cavities of air or water under them, while others collapsed to leave valleys. (The feasibility of this suggestion is illustrated by the pockmarked surface of the moon.) When the vaults enclosing the water were broken, inundations would occur, and the resulting rubbish would be deposited in various places as a sediment. The continued destructive operations of exploding gases, water, and corrosion continued the process of sedimentation until many beds had been superimposed on the face of the earth. The result was a double origin of solid bodies, "at first by their cooling after the igneous fusion, and then, by the new aggregations after their solution in the waters."[95] It was not necessary to believe that stones arose only from fusion, Leibniz took pains to point out. It was the first masses and the base of the earth that had an igneous formation, while other stone was formed by the sedimentation and hardening of materials deposited by water in the superimposed beds. He suggested that when the curiosity of men had led them to examine and describe the terrain and strata of various countries the details of formation would be better understood.

After the separation of light from darkness by veiling the fiery earth with a crust, the earth was covered by waters. This was supported, Leibniz held, by Scripture, ancient tradition, and the traces the sea has left in the middle of the land, such as shells, amber, and *glossopetrae*. To explain the causes of the Deluge he discounted those theories which were in opposition to Scripture, "from which we must not deviate," and suggested:

[95] *Ibid.*, p. 9.

we can certainly help ourselves with some reflections of an
ingenious author who has recently given the sacred Theory of
the earth, and who considers the mountains and valleys as
formed by debris, and we are not neglecting the writings of
the savants whom he has provoked to research; but already,
Steno, after having visited a notable part of Europe and collected from diverse sides observations on the composition of
the terrestrial crust, had conceived, touching the debris of the
first ages and the sediments left by the waters, ideas which differed little from theirs.[96]

Leibniz was willing to admit some kind of collapse of vaults
into depths of water as the cause of the Deluge, borrowing from
Steno and Burnet, but he had little conviction as to the correct-
ness of the view. It was a hurdle in cosmology which he had to
make for the sake of consistency with Scripture. Leibniz's cos-
mical theory, in the judgment of Karl Alfred von Zittel, was
"strained on account of the author's conscientious effort to present a historical account of the earth's surface that should be in
harmony with the Mosaic genesis."[97] His handling of the Deluge
bears out Zittel, but the remainder of Leibniz's essay is one of the
outstanding works on geology and paleontology of the century.
Like Leonardo da Vinci's earlier work on fossils, it was unfortu-
nate that the *Protogaea* was not more extensively known at the
time of its writing. Leibniz's voice in support of Steno's would
have gone a long way in dispelling the belief that fossils were
sports of nature, and his picture of repeated inundations in Northern Europe would have hastened the recognition of his conclusion that nature "fills up the gaps of history for us."[98] The rich
content of natural evidence and natural operations which Leibniz
wove around the Cartesian-Mosaic framework of cosmic evolution tied natural history—then a term which had little more than
a descriptive meaning—to historical process. The genealogy of

[96] *Ibid.*, p. 18.
[97] *History of Geology and Paleontology* (London, 1901), p. 28.
[98] *Ibid.*, p. 133.

the House of Brunswick had been extrapolated back to the Creation.

Although the influence of *Protogaea* was not widespread, it was profound at a later date on the thinking of Buffon, whose *Epochs of Nature,* as we shall see, attempted to establish a chronology of cosmic evolution. Leibniz's natural history researches may have had an effect on the formulation of his concepts of the chain-of-being, the doctrine of continuity, and the monad, and the association seems to have been indirectly amplified as these concepts were developed in the eighteenth century in connection with living nature by Buffon and Maupertuis. The intellectual heritage, from which Leibniz could have drawn these ideas, reaches back to the scholastics, but it is quite possible that the organic approach to nature expressed by so many others in the ancient heritage seemed convincing to Leibniz in part because of his study of fossils. The sheer mass of remains of organic matter which had come to his attention may have emphasized in his mind the productive power of living nature, and this at a time when the mechanical philosophers were preoccupied with abstract "dead" matter and motion. Also, Leibniz had recognized in the fossil masses extinct species and the fine gradations between species, which presented an observational confirmation of the continuities in the chain of being, with the loss of some species explaining the existing gaps.

Although Cartesian cosmology was destined to be displaced by Newton's system, Newton brought strong logical evidence to the support of the essential idea in Cartesian cosmogony that the earth had been evolved, and at the same time suggested something analogous to the Cartesian theory about the constitution of the inner earth. The subterranean world had always been the subject of the wildest flights of fancy and imagination. The view of Lucretius was well known:

> Now come, and what the law of earthquakes is
> Hearken, and first of all take care to know

> That the under-earth, like to the earth around us,
> Is full of windy caverns all about;
> And many a pool and many a grim abyss
> She bears within her bosom, ay, and cliffs
> And jagged scarps; and many a river, hid
> Beneath her chine, rolls rapidly along
> Its billows and plunging boulders. For clear fact
> Requires that earth must be in every part
> Alike in constitution.[99]

Seneca's picture of the subterrannean world was similar to that of Lucretius and was influential throughout the Middle Ages and Renaissance:

> Beneath the earth likewise there are laws of nature, less familiar to us, but no less fixed. Be assured that there exists below everything that you see above. There, too, there are antres vast, immense recesses, and vacant spaces, with mountains overhanging on either hand. There are yawning gulfs stretching down into the abyss, which have often swallowed up cities that have fallen into them, and have buried in their depths their mighty ruins. These retreats are filled with air, for nowhere is there a vacuum in nature; through their ample spaces stretch marshes over which darkness ever broods. Animals also are produced in them, but they are slow-paced and shapeless; the air that conceived them is dark and clammy, the waters are torpid through inaction.[100]

A straightforward analogy between the inner earth and its outer surface was the characteristic of these classical views, but there was also the theological conception of the fires of hell and the damned. Dante's representation of the infernal regions in the *Divine Comedy* is perhaps the best known of such schemes. Whatever value the classical or theological schemes of the underworld may have had in satisfying curiosity or frightening sinners, they were not useful from a scientific point of view.

[99] *Of the Nature of Things,* tr. William Ellery Leonard (New York: Everyman's Library, 1950), Book VI, ca. line 1032.
[100] John Clarke, *Physical Science in the Time of Nero, being a translation of the Quaestiones Naturales of Seneca* (London, 1910), pp. 128-9.

It can hardly be maintained that the subterranean worlds of Lucretius, Seneca, or Dante were any more imaginary than that of Descartes, but the Cartesian earth was constructed in a regular fashion out of a homogeneous matter differentiated into concentric layers according to fixed principles. Though essentially fluid at its commencement, the earth was a compacted globe of matter at its completion, devoid of all the mythical inhabitants and foliage of previous systems. The only irregularities in the globe—and these corresponded with observation—were those of the outer crust. Sir Isaac Newton utilized the idea of a primitive fluidity of homogeneous material in framing his theory of gravitation, and then his theory of gravitation furnished confirmation that the earth had been originally in a fluid state and that it was increasingly dense toward its center. These mathematical results in turn left no doubt that the earth had undergone a series of changes from a point of creation to the present.

When Newton first conceived the idea of gravitation in 1666 and applied it to the mutual attraction of the earth and moon, he encountered difficulties which led him to set aside his theory. The traditional story is that he based his estimate of the size of the earth, and consequently the amount of gravitation force in its mass, on a mistaken calculation of the length of an arc of meridian.[101] When he wrote his *Principia* he had available an accurate measurement of such an arc made by Jean Picard under the direction of the Académie Royale des Sciences.[102] In addition, he benefited by another result of a surveying expedition.

In 1671, Jean Richer was sent to Cayenne to make astronomical observations, and here he noted a curious discrepancy in the pendulums of his clocks, which had been very carefully adjusted

[101] See Florian Cajori, "Newton's Twenty Years Delay in Announcing the Law of Gravitation," in *Sir Isaac Newton, 1727-1927* (Baltimore, 1928), pp. 127-88.

[102] For a history of the surveys made to establish an accurate measurement of a degree of longitude, see Lloyd A. Brown, *The Story of Maps* (Boston, 1949), chapters VIII and IX.

in Paris. In order to make them keep time properly he had to shorten the pendulums a line and a quarter (about a twelfth of an inch). A regular check on the pendulums several times a week between April, 1672, and May, 1673, confirmed the necessity of this adjustment.[103] Why should a pendulum have to be shorter to measure a second of time near the equator than in Paris? Reading about it, Newton immediately grasped the significance of Richer's discovery.

It had already been observed by Cassini, Flamsteed, and other astronomers that Jupiter appeared to be slightly elliptical instead of spherical. This accorded well with Descartes' theory of elliptical orbs and did not create much excitement. In the meantime Huygens had made some important studies of centrifugal force in hydrostatics, in addition to his invention of the pendulum clock itself. Pulling together these apparently unrelated bits of information and combining them with his theory of gravitation, Newton boldly pronounced that the earth, like other planets, must be an oblate spheroid in shape.

By assuming that the earth was a fluid, homogeneous substance at the time of its formation, Newton calculated some of the basic principles which would govern its form. To simplify the data sufficiently for the application of mathematical formulas, he supposed that the polar and equatorial axes were canals filled with fluid. Impose rotation around the polar axis and it can be seen that the polar canal would rotate in a smaller arc than the canal intersecting the equator. The liquid parts near the surface of the earth on the axis of the equator would thus be subjected to a much greater tendency to fly off from the body of the earth according to the laws of centrifugal force. To reach an equilibrium between gravitational and centrifugal forces, the mass of material would have to be distributed so that the equatorial canal would be slightly longer than the polar canal. On the basis of this hypothe-

[103] Jean Richer, "De la longeur du pendule à secondes de temps," *Académie Royale des Sciences Mémoires*, VII (1666-1699), pt. I, p. 320.

sis and the size of the earth provided by Picard's measurements, Newton estimated that the excess of the axis of the equator over the axis of the poles was about sixteen miles.

> The equal gravitation of the parts on all sides would give a spherical figure to the planets, if it was not for their diurnal revolution in a circle. By that circular motion it comes to pass that the parts receding from the axis endeavour to ascend about the equator: and therefore if the matter is in a fluid state, by its ascent towards the equator it will enlarge the diameters there, and by its descent towards the poles it will shorten the axis. So the diameter of Jupiter (by the concurring observations of astronomers) is found shorter betwixt pole and pole than from east to west. And, by the same argument, if our earth was not higher about the equator than at the poles, the seas would subside about the poles, and, rising towards the equator, would lay all things there under water.[104]

Newton's assumption of a bulge at the equator cleared up the mystery of the necessity for shortening the pendulums on Richer's expedition to Cayenne, and, at the same time, Newton's gravitational theory was given strong observational confirmation by Richer's pendulum measurements. An object on the equator was at a greater distance from the locus of gravitational attraction at the center of the earth, so the force of gravity would be accordingly lessened. The force pulling a pendulum downwards in its swing would thus be weaker at the equator, necessitating a shortening of its arc of oscillation in order to describe a full swing in the same length of time as a pendulum situated in Paris. Also, the bulge at the equator explained the age-old riddle of the precession of the equinoxes.

Although the rate of precession had been measured as early as the second century before Christ and had formed an astronomical basis of the idea of a Great Year, or Platonic Year of 36,000 years, in chronological theories, the cause had remained hidden from

---

[104] *The Mathematical Principles of Natural Philosophy*, Motte translation of the 3rd ed. (New York, 1846), p. 405. (Book III, Prop. 18, Theor. 16.)

astronomers. Newton showed how it took place as a consequence of the attraction of the sun and moon on the earth's equatorial bulge which tended to twist the axis of the earth's rotation and forced the polar points to revolve in a small circle at the rate of 50.2 seconds of arc a year or about 25,800 years for a complete revolution. To an observer on the earth this movement becomes projected to the equinoctial points in the heavens as an almost imperceptible westerly rotation. There was then no great revolution of the heavens.

Most important, the bulge was one point in Newton's whole hypothesis of gravitation which could be put to an empirical test. Either the earth was oblate by actual measurement or it was not. Although the triumph of Newton in England was achieved quickly, on the Continent the situation was different. Cartesianism ruled supreme among the pedants and was taught widely in the schools. In a broad sense Newton placed the keystone in the Cartesian arch of a mechanistic universe, but he made a frontal assault on specific details of Cartesian cosmology. He resurrected the void in outer space, denied the principle of the vortex in the heavens, and substituted attraction for impulsion, to mention only a few of his heresies. What was this attraction? It operated over long distances without physical contact, and Newton himself would not, could not, explain its cause. After Descartes had driven the spirits out of science and moved bodies by impact with other bodies, Newton was bringing back supernatural forces again in the guise of attraction: it was another medieval occult celestial influence, thought many Cartesians.

Among the savants of the Académie Royale des Sciences there was a natural prejudice for the French cosmology, but there is no reason to suppose they would have held out against demonstrable facts, and the truth is that the scientific surveys they were carrying out actually supported the Cartesian view that the earth was a spindle-shaped ellipse with the long axis running through the poles, instead of being flattened at the poles as Newton claimed. If there were no bulge at the equator, but rather a narrowing, the *Principia* would be reduced to one more fabulous system. On the single problem of "la figure de la terre" the fate of Newton's theory of gravitation hung suspended in Europe. It was the French who, in spite of their resistance to it, verified the Newtonian system. In 1735 Louis XV authorized expeditions to the Gulf of Bothnia near the Arctic Circle and to Peru near the equator to settle the shape of the earth for the scientists. Precise measurements of arcs of meridian were carried out, and the result was an unequivocal victory for Newton's oblate spheroid. Once the truth of the gravitational theory had been confirmed by the figure of the earth, the French took a leading part in extending the applications of it. Alexis Claude Clairaut, for instance, demonstrated mathematically what Newton could only assume, that a rotating fluid mass would take the figure of an oblate spheroid. Further, he devised a method of mathematically determining the figure of the earth on the assumption it was composed of heterogeneous strata, as would be the case when the density of the strata increased from the surface to the center.[105] This was a problem Newton had been unable to solve, although he had pointed the way.

When Newton used the canals-of-fluid premise to arrive at the figure of the earth, he was well aware that the earth was not now constituted of a simple homogeneous substance and that somewhere in the transition between such a state and the present one there had been a differentiation of materials, to some extent in accordance with a difference in specific weights of the earth's masses. The gravitation theory offered a glimpse of the first principles in the evolution of the earth. Newton summed them up in the *Principia* as follows:

> But that our globe of earth is of greater density than it would be if the whole consisted of water only, I thus make out. If

[105] See Isaac Todhunter, *A History of the Mathematical Theories of Attraction and the Figure of the Earth, from the time of Newton to that of Laplace,* 2 vols. (London, 1873), I, 82ff.

the whole consisted of water only, whatever was of less density than water, because of its less specific gravity, would emerge and float above. And upon this account, if a globe of terrestrial matter, covered on all sides with water, was less dense than water, it would emerge somewhere; and, the subsiding water falling back, would be gathered to the opposite side. And such is the condition of our earth, which in a great measure is covered with seas. The earth, if it was not for its greater density, would emerge from the seas, and, according to its degree of levity, would be raised more or less above their surface, the water of the seas flowing backward to the opposite side. By the same argument, the spots of the sun, which float upon lucid matter thereof, are lighter than that matter; and, *however the planets have been formed while they were yet in fluid masses, all the heavier matter subsided to the centre.* Since, therefore, the common matter of our earth on the surface thereof is about twice as heavy as water, and a little lower, in mines, is found about three, or four, or even five times more heavy, it is *probable that the quantity of the whole matter of the earth may be five or six times greater than if it consisted all of water;* especially since I before shewed that the earth is about four times more dense than Jupiter.[106]

The Cartesian system of cosmic evolution pictured the finest and lightest particles at the center of the earth with progressively grosser particles extending from the center outwards. The Newtonian system reversed this order and put the heavier substances at the center. Estimates today agree with Newton's earlier suggestion that the density of the earth, from its known total mass and volume, is about five and one half times greater than water. The core of the earth, since the surface rocks are only about 2.7 times the density of water, must then be about ten times the density of water. The logical assumption, still widely held today, is that the separation of materials according to their specific gravities must have been due to gravity, and must have taken place when the earth was still entirely liquid so as to permit the easy circulation

---

[106] *Principles, op. cit.*, p. 100. (Book III, Prop. 10, Theor. 10.) Italics not in text.

of matter between the earth's center and the surface. Here then was scientific evidence from Newtonian physics and astronomy that the earth did have a beginning and went through a series of stages evolving from a homogeneous fluid mass to a more solid state with concentric layers of increasing density from the surface to the center. Granite, heavy as it is, is still only half as heavy as the mean density of the earth and less than a third as heavy as the core, so the existence of huge caverns in the earth was unlikely, nor could water form any substantial part of the earth's inner constitution since it was only a tenth as heavy as the core.

After Newton, almost all cosmogonists took into consideration the principle of the oblate spheroid and the evolution of the earth out of a primitive fluid mass, but the nature of the fluidity remained an unresolved problem. Newton was explicit about the limitations of water as an important element of the inner earth's structure, but water remained a favorite medium in cosmogony since it was mentioned in Genesis. Woodward, the self-professed Newtonian, for instance, had asserted: "That there is a mighty *Collection of Water* inclosed in the *Bowels of the Earth*, constituting a *huge Orb* in the *interiour* or *central* Parts of it; upon the Surface of which Orb of Water the *terrestrial Strata* are expanded."[107] This Orb of Water, "which Moses calls the Great Deep," was untenable, of course, under the principles of Newton, and Woodward's successor in explaining the Deluge, Whiston, tried to save the waters of the Deluge by assuming that they were composed of a dense fluid much heavier than water or earth.[108] As an added safeguard for the reconciling of Newton with Moses, he premised that the earth's core was a solid nucleus that had once been the center of a comet and had retained some of its heat. In this theory, he had the support of Newton.

Newton was content to work in the old familiar context of

[107] John Woodward, *An Essay Towards a Natural History of the Earth*, 2nd ed. (London, 1702), p. 116.

[108] William Whiston, *A New Theory of the Earth*, 2nd ed. (Cambridge, 1708), p. 419.

Mosaic history, unraveling the prophecies of Daniel, the apocalypse of St. John, and scriptural chronology, instead of grappling with the metaphysics of the new cosmology he had brought forth. But however much Newton might prefer to trace out Biblical chronologies, the philosophers wanted answers to big questions. What is gravitation? What is absolute space and time? What is their relationship to God? Is the Newtonian system deterministic? Newton in his letters to Richard Bentley and his replies to Leibniz through the pen of Samuel Clarke tried to clarify such questions. Newton and Leibniz each tried to escape determinism, but contributed to it. Newton started out with a clock-work mechanism created by a Biblical God, a clock which required a constant renewal of God's energy to keep it from running down. Leibniz criticized such a conception of craftsmanship on the part of God, so clumsy that the machine need be constantly wound up, and as the eighteenth century went on: "Every progress of Newtonian science brought new proofs for Leibniz's contention: the moving force of the universe, its *vis viva*, did not decrease; the world-clock needed neither rewinding, nor mending."[109]

As the astronomical revolution penetrated the thought of the seventeenth century, the age was staggered by the immensity of the universe and felt contemptuous of that grain of sand in the total creation reserved for man. This had again raised the question of eternity in an infinite universe, and attention was centered more on the philosophical question of how there could be a created world in an eternal universe than on the actual historical details of this world. Still, as we have seen, the work of bridging the gaps in the history of a world which was assumed to have been created went forward. The men of genius had contributed to it, almost as a by-product, working from the point of Genesis down to the present. Naturalists had contributed to it by filling out what they thought was the divine narrative of history, while

[109] Alexandre Koyré, *From the Closed World to the Infinite Universe* (Baltimore, 1957), p. 276.

historians and Biblical exegetes were closing the gap by pushing human history back farther into the past. In many cases all these approaches were combined in the same people.

THE DECLINE OF ANTIQUARIANISM

In England there was a flowering of historical studies in the seventeenth century and many of the great county histories were then first written. The interest in genealogy, local history, and legal precedents (especially in connection with the Civil Wars) sent scholars into old records—ledger-books, manuscripts, charters, parish accounts, inscriptions on tombs, and arms. It even took them into the countryside searching for unusual natural history objects in particular counties. Edward Lhywd, for instance, was interested in Welsh, Irish, and Celt origins, old words, charters, customs, fossils, coins, inscriptions, genealogy, castles, old cathedrals, ruins, and monuments. The activity of the local antiquarians was matched by that of the virtuosi exploring the ruins of the ancient civilizations and pondering over hieroglyphics. The extent of this historical activity and its connection with geology has been indicated by Cecil Schneer, who writes: "An early tradition of antiquarianism and of painstaking historical scholarship had coupled with natural history in the late seventeenth and early eighteenth centuries, and an historical attitude for a science of the earth was the issue."[110]

"Between 1660 and 1730 a long succession of highly distinguished Englishmen brought to its proper culmination the best sustained and the most prolific movement of historical scholarship which this country has ever seen. Today, they are known to professed students of history mainly through stark references to

[110] "The Rise of Historical Geology in the Seventeenth Century," *Isis* XLV (1954), 256-68.

their names in the footnotes of learned works, and to others of their countrymen they are known scarcely at all."[111] So writes David C. Douglas, who shows the connection of the antiquarianism of his countrymen of that period to political and constitutional events, as well as their other varied interests in the ancient and medieval studies. But as the seventeenth-century scholars died out in the early eighteenth century, the movement suddenly came to a halt. On the Continent, too, there had been a great movement in antiquarian and historical studies, but this too withered on the vine.

Since the breakdown of story-book Mosaic history had begun with the scholarship of exegetes and historians pursuing natural and civil history alike, and developing a sense of process and change which carried them outside Biblical chronology again and again, it is to be expected that the decline of the sense of historicism at the end of the century would affect the outlook on historical time. Douglas notes the disdain in the Enlightenment for the past and those who explored it. The Georgian Age of classical interest found the Middle Ages ignoble and a waste of time; the man of taste and fashion was more interested in wit and elegance than in learning, having nothing but contempt for erudition and antiquarianism which he deemed to be the pursuit of men of low genius; and in the Anglican ministry there was a negation of "monkish owl-light" and "monkish historians."

Douglas thought that some of the antiquarianism had arisen out of the need to buttress the Reformation and the Civil Wars, and after the Restoration this need declined. There was a change of attitude about political and social foundations too. The British constitution under the theories of social contract made historical precedents unnecessary, since the social contract was incapable of historical proof, while English satisfaction with the constitution left little room for questioning it. Along with the social contract went the idea of the common and universal consent of mankind,

[111] *English Scholars*, 1660-1730 (London, 1951), p. 13.

and as this idea spread, diversity of origins and national differences seemed less important than the things held in common by all mankind. The growth of scepticism and the attacks on miracles also laid the testimony of witnesses open to question, not only in the case of miracles, but for any historical event not attested to by more than one witness. The endless exegetical controversies had grown wearisome too—Lord Bolingbroke, for instance, expressed his open contempt for all the systems of chronology and history that we owe to the immense labors of a Scaliger, a Bochart, an Ussher, or even a Marsham. For the philosophic mind the massive, undigested, accumulations of the antiquarian were found boring —such details Voltaire called "the vermin which destroy books."

In discussing the change of outlook in Europe between 1680 and 1715, Paul Hazard also emphasizes that the modern man of this period was fascinated by novelty and absorbed with the present. The cult of antiquarianism, in which national and local history were eulogized, was out of step with the new cosmopolitanism and its search for consensus. With the great increase in travel came a knowledge of non-European cultures and a criticism of the customs, traditions, and beliefs of Christendom.[112] Instead of being the seat of ultimate truths, the Christian community was seen as the product of history, a society in the grip of ancient mores and institutions. The drive for reform which grew up in the eighteenth century did not look to actual history for succor, but to an idealized, utopian history in which models could be found of the common and natural principles underlying all human behaviour. The search was for a kind of Newtonian system for mankind, hence the preoccupation with *natural* (primitive) man, *natural* religion, *natural* law, *natural* rights, and *natural* economic laws. History deals with the unique event, but the age was in quest of universals. Nevertheless, in spite of its non-historical thinking, and in spite of the neglect of the older historicism, there

[112] *The European Mind, The Critical Years* (1680-1715), tr. J. Lewis May (New Haven, 1953), or *La crise de la conscience Européenne* (Paris, 1935).

was a new spirit of progress and advancement in the air, a new interest in civilization, and a new interest in finding the underlying web of history, rather than its details. A sense of historical process, well illustrated in the work of Herder, began to transform the view of history from a static chronology of events, or a lesson book from which morals could be drawn, into a vital, organic, moving force. In this, it was a part of a general eighteenth-century movement towards replacing the model of a mechanical universe with an organic one.

III

TIME AND WORLD PROCESS IN
THE EIGHTEENTH-CENTURY OUTLOOK

FOSSILS AND THE WORLD-MACHINE

Considerable attention was given to motion, movement, change, in the early Scientific Revolution. The men of science were interested in the dynamics of nature, whether it was the analysis and measurement of the motion of projectiles and falling bodies, or the changes in the earth and history. It is as though the tremendous outburst of activity on all fronts of life—economics, politics, religion, art, letters, technology, and science—had induced the age to seek in the universe a reflection of its own energy. That sixteenth-century pioneer in the investigation of fossils, Bernard Palissy, who was a devout Calvinist and an ambitious potter, reminded his readers that God did not create things to leave them idle. The stars and planets are not idle, the sea wanders from place to place and labours to produce profitable things, and the earth likewise is never idle.[1] Armed with such an outlook towards nature, he had no difficulty in recognizing that the earth is always undergoing changes.

For the men of the early seventeenth century, the natural world had become as active as their commercial cities, and not merely busy, like the Aristotelian earth which was in a constant state of

[1] *Oeuvres*, ed. Benjamin Fillon (Niort, 1888), I, 46.

flux, but busy laboring towards goals. It was not enough for Descartes to fill the universe with moving particles of matter in his system—this the ancients had already done. He also gave direction to the movement through a machinery of natural laws. Though most of the men of genius were able to transcend a simple anthropomorphic teleology, they could not escape the premise that there was a design in nature and that it had a purpose, though perhaps known only to God. And increasingly towards the end of the century, that design tended towards mechanism rather than organism in the outlook on nature.

With the growth of tolerance and cosmic optimism in the eighteenth-century intellectual world, the hard-working universe gave way to one in which the operations were harmoniously arranged to maintain all movements in equilibrium—everything had its proper place and function. The clock became the symbol of the Newtonian universe. Gone was the angry, personal Jahweh who stuck his fingers in the works. A Master Craftsman had contrived the world-machine and set it in motion, and it was so ingeniously contrived that it would run on indefinitely without any need for adjustment from the hand of the Maker.

There was plenty of motion in the world-machine, but little room for development. And as the Newtonian system was taken over by the deists and popularizers of natural theology, a simple anthropomorphic teleology was given to it. The purpose, or final cause, of the Great Contrivance was the convenience and utility of man. This was made explicit by the writers in the natural theology movement, but implicit was the pride of workmanship. Certainly the pious writers would not accuse God of being vain, but as they extolled the Spectacle of Nature and the fine workmanship everywhere displayed in it, the attitude can be detected that they thought God had done some showing off to dazzle man with His great powers, thereby insuring respect and subservience. In return, it was man's duty to recognize and admire His ingenuity.

Homage to the truths of revelation became increasingly hollow in natural theology as its advocates turned to evidences of design in nature for a proof of deity. Natural theology thus became an apology for the new mechanical philosophy, and as the utilitarianism of secular life asserted itself, it gave a strong religious sanction to the pursuit of scientific inquiry, a pursuit which had no apparent practical benefits. This dual role is expressed by William Derham in his exceedingly popular *Physico-Theology* in the following manner:

> Many of our useful Labours, and some of our best modern Books shall be condemned with only this Note of Reproach, That they are about trivial Matters, when in Truth they are ingenious and noble Discoveries of the Works of GOD. And how often will many own the World in General to be a Manifestation of the Infinite Creator, but look upon the several Parts thereof as only Toys and Trifles, scarce deserving their Regard? But in the foregoing (I may call it) transient View I have given of this lower, and most slighted Part of the Creation, I have, I hope, abundantly made out, that all the Works of the LORD, from the most regarded, admired, and praised, to the meanest and most slighted, are Great and Glorious Works, incomparably contrived, and as admirably made, fitted up, and placed in the World. So far then are any of the Works of the LORD, (even those esteemed the meanest) from deserving to be disregarded, or contemned by us, that on the contrary they deserve . . . to be *sought out, enquired after,* and *curiously,* and *diligently pryed into* by us; as I have shewed the Word in the Text implies.[2]

As the Works were pryed into, the enormity and complexity of the Creation rapidly emerged before eighteenth-century man, and he was staggered at the infinite pains the Master Craftsman had taken in outfitting his abode. It is small wonder that hymns of praise were sung about the Benevolence of the Creator—"upon a transient View of the Animal World in General only, we have such a Throng of Glories, such an enravishing Scene of Things

[2] *Physico-Theology, or a Demonstration of the Being and Attributes of God, from His Works of Creation,* 15th ed. (Dublin, 1754), p. 431.

as may excite us to Admire, Praise, and Adore the Infinitely Wise, Powerful, and Kind Creator. . . ."[3] In surveying the largess, however, it would have been most ungracious of man to carp about flaws in it. There were no "rude bungling Pieces" in Nature, "And so far are we from being able to espy any Defect or Fault in them, that the better we know them, the more we admire them; and the farther we see into them, the more exquisite we find them to be."[4] Turning to the Principal Fabrick, the Terraqueous Globe, we find this attitude expressed by Derham:

> And so for all the other parts of our Terraqueous Globe, that are presumed to be found Fault with by some, as if carelessly order'd, and made without any Design or End; particularly the Distribution of the dry Land and Waters; the laying of the several Strata, or Beds of Earth, Stone, and other Layers before spoken of; . . . I have before shewn, that an Infinitely Wise Providence, an Almighty Hand was concerned even in them; that they all have their admirable Ends and Uses, and are highly instrumental and beneficial to the Being, or Well-being of this our Globe, or to the Creatures residing thereon.[5]

Nature became a sanctuary in natural theology—"The World thenceforth becomes a Temple and life itself one continued act of adoration."[6] Innumerable theologians took up the study of natural history, and under the influence of natural theology, they regarded the Creation as a completed mechanism. Their work, marked by a passive-minded wonderment, was concerned with gathering examples of design in the contrivances of nature, contrivances which were doing exactly what they had been designed to do. The admirable ends and uses of fossils were somewhat elusive, but in the uncritical spirit of the orthodox naturalists, it

[3] *Ibid.*, p. 265.
[4] *Ibid.*, p. 38.
[5] *Ibid.*, p. 82.
[6] William Paley, *Natural Theology*, 1st ed., 1802 (Boston, 1837). This statement appears as a legend under a frontispiece picture showing a pious man standing on an eminence with Bible in hand, gazing worshipfully at the spectacle of nature extending out before him.

was easy to assume that they were Reliques of the Deluge or Medals of Creation, as fossils were called, serving a moral function by reminding man of his early transgressions and punishment.

Orthodox naturalists became all the more anxious to discover in fossils a scientific corroboration of the testimony of Moses as the *philosophes* attacked supernaturalism in the Old Testament. Almost instinctively, they adopted a doctrinaire philosophy of empiricism which had become rampant as the ideas of Newton and Locke saturated the fabric of eighteenth-century thought. They condemned system-making, never doubting for a moment that Mosaic cosmogony in its garb of natural theology was among the self-evident truths of science, and they contented themselves with the naming and cataloguing of the artifacts in the temple of nature.

The tendency to use empiricism to close off inquiry into fundamental questions was well illustrated in the work of the Abbé Noël Antoine Pluche, the leading French popularizer of natural theology. His *Spectacle de la nature*, first published in 1732 and often republished, was perhaps the most widely read book of its kind in France during the eighteenth century.[7] Pluche undertook the refutation of the entire range of speculation on the origin of the world which conflicted with Mosaic cosmogony in his *Histoire du ciel* (1743-1753), forcefully emphasizing the sufficiency of the empirical method in science, utility as the goal of science, and the vanity of trying to unlock all of nature's secrets. He singled out the fossil enigma as a particularly mischievous source of false systems, and, with an air of finality, he assigned the origin of fossils to the Flood, about four thousand years ago. He closed the discussion with the observation:

> The natural conclusion of the comparison we have made of the thoughts, either of the ancients or the moderns, on the origin and end of all things, with what Moses teaches us is that NOT

ONLY IN RELIGION, BUT ALSO IN PHYSICS, WE MUST RESTRICT OUR-
SELVES TO THE CERTAINTY OF EXPERIENCE AND THE MODERATION
OF REVELATION.[8]

Experience, the great touchstone of the physical sciences, needed the analogy of historical process before it could become fruitful in the reconstruction of a world which lay completely outside experience, but it was precisely this historical process which the timeless world-machine view of the universe excluded. As a result, many *philosophes* and deists were in the same camp with the proponents of natural theology, despite the mission of the luminaries to rid the world outlook of anthropomorphism, supernaturalism, and final causes. Voltaire, for instance, did all in his power to combat the idea of development in nature. In 1749, he sent to the Academy of Bologna a *Dissertation sur les changemens arrivés dans notre globe, et sur les pétrifactions qu'on prétend en être encore les témoignages* in which he accused the natural philosophers of wanting great changes in the scene of the world much as the people craved spectacles. It seemed to Voltaire a complete inversion of reason and experience to elaborate a great system of earth changes in order to explain a shell, like those in the seas of the Indies, which might be found in the mountains of Europe. Instead of trying to get the seas up into the mountains, it was more reasonable to question the identity of the shell. As for Ammonites, known for ages as serpent stones, it was obvious that they were coiled snakes which had been petrified, or stones which had been formed in such a shape. The small shells found in the mountains of France and Italy, resembling those in the seas near Syria, had probably been dropped by pilgrims and crusaders who had the custom of wearing shells in their hats. Where there were masses of shells, he suggested that mountain lakes had dried up. Rearranging the earth to account for a few shells was nonsense. The mountains were not, as Burnet had said, a ruins. "This chain

[8] *Histoire du ciel considéré selon les idées des poetes, des philosophes, et de Moïse*, Vol. II (The Hague, 1740), pp. 476-7.

of rocks is an essential piece in the machine of the world."[9] Nor could marble and metals be dissolved by the Deluge as Woodward claimed, while a shift in the axis of the earth, pretended by so many, was disproved by the astronomical observations on precession.

> There is then, no system which can give the least support to this idea so widely prevalent that our globe has changed its face, that the ocean has occupied the earth for a very long time, and that men have formerly lived where porpoises and whales are today. Nothing which vegetates or which is animated changes; all the species have remained invariably the same; it would be very strange that the grain of the millet had eternally conserved its nature, and the entire globe varied its.[10]

Voltaire may have been prompted to write the dissertation to refute *Telliamed, ou entretiens d'un philosophe indien sur la diminution de la mer avec un missionnaire français* (1748) by Benoît de Maillet, judging from internal evidence in this piece of Voltaire's and explicit attacks on Maillet in subsequent ones.[11] Maillet had projected an eternalistic system on the basis of fossil evidence and speculation, and Buffon elaborated many geological theories similar to Maillet's in his *Theory of the Earth* (1749), a part of the *Natural History*, which refuted the anonymous *Dissertation* of Voltaire. Maillet and Buffon threatened the whole concept of Voltaire's Newtonian world-machine, and he returned to the attack on system-building on the basis of fossils numerous times.

In his *Singularités de la nature*, Voltaire scorned the method of giving a name to an object, and then assuming that the object corresponded fully to the name. Some gallant, for instance, had

[9] *Oeuvres complètes de Voltaire*, Kehl ed., xxxi (1785), 384.

[10] *Ibid.*, pp. 385-6.

[11] Although Charles Lyell in *The Principles of Geology*, 9th ed. (New York, 1857), pp. 54-5, accused Voltaire of bad faith and inconsistency in the treatment of fossils, Voltaire's opposition to systems of cosmic evolution, and these were supported by fossil evidence, seems sincere enough. Voltaire's editor thought so, too, and he remarked that Voltaire never changed his mind on the ideas he first put forward in the *Dissertation*. (*Ibid.*, p. 18).

given the name *Conchae Veneris* to a shell of a particular shape, but this hardly proved that the shell was the remains of a lady. Similarly, giving the name of Ammonite or Nautilus to a shell did not mean that it really was the remains of such a species. He also ridiculed the thesis of Maillet and Buffon that mountains were formed by the flux and re-flux of the seas over thousands of centuries.

What then is the true system? the one of the great Being who has made all, and who has given to each element, to each species, to each genus its form, its place, and its eternal functions. The Great Being who has formed the gold and iron, the trees, the plants, man, and the ant, has made the ocean and the mountains. Men have not been fish, as Maillet says; all is probably what it is by immutable laws. I cannot repeat too often that we are not gods who can create a universe with a word.[12]

Voltaire continued his assault on the system-makers in a long article, "Des coquilles, et des systèmes bâtis sur des coquilles," in the *Dictionnaire philosophique* and in the "Dissertation du physicien du Saint-Fleur," in *Les Colimaçons*, belaboring Buffon and Maillet for their opinion that calcareous stone was comprised of the remains of marine shells. He also poked fun at the system of Bernard Palissy, who maintained the same thing, and impugned his motives. The character of Palissy was revealed in the title of his book, *Le moyen de devenir riche*, Voltaire sneered, and, he was, like the rest of the system-makers, a charlatan.[13] The high priest of the Enlightenment was annoyed to see the wonderfully simple, precise system of the Newtonian world-machine, which he had done so much to establish among the French, challenged on the basis of some old shells.

Telliamed (de Maillet spelled backwards) marked the summation of the seventeenth-century progress in geology and the point of rupture with the attempts to bypass the conclusion that fossils

[12] *Ibid.*, p. 418 ("De la formation des montagnes").
[13] *Ibid.*, p. 486. See also "Coquilles" in *Dictionnaire philosophique, ibid.*, XXXIX, 140ff.

were the product of a process in time. Maillet (1659-1738) was a
Cartesian (his work was published posthumously). He was well
read in ancient literature and the leading works on fossils, had
traveled widely in the Mediterranean regions, and had apparently
done some original investigation into the processes of sedimentation. His literary style was successfully modeled after Fontenelle's
Conversations on the Plurality of Worlds. Speaking through his
Indian philosopher, Telliamed, in a series of conversations with a
Christian extending through six days, Maillet unfolded his system.
It was remarkably free of final causes, anthropomorphism, and
supernaturalism, but filled with Cartesian fantasy and with cre-
dulity.

Maillet assumed that the universe was eternal and that there
was a constant transmigration of matter throughout the various
whirlpools of the Cartesian system. Our earth had taken its origin
from the gatherings of the ashes of other celestial bodies at the
center of a whirlpool. Eventually it picked up bodies of waters
from the outer regions, and these covered its surface. The waters
circulated over the earth for countless ages, drifting the fine ash-
like material, and finally giving shape to the primordial mountains. The waters were, however, steadily evaporating back into
the outer regions, and after a long time the mountains emerged
above their surface. Life then appeared in the shallow coastal
waters, plants began to grow on land, and, after repeated failures,
sea animals trapped in the marshes mastered flight and walking to
give rise to birds and land animals. Maillet pointed to the basic
similarity in the anatomy of some sea, land, and air species which
made it likely that such a development had occurred through a
specialization of parts. As the waters continued to lower after
the emergence of land, the debris of erosion and the remains of
organisms were deposited on the bed of the sea, forming the
fossil strata.

The system of Maillet had been instigated by observing fossil
shells in the hills when he was in Egypt, and the core of *Telliamed*

was concerned with geological proofs of the diminution of the sea. Around this core he fabricated much speculation in order to make the diminution reasonable. Maillet worked in catastrophes, such as the taking on of additional bodies of water from outer regions, and the shifting of the earth's axis, but his geology was essentially uniformitarian. At one point dealing with the slowness of the process and the time it would require, he made the statement (later echoed by Hutton and Lyell), "But, continued Telliamed, not to enter upon a question, which you look upon to be necessarily connected with your religion, . . . let us be here content not to fix a beginning to that which perhaps never had one. Let us not measure the past duration of the world, by that of our own years." [14]

Maillet recognized in the succession of strata the progression of life, suggesting that the first appearance of a species could be approximately dated from his estimate that the sea had diminished at the rate of three feet four inches every thousand years. Unfortunately, after several pages of provocative general discussion on the origin of man and animals through evolution, in his last chapter, he appended as proofs of evolution many far-fetched stories of the simple transformism of men and animals out of sea animals. His mermaids and mermen proved only his gullibility and brought ridicule upon his whole system.

The reaction to *Telliamed* was violent. The orthodox were scandalized by it and gave a stock retort, like that of Dezallier d'Argenville, author of books on fossils and subsequently a contributor to the *Encyclopédie:* "What a folly in this author to substitute Telliamed for Moses, to bring man out of the depths of the sea, and, for fear that we should descend from Adam, to give us marine monsters for ancestors! Only a kind of godlessness could

[14] *Telliamed, or, The World Explain'd . . . —A Very Curious Work* (Baltimore, 1797), p. 194. A careless edition was published in 1748 at Amsterdam by Jean Antoine Guer. The best French edition was published at The Hague in 1755 by the Abbé le Mascrier, who had custody of the original manuscript.

invent such dreams."[15] However, *Telliamed* was a fascinating book, and it was well publicized by its opponents. It brought into sharp focus the concept of the evolution of the earth and organic life through the slow operation of natural forces, in spite of its cosmological trappings and the appendage of fantastic reports of transformism, and it was still being refuted in the middle of the nineteenth century by anti-evolutionists.[16] Henceforth the ortho- dox regarded fossils with suspicion, for they had now seen how fossils could be used to promulgate views in direct opposition to their belief in the finished Creation of Mosaic cosmogony and natural theology. However, of all the phenomena presented by natural history, none attracted the attention of naturalists more than the prodigious quantity of marine shells to be found in the depths of the earth and in the highest mountains, Baron d'Holbach observed in his article *"Fossiles"* in the *Encyclopédie* (1757),[17] a comment also made by others in the literature of natural history around the middle of the eighteenth century. Holbach noted that there was a multitude of works on fossils, but that naturalists, even some who were otherwise enlightened, continued to be par- tisans of plastic forces or the Noachian Deluge in explaining them, despite observational evidence which controverted both views.

In speculating about the fossil enigma, the position of religious officials, Protestant and Catholic alike, was a strong deterrent to moving outside the accepted bounds of orthodoxy, but the con- servatism of the generality of naturalists seems to have left them as austerely orthodox as the guardians of dogma, perhaps because so many were in theology. The combined effect placed Mosaic history directly across the path of the investigators of fossils, and

---

[15] *L'Histoire naturelle eclaircié dans une de ses parties principales, . . . conchyliologie* (Paris, 1757), p. 74.

[16] For example, Hugh Miller, *The Foot-Prints of the Creator,* 3rd ed. (Boston, 1856), pp. 243-4.

[17] *Encyclopédie,* VII, 209-11. Articles by Holbach were indicated by the mark (—).

rather than push on, they scurried off in strange directions, or returned to earlier positions. Virtually every suggestion which had ever been made to explain the origin of fossils found some advocates in the early eighteenth century. Careful, but pious, naturalists could not find a natural means of accounting for fossils and fossil strata which would fit Mosaic history, and they tried to avoid the premise of a slow deposition in the process of time which would conflict with Mosaic history.

One course of compromise was to avoid the Deluge altogether and place the origin of fossils at the time of Creation. This had the merit of lending to the fossil strata the appearance of a natural origin without the necessity of explaining their deposition as a process of time. Elias Camerarius in 1712 suggested that God had supplied the varied forms of fossils at creation to furnish the interior of the earth with foliage to correspond with that on the exterior. Theodore Arnold in 1733 ventured the opinion that at creation infinitesimal particles were brought together to form the outlines of all the creatures and objects destined to occupy the earth—a sort of trial run.[18] There were many such attempts at this kind of compromise, but one of the most philosophical was that of Father Bertrand in 1765. He had an intimate knowledge of the history of thought on fossils, which he presented in his *Recueil de divers traités sur l'histoire naturelle de la terre et des fossiles*, (Avignon, 1766) but he was forced to reject all previous theories because they failed to conform to either observed data or scriptural history. Aristotelian alternations of land and sea would not have left uniform strata, and they would have required an enormous course of centuries in any case. The Flood, on the other hand, was not long enough, for the strata were not the work of a cataclysm. Plastic forces could not imitate nature down to such details as the worn teeth of fish, while shells were an integral part of the stone in which they were found, so both must have

[18] See Lester F. Ward, "Sketch of Paleobotany," *Fifth Annual Report, U. S. Geological Survey* (1883-4) (Washington, 1885), p. 363ff.

been formed together. But there simply was not enough time in the history of the earth for the natural production and orderly deposition of the masses of shells and their solidification into stone. Father Bertrand suggested weakly that the Creator had arranged the fossils in their places for some impenetrable purpose in the Great Design of Nature.

The persecution of Buffon probably discouraged some curious souls from proceeding outside of scriptural history for the answer to the fossil enigma. In his *Theory of the Earth* (1749), Buffon had described the formation of mountains through the action of the flux of tides and the deposition of fossils to form strata, when the earth was still beneath the sea. The processes he described were slow, steady, transformations. He reviewed the previous attempts of Leibniz, Burnet, Whiston, Woodward, Bourguet, Scheuchzer, Steno, and Ray to explain the presence of shells on the continental lands, and he attributed their failure to a reliance on the authority of Scripture, adding, "The notion, that the shells were transported and left upon the land by the deluge, is the general opinion, or rather superstition, of naturalists."[19] The universal deluge was an established fact, he continued, but it was the direct operation of the Deity, not the effect of a physical cause, and should not be blended with bad philosophy. With this genuflexion, Buffon proceeded to explain how a comet had struck the sun obliquely and knocked off a mass of material which separated out according to the laws of gravitation, becoming our planetary system. After the formation of the earth, the rotation of the waters elevated land in the equatorial parts (thus explaining how the bulge was brought into existence) and sculptured the continents in the course of time.

The Faculty of Theology at the Sorbonne instituted action designed to suppress Buffon's heresies and in 1751 furnished Buffon with a list of reprehensible statements in his cosmogony. Buffon agreed, in lieu of punitive proceedings by the Faculty, to publish

[19] *Natural History*, ed. William Smellie (London, 1791), I, 130-1.

a retraction of these statements, which he did in the fourth volume of his *Natural History*, saying that he believed very firmly
in the text of Scripture and all that is reported in it about creation, both as to order of time and matters of fact.[20] But in spite
of his abjuration, Buffon continued on his way towards a new
theory of the earth, even more reprehensible from an orthodox
point of view, in which he formulated for the first time a system
of geological epochs covering the prehistoric period.

BUFFON'S 'EPOCHS OF NATURE'

Until the works of Leibniz were published in full by Louis
Scheidt in 1749, Buffon knew of his theory of the earth only
through brief summaries, but when the complete *Protogaea* was
thus made available, Buffon was stirred to a reconsideration of the
role of igneous forces in the shaping of the earth. In the meantime, there was considerable interest among various scientists in
the experimental verification of the premise that the earth contained a residual heat. One of the leading workers on this problem
was Jean Jacques Dortous de Mairan, who published his first essay
on the subject in 1702, and in 1749 in his *Dissertation sur la glace*
brought more than fifty years of measurements to the support of
the principle of a residual, central heat in the earth.[21] The measurements utilized by Mairan were made on the atmosphere, the
heat of mines and hot springs, and the formation of ice in bodies
of water on the earth's surface.

Once the existence of a residual heat was established, the next
step in connecting it with a theory of the evolution of the earth
out of a molten state was to establish that this heat was also vesti-

[20] *Oeuvres complètes de Buffon*, ed. Pierre Flourens (Paris, 1853-4), XII,
350-3.
[21] *Académie Royale des Sciences Mémoires*, 1702, pp. 161-80; 1719, pp.
104-135; 1765, pp. 143-266.

gial. Buffon accepted the work of Mairan as sound and proceeded in the direction of finding experimental evidence on the *duration* of the process of cooling. His experiments had as their point of departure the statement of Newton in his *Principia* on the time it would take for a mass of hot iron the size of the earth to cool. The statement occurred in connection with Newton's speculations on a comet.

> This comet, therefore, must have conceived an immense heat from the sun [at its perihelion], and retained that heat for an exceeding long time; for a globe of iron of an inch in diameter, exposed red hot to the open air, will scarcely lose all its heat in an hour's time; but a greater globe would retain its heat longer in proportion of its diameter, because the surface (in proportion to which it is cooled by the contact of the ambient air) is in that proportion less in respect of the quantity of the included hot matter; and therefore *a globe of red hot iron equal to our earth,* that is, about 40,000,000 feet in diameter, would scarcely cool in an equal number of days, or in above 50,000 years. But I suspect that the duration of heat may, on account of some latent causes, increase in a yet less proportion than that of the diameter; and I should be glad that the true proportion was investigated by experiments.[22]

Buffon set up a laboratory in a cellar which was deep enough and cool enough, he thought, to be free from the influence of solar heat. He fashioned two series of balls, ranging in diameter from one to five inches, for each of the principal materials out of which the earth was composed and then proceeded to heat and cool them under "controlled" conditions to determine their rate of cooling from incandescence to room temperature. The experiments were crude. The first stage of measurements, executed in the dark, were observations on the rate of change from white heat to red heat, then to the absence of glow. In the second state of measurements, Buffon with one hand tried to ascertain first at what point the heated ball was cool enough to hold, and secondly,

[22] *Principles,* Book iii, Prop. 41, prob. 21.

when it reached room temperature. In the other hand he held the
mate of the heated ball as a standard of comparison.

As his experimental work progressed, Buffon kept in touch with
Mairan, who announced in 1765 that his researches pointed clearly
to the conclusion that there is a central heat, that it is residual,
that it is a vestige of the progressive diminution of heat from a
primitive molten stage of the earth, and that, barring supernatural causes, it indicated that the earth had passed through successive changes.[23] As we now know, Mairan's hypotheses were
not conclusively demonstrated at all, but they were convincing
enough for Buffon to accept them without question as a foundation in his own system, and in his *Introduction to the History of
Minerals* (1774), Buffon published the results of his own research
on the laws of the progress of heat in different bodies.

As Flourens correctly points out, in all these experiments on
heat undertaken by Buffon, finding the *duration* of the cooling of
the terrestrial globe was his "grand objet et son but final."[24] Logically, but naïvely, Buffon extrapolated the measurements made on
the tiny balls to the planetary bodies. He thus calculated more
than 42,964 years for a mass of molten iron the size of the earth
to cool to the point where it was no longer incandescent and
96,670 years to cool to the present temperature of the earth.[25]
Since the earth obviously was not composed entirely of iron,
Buffon worked out a resultant of cooling rates from a variety of
substances which were compounded in the earth.[26] He also tried
to find the time necessary for the surface of a fused body to become hardened, the rate of cooling inside the hardened shell, and
to what extent the inside would remain liquid after an outer crust
had formed. A number of ingenious devices were invented by
Buffon to carry out these investigations. For instance, to find out

[23] Buffon to Mairan, Oct. 31, 1767, A. L. S., Franklin Papers, Yale University.
[24] *Oeuvres complètes de Buffon*, IX, 82, nl.
[25] *Ibid.*, IX, 89.
[26] *Ibid.*, IX, 97ff. and 154ff.

if the inside remained incandescent after the outside of the molten mass had hardened, Buffon inserted a coil of wire in the substance and in his darkened room observed how much longer the wire glowed after the crust had become opaque.

On the basis of his researches, Buffon attempted to construct a chronology of the cooling of the earth from a primitive incandescence to its present and future temperatures.[27] He allowed one day for the surface to consolidate, much too short a time, he felt, because of the disturbing influences of centrifugal forces and a variety of other factors for which he could make no measurable compensation. Commencing with this initial stage in the formation of the earth as the first year, Buffon dated the successive epochs in the history of the world as follows:

2,936	The earth is consolidated to the center.
34,270	The earth is cool enough to be touched.
35,983	The beginning of organic life.
74,832	Temperature of the present (c. 1800) reached.
168,123	End of organic life.

The exposition of Buffon's experiments proceeded detail by detail and computation by computation. His results were frequently expressed in months and days. Doubters could follow his observations and reasonings step by step, and Buffon even went so far as to divide the "experimental" part of his work from the "hypothetical" part in his *Introduction*. All had the air of precision about it, but there was a considerable amount of window-dressing in the whole treatise on the cooling of the earth. Buffon knew that more time was needed in his chronology than he had outlined, but even the most conservative period of duration that he could present to his contemporaries was an enormous extension of the time allowed by Scripture for the history of the earth. Speaking of his chronology, Buffon confessed that the time, considerable as it is, was not long enough for certain successive alterations that natural history demonstrates to us, and which seem

[27] *Ibid.*, IX, 305.

to have required a succession of centuries even longer. In reality, he believed, this time indicated for the duration of nature must be increased, perhaps doubled, if all the phenomena are to be readily explained, but he held to the least terms and restricted the limits of time as much as possible without contradicting facts and experiments.[28]

Buffon's thoughts on chronology were extended a few years later in the *Epochs of Nature* (1778). This work was Buffon's masterpiece. According to Flourens, it was a profound resumé of all that a full life of meditation and study had revealed to him of what was most worthy of being transmitted to posterity touching the great history of the earth.[29] A contemporary, Grimm, reported that Buffon had regarded this work as the most valuable monument of all his studies and researches; Cuvier said that Buffon reworked it eleven times while Herault de Sechelles said that Buffon admitted working it over eighteen times.[30] The *Epochs* was Buffon's last will and testament as a naturalist, and there is no doubt he intended it as such. He labored over style as much as scientific content, for it was a tenet of Buffon's that only well-written works would or should be passed on to posterity.[31] More than a century after it was published, Lucien Picard selected the *Epochs* for use in the French secondary schools because of its claim to being a classic of French prose. Picard thought it comparable to the *De Natura Rerum* of Lucretius in the grandeur of its cosmogony, and though apparently lacking the feeling of Lucretius's work, the *Epochs* made up for it in constant serenity of thought, beautiful arrangement and pure nobility of style.[32]

Modern critics might hesitate to go so far as Picard in extolling

---

[28] *Ibid.*, IX, 443-4.
[29] *Ibid.*, IX, 454.
[30] *Ibid.*, IX, 454.
[31] "Discours sur le style, prononcé à l'Académie françoise le 25 août, 1753." The catalogue of the *Bibliothèque nationale* lists 54 editions down to 1901, a measure of its importance in the French literary tradition.
[32] *Des Époques de la Nature*, ed. Lucien Picard (Paris, 1894), Intro.

the style of Buffon's *Epochs*, but its literary excellence cannot be denied; it was his style that enabled Buffon to sweep through opposition and spark the imagination of his readers. The *Epochs* was a stirring manifesto for the rising workers in prehistory and itself marks an epoch in the emancipation of Western man's outlook on the scope of history in nature, even though in detail after detail its scientific theories proved fallacious. It was the grandeur of his conception that was important, for it was that which was most needed to integrate the knowledge coming from the fossil-grubbers and stone-chippers on the one hand, and the historians, on the other hand. Buffon tried to knit together human history and earth history in one connected series, and opened his work with the declaration:

> As in civil history written documents are consulted, medals studied, ancient inscriptions deciphered, to determine the epochs of human revolutions and to establish the dates of moral events, so in natural history it is necessary to rummage through the archives of the world, to draw from the bowels of the earth old monuments, collect their debris, and assemble in a body of proofs all indications of the physical changes which can carry us back to the different ages of nature. It is the only means of fixing points in the immensity of space and of placing a few milestones on the eternal path of time. The past is like distance, our view of it would diminish and disappear if history and chronology had not placed beacons and torches at the darkest points; but in spite of these lights of written tradition going back a few centuries, what an uncertainty of facts! what errors about the cause of events! and what deep obscurity surrounds the time before this tradition! Besides, only the exploits of a few nations have been transmitted to us, that is to say, the acts of a very small part of mankind; all the rest of the people mean nothing to us, nothing to posterity: they have passed away like shadows leaving no traces.[33]

Civil history, Buffon continued, was bounded by darkness on all sides except where a few peoples mindful of their tradition

[33] *Oeuvres*, IX, 455.

preserved a record of their exploits, but natural history embraced all places, all times, and had no other limits than those of the universe. Nature being contemporaneous with matter, space, and time, its history is that of all substances and all ages, and though it may seem at first sight that the great works of nature never alter or change and that its most fragile productions constantly reappear fashioned after the first models, the course of nature is not absolutely uniform. Sensible variations can be recognized, alterations steadily take place, new combinations occur, and, much as nature appears fixed as a whole, it is changeable in all its parts. When we see it at full length we cannot doubt that "it is very different today from what it was at the beginning and from what it has become in the process of time. It is those changes which we call epochs. Nature has successively taken different forms; the skies themselves have varied, and all things in the physical universe, like those of the moral world, are in a continual movement of successive variations."[34]

Here in the opening pages of the *Epochs* Buffon has set the tone for his conception of history, and a modern one it is indeed. The written inheritance of Greeks, Romans, and Hebrews he saw as only a marker placed not far from us by a handful of people among the multitudes who have lived and passed away, while time rolled back to immense distances. To find the signposts of these past ages which have witnessed so many changes in nature we must study nature itself and reconstruct the revolutions in nature from their vestiges. In the vast ages of time a steady succession of variations has taken place in nature from the beginning to the present: the world and its productions have been in a process of evolution. The seven epochs Buffon outlined in his work were periods of what we would now call geologic time during the evolution of the earth to its present state.

To unravel the evolution of the earth, Buffon proposed using three types of evidence: (1) facts which can bring us closer to

[34] *Ibid.,* ix, 456.

the origin of nature; (2) monuments which can be considered as witnesses of the first ages; and (3) traditions which might give us some hints about subsequent ages. When the whole was tied together with some analogies, he hoped to form a chain which would descend from the summit of the scale of time down to the present. The facts he planned to use were the oblateness of the earth, evidence of interior heat, the inadequacy of the sun by itself to support life, the vitreous nature of the materials of earth, and the presence in the structure of the earth of immense quantities of marine fossils. His monuments proved to be mostly fossils. Of the traditions, the most important was Plato's Atlantis.

After a brief preview of his epochs, Buffon paused, saying, "But before going further, let us hasten to anticipate a serious objection which may even degenerate into a charge."[35] The allusion was to the previous difficulty he had had with the Sorbonne.

> How do you reconcile, it will be said, this high antiquity that you give to matter with the sacred traditions which give to the world only six or eight thousand years? However strong your proofs may be, however well-founded your reasonings may be, however clear your facts may be, are not those reported in the sacred books still more certain? Is it not unfaithful to God who has had the goodness to reveal them to us to contradict them? [36]

Like other cosmogonists of the seventeenth and eighteenth centuries, Buffon had to come to grips with Genesis—to make a reconciliation between theology and science. He undertook a literal analysis of those parts of Genesis dealing with the creation. The first paragraph should read, he maintained, "In the beginning God created the *matter of the* heaven and earth." The immediately following words of the text supported two periods of time, one between the creation of matter and the creation of light, and one between the creation of light and its separation from darkness, and these periods were of considerable length, Buffon thought.

[35] *Ibid.*, IX, 472.
[36] *Ibid.*, IX, 473.

Buffon's literalism soon led him into the opposite camp of allegorical scriptural interpretation:

> What can we understand by the six days the sacred writer designates so precisely by counting them one after the other, if not six spaces of time, six intervals of duration? And these spaces of time indicated by the name of *days*, for the lack of other expressions, could not have any relationship to our actual days, since three of these successive days had passed before the sun had been placed in the sky.[37]

What the scriptural writer "meant" was six periods of time, according to Buffon, in the best allegorical tradition. Why then cry out so loudly over this borrowing of time which we are forced to make by knowledge derived from the phenomena of nature? Why wish to refuse us this time since God gives it to us by his own Word, and what a contradiction and unintelligibility would it not be to admit the existence of this first time before the formation of the world *such as it now is?*[38] Buffon took his cue from Burnet and maintained that all truth comes from God equally, there being no difference between the revealed truths and those he has permitted us to discover by our observations and researches. Following Burnet, who had himself only expressed a thought growing in popularity, Buffon stated that the divine interpreter spoke to a primitive people who would have been unable to understand a true system (like the *Principia*), and had to gauge his words to their limited understanding about the world.[39] The sole purpose of Moses' narrative was to instruct these rude intellects in the all-powerfulness and beneficence of the Creator. The truths of nature could only appear gradually with the growth of knowledge, and the Sovereign Being had reserved this growth

[37] *Ibid.*, IX, 475-6.
[38] *Ibid.*, IX, 476.
[39] This is called the "theory of accomodation" by Heinrich Meyer, who traces it in Biblical exegesis with copious illustrations, and who shows its importance in the history of ideas, in his *Age of the World* (Muhlenberg College, Allentown, Pa., 1951).

as a means to recall man constantly to the worship of Him. In the course of centuries man would become accustomed to the spectacles of nature and his faith would decline, if from time to time the idea of God was not reaffirmed and expanded in his spirit and heart. Now each new discovery produced this great effect, since each new step we take in unfolding the secrets of nature brings us closer to the Creator. "A new truth is a kind of miracle," differing from a true miracle only in the manner of its unfolding, and God draws man to Him by new contemplations of his power, not only by actual spectacles, but also by the successive development of his works. This was Buffon's appeal to the Christian rationalist. For the literal dogmatist, particularly the doctors at the Sorbonne, he had another approach.

> Besides, I have allowed myself this interpretation of the first verses of Genesis only with a great good in mind—to reconcile the science of nature with that of theology once and for all. They cannot be, I believe, in contradiction except in appearance, and my explanation seems to demonstrate it. But if this explanation, though simple and clear, seems inadequate or even improper to some spirits too strictly attached to the letter, I beg them to judge me by intention, and to consider my system on the epochs of nature as being purely hypothetical. It is harmless to revealed truths, which are so many immutable axioms, independent of all hypothesis, to which I have subordinated and now subordinate my thoughts.[40]

Through the allegorical interpretation of the days of creation Buffon hoped to ward off some of the theological criticism which his time scale was certain to arouse. The world *such as it is* was the seventh epoch in Buffon's system, and it came after the progressive work of creation had been finished. The other six epochs corresponded to the days of creation and were thus outside Biblical genealogy, as long as the Biblical day was interpreted as a period of time. Once this concession was granted to Buffon, he was willing to defend Biblical chronology. "It is correctly said,

[40] *Oeuvres*, IX, 478.

and even rigorously maintained, that since the last period, since the end of the works of God, that is, since the creation of man, only six or eight thousand years have passed, because the different genealogies of mankind after Adam indicate no more. We owe this faith, this mark of submission and respect to the oldest, the most sacred of all traditions. We owe it even more, we must never permit ourselves to deviate from the letter of this holy tradition except when the latter is self-contradictory. . . ."[41] In Buffon's cosmic evolution the need for time was in the period of the pre-history of man and by the device of considering the revolutions in nature as part of the creative act of God, he thought he might avoid entanglement with the scriptural genealogy.

Ending cosmic evolution with the creation of man did not mean, however, that the process of evolution stopped at this point in Buffon's system. He had no sympathy whatsoever with the primitivism of Rousseau and regarded man's progress as an upward struggle out of barbarism. With the advent of man in the world, a new force in the creative process was added—civilization. Through the arts and sciences man was given the possibility of bringing the earth under control and developing its potentialities. It would not be too much to say that Buffon felt God had turned over the work of creation to his first lieutenant, or to avoid bringing a capricious spiritual connotation into the naturalistic work, man became Nature's agent. Herault de Sechelles said that Buffon no longer dared to use the word God and put in its place the power of Nature.[42] Flourens disagreed with Sechelles, but it seems evident that Buffon used Nature in the sense of God as well as in the number of other active and passive meanings of the eighteenth century. In either cosmic cause, God or Nature, man became a shaping force in the seventh epoch, entitled, "When the Power of Man Assisted that of Nature."

[41] *Ibid.*, IX, 476.
[42] Marie Jean Pierre Flourens, *Buffon. Histoire de ses travaux et de ses idées* (Paris, 1844), pp. 252-5.

The epochs corresponding to the days of creation were: (1) when the earth and planets took their form; (2) when the matter, being consolidated, formed the inner rock of the globe, as well as the great vitrifiable masses on its surface; (3) when the waters covered our continents; (4) when the waters retreated and volcanoes began to act; (5) when the elephants and other southern animals inhabited the northern lands; and (6) when the continents were separated. It would not serve our purposes here to go into a detailed analysis of the various epochs other than where they touch upon chronology and its ramifications.

There was little in the first epoch that Buffon had not described in his essay on the formation of planets. A comet struck the sun a glancing blow, forcing off torrents of incandescent solar material. The lightest parts of the detached material were flung to the greatest distances, spreading the solar material out into a plane around the equator of the sun. Mutual attraction between the particles then pulled the masses of matter into globes, our planets, but when the globes commenced rotating around their own axes, gravitational force could not hold all the matter in equilibrium, and centrifugal force caused the excess matter to be cast off and to become satellites. This simultaneous origin of the planetary system enabled Buffon to explain the common plane in which the planets revolved, their similar direction of revolution, their order of decreasing densities away from the sun, and most important of all for his system, the source of their molten fluidity.

That the earth was once in a primitive state of original fluidity, Buffon thought, was demonstrated by physics, gravitation, and pendulum experiments. Since water could not dissolve the bulk of the earth's matter, and if it could, there was too little of it to make a solution out of the dry materials, Buffon found moltenness to be the only possible kind of fluidity. This was the first great fact in Buffon's system. The second was cooling, or loss of heat. Once the globes of molten material had arrived at an equilibrium between gravitational and centrifugal forces and assumed their oblate spheroidal shapes, the dissipation of heat commenced the process of solidification at the surface. As soon as a crust had been formed on the molten mass, it impeded the rate of heat loss and put a barrier between the globes and the volatile parts of the surrounding atmosphere.

A period of stress and strain set in with the solidification of the outer crust. The cooling continued, but the mass was still incandescent and sent the atmospheric elements exploding back as steam and vapor when they came in contact with it. Explosions, eruptions, cracking, and other disturbances wracked the surface of the earth, giving rise to the original mountains and valleys of the world, like those still to be seen on the surface of the moon and some of the other planets. The first epoch was brought to a close with the solidification of the earth to its center and the loss of incandescence after a period of 2,936 years.

The three thousand years of his first epoch was still an insignificant part of the time scale Buffon was developing, and before proceeding to the second epoch he thought it desirable to try again to remove some of the prejudice against his enlarged view of the history of the earth.

I must reply to a kind of objection that has already been made on the very long duration of time. Why throw us, it has been said, into space as vague as a duration of 168,000 years? because, from your system, the earth has aged 75,000 years, and living nature must subsist for 93,000 more. Is it easy, is it even possible to form an idea of the whole or of the parts of such a long course of centuries? I have no other reply than the exposition of the monuments and the consideration of the works of nature. I will give the details and the dates in the following epochs, and it will be seen that far from having unnecessarily increased the duration of time, I have perhaps shortened it far too much.

And why does the human mind seem to get lost in the space of duration rather than in that of extension, or in the consideration of measures, weights and numbers? Why are 100,000 years more difficult to conceive and to count than 100,000 pounds of money? [43]

Was it difficult to envisage large tracts of time, Buffon asked, because we have never experienced them ourselves or seen them take place? Was it because in our own short existence a hundred years seems like such a long time that we have difficulty in grasping the extent of a thousand years? The way to grasp the idea of a long stretch of time was to divide it into parts and to compare the parts with events taking place within them, he recommended. Envisage the number of centuries needed to produce all the shelled animals of the earth, then the number necessary for depositing their remains at the depths where we find them, and again, count the centuries necessary for the petrifaction of these materials. The slow, steady building of these deposits alone would add up to an enormous period of time, and Buffon repeated that he had restricted the limits of time as much as he possibly could without contradicting "the facts deposited in the archives of nature." [44]

In the second epoch the basic skeleton of the earth's surface was formed. As the earth contracted from cooling, mountains arose, subterranean cavities were enlarged and the chemicals of the earth were sublimated. Buffon believed that the great mountain chains dated from this period, and he pictured them as standing with sharp peaks, untouched by the destructive action of water. The second epoch lasted from 30,000 to 35,000 years, and in that time the earth cooled to the point where it could have been touched by the hands of a man. The water vapors of the atmosphere could then condense on the crust without being converted back into steam, and the third epoch commenced with the falling of waters onto the earth's surface.

Torrential rains beating down on the pristine vitreous masses

[43] *Oeuvres*, IX, 493. In the manuscript, Buffon had written 400,000 or 500,-000 instead of 168,000. (See Picard's edition of *Époques*, p. 64.)
[44] *Ibid.*, IX, 495.

commenced a revolution in the structure of the earth's surface. Rains, floods, torrents, waves, and the action of water in general "gave a second form to the greatest part of the surface of the earth." The waters dissolved, broke, and wore down the exposed parts of the primitive earth, and eventually the waters and the detritus covered all but the highest parts of the earth. Clays and sands began to accumulate in beds on the floor of this ocean and in the hot waters appeared the earth's first life, shell-fish and plants.

The warmth of the waters and a primeval fertility, Buffon thought, added force to the first life and produced on the land large tropical plants and in the seas huge ammonites. For about 20,000 years these shell-animals and plants multiplied prodigiously. The earth's many deep beds of calcareous materials were formed out of the remains of the marine life and our coal deposits from the vegetable remains. The building up of these beds as well as the formation of marble and other sedimentary stone, testified to the long duration of the third epoch. Again Buffon reminded his readers, "This long course of centuries, this duration of 20,000 years, seems to me much too short for the succession of events that all these monuments demonstrate to us."[45]

A period of violent volcanic activity marked the fourth epoch. Large cavities were opened up in the earth, and there was a retreat of the seas as the waters filled them. As the waters slowly withdrew from the continents they sculptured out the valleys and contours of the land, a process interrupted only by the eruption of volcanoes on the continents. Gradually, the volcanoes became quiescent. The violent explosions, inundations, earthquakes, and catastrophes subsided about 60,000 years after the earth's formation, and in the period of relative calm following this epoch terrestrial animals appeared on the earth.

The first land animals which were to dominate the earth during the fifth epoch, like the first marine animals, were larger than

[45] *Ibid.*, IX, 519.

those of today because of the primitive fertility and heat of the
earth. Since the earth was oblate, Buffon supposed that the cooling
of a thicker equatorial region would be several thousand years
behind that of the northern regions, so he thought that animal
life made its first appearance near the Poles. The discovery of
mastodon fossil bones in Siberian lands convinced Buffon that the
dominant species of the period were huge elephants, rhinoceroses,
and hippopotamuses who lumbered through steaming tropical
jungles in Siberia.

As the earth continued to cool, the tropical plants and animals
began to migrate slowly toward the equatorial regions, and at the
same time, the continents began to separate as a result of the movement of waters in the oceans and continued land disruptions. The
process of separation, Buffon's sixth epoch, lasted 5,000 years.
Some 70,000 years had now transpired in the history of the earth,
and at this point the work of creation was ended with the appearance of man. The earth was now ready to be inhabited by God's
noble creature. "Thus we are persuaded, independently of the
authority of the sacred books," Buffon assured his readers, "that
man has been created last, and that he arrived to take the scepter
of the earth only when it was found worthy of his empire." [46]
Nature had not really ended her work of creation, as Buffon goes
on to show in his seventh epoch, but rather she changed her instrumentality from brute forces to intelligence, from the physical
to the cultural, and henceforth evolution was to be centered
around the activities of man.

Men first appeared on the high steppes of Asia, according to
Buffon, just in time to witness the last convulsive movements of
the earth. Having only a few mountains for refuge from inundations, they were often driven from these asylums trembling with
fear from the trembling under their feet caused by earthquakes.
Naked in mind and body, exposed to all the ravages of the elements, the prey of ferocious animals, these primitive men were

[46] *Ibid.*, ix, 560.

driven by terror and necessity to work together for common defense and an improvement in their way of life. Slowly civilization emerged. This conception of the rise of civilized man was as old as Lucretius and was often reiterated in the seventeenth and eighteenth centuries, but Buffon traced it out in more detail and added several twists which stamp the *Epochs* as the work of an eighteenth-century *philosophe*.

At the outset of his *Epochs*, Buffon had taken over the interpretation that Genesis was written for the vulgar mob in terms it could understand, and he had used this interpretation to expand the days of creation. Now that he had reached the advent of man on the earth, Buffon claimed that all the great deluges had occurred in a previous epoch, hence the universal flood was prior to the creation of Adam by about 35,000 years. The Biblical Flood was only a local inundation, in his view, and there were many such flood traditions among various peoples. Buffon proceeded to explain why, and the Sorbonne must have shuddered at his exegesis, for he reduced the traditions to a kind of superstition.

Although the lot of man became easier with the development of civilization, in Buffon's theory, the calamities of his first state left an indelible mark on his mind. The idea that he must perish by a universal deluge or by a general conflagration; the respect he had for certain mountains which had proved to be a safe retreat from inundations; his horror of volcanic mountains throwing forth terrible fires; his fear and superstition based on the belief that there were evil spirits in nature—all these sentiments founded in terror were from then on imprinted in the mind and heart of man. By implication, the Flood of Noah had been exaggerated in the memory of terror-ridden minds, and Mount Ararat, once a refuge from natural disasters, was endowed with superstitious respect. Buffon's approach to primitive folklore was good cultural anthropology, but devious orthodoxy. There was no fall from grace, no departure from paradise, in Buffon's conception of primitive man. The *philosophe* looked to man's perfectibility in the future through the use of intelligence: "who knows to what degree man would be able to perfect his nature, both morally and physically?"[47] Through Reason man could perfect his society, establish equality among men, abolish war and find peace. Man had only to follow the path of science and culture. Fortunately for his peace of mind, Buffon died just before the greatest blood-letting in French history, which claimed his own son, and his close friend and enthusiastic supporter, Jean Sylvain Bailly, the ill-fated acting mayor of Paris from 1789 to 1791.

In explaining the early history of man, Buffon conjectured that a high stage of civilization was reached on the steppes of Asia prior to the early history of Babylonia, Greece, and Egypt which is documented by our records. These early civilizations were remnants of an earlier civilization which had reached a high stage of development on the steppes of Asia, but which also had suffered some kind of a disaster. The advantage of such a theory to the philologists and the incipient anthropologists who were seeking an older but unitary origin for the languages and races of man is obvious. Buffon's friend, Bailly, had already given this aspect of Buffon's thought considerable publicity through a history of ancient astronomy, published in 1775, wherein he maintained that there had been a people of great learning prior to the Chinese, Hindus, Chaldeans, Egyptians, and Greeks. In studying the history of astronomy before Hipparchus and Ptolemy he thought he had found a number of great but isolated truths towering above the general ignorance of astronomy in the period. When these were all gathered together, they had the appearance of remains from a mass of knowledge that had been destroyed and scattered in fragments.[48] The general understanding of astronomy after recorded history began was inadequate to have enabled the users of the astronomical knowledge to have formulated it, he

[47] *Ibid.*, IX, 594.
[48] *Histoire de l'Astronomie ancienne* (Paris, 1775), p. 16ff.

thought. The wide dispersal of the bits of information which properly belong together, added to historical traditions such as Plato's Atlantis and the existence of a learned, dead language like Sanscrit among the Hindus convinced Bailly a culture of great antiquity had existed somewhere on the steppes of Asia and had been the fountainhead from which the Hindus and Chinese had received their knowledge of astronomy. When the culture of the "lost people" fell, the source of astronomical knowledge was dimmed in the memories of the transmitters, and they claimed the credit for originating the knowledge, though they proved incapable of adding to it.

After the publication of Buffon's *Epochs* which contained an elaboration on the idea of a lost people of high culture on the steppes of Asia, Bailly sent to press a series of letters exchanged between himself and Voltaire on Plato's Atlantis.[49] The letters were written to convert Voltaire to the view that there had been a lost people of greater antiquity than the Brahmins. The first letter in the series was from Voltaire thanking Bailly for a copy of the history of astronomy, December 15, 1775, and stating his agreement that the knowledge, superstitions, and fables of the different nations had been derived from a primitive nation. However, he had long been accustomed to think that this primitive nation was the ancient dynasty of the Brahmins, "The Old Invalid" assured Bailly. In a subsequent letter he asserted: "The notion, that our poor globe was once hotter than it is at present, gives me little concern. I have never read the Central Fire of M. de Mairan; but since we have renounced our belief in Tartarus, I apprehend the doctrine of central fire can obtain but little credit."[50] Furthermore, he doubted if civilization could have commenced in the colder climates above the Indian lands of the Ganges region.

[49] *Lettres sur l'Atlantide de Platon* (Paris, 1779)
[50] *The Ancient History of Asia and Remarks on the Atlantis of Plato*, 2 vols. (London, 1814), I, 49.

The interest Voltaire showed in the question of his "lost people" moved Bailly to a passionate desire to convince the philosopher of Ferney. In ten long letters written in 1776 Bailly poured out his arguments to Voltaire on the proofs and evidences of there being a lost people of great antiquity. The ninth letter dealt with the central fire, or the internal heat of the globe.[51] Tartarus, he pointed out, had nothing to do with the central fire discovered by Mairan. He repeated Mairan's conclusions that the heat of the sun by itself was inadequate to sustain life on the face of the globe and gave the supporting series of thermometric investigations of cold made by Amontons, Mairan, and others. The tenth letter dealt with the refrigeration of the earth, or the decrease of the native heat of the globe, and here he enthusiastically introduced the ideas of Buffon on the cooling of the earth over a long period of time. This evoked another reply from Voltaire, who wrote that he still doubted that there was a people more ancient than the Brahmins, but:

> The artichokes and asparagus which I have eaten this year, in the month of January, in the midst of frost and snow, and which were produced without one ray of the sun, or an atom of artificial fire, sufficiently convince me that the earth contains a very strong intrinsic heat. What you observe in your Ninth Letter, has afforded much more instruction than I derived from my kitchen-garden.[52]

Bailly failed to get across to Voltaire his main point on a lost people, but captured his interest with the idea of heat in the earth. Bailly continued to exercise his persuasive powers in another series of letters and called upon Voltaire "to believe in the refrigeration of the earth, in the same manner as you believed in the attraction of Newton. You are the French apostle of this sublime truth. I present you with another, which is entitled to the same homage. By defending the latter as you have done the former, you will

[51] *Ibid.*, I, 228-52.
[52] *Ibid.*, II, 5-6.

acquire equal glory."[53] Written only two weeks before Voltaire's death, it is doubtful if he ever read the appeal. Publication of the letters, however, gave more publicity to Buffon's theory of refrigeration.

Much of the reaction to central heat and the principle of the earth's refrigeration was hostile. Romé de l'Isle expressed the sentiments of a large number of the naturalists in a diatribe against Buffon, Bailly, and Mairan in 1779.[54] Nothing is more injurious to physics and the progress of human knowledge in general than to give as genuine facts, he wrote, some hypotheses sustained with a display of calculations, while contradictory facts are passed over in silence. "The evil is even greater when such suppositions are given to us with the tone of the greatest conviction by men truly eloquent, by great intellects whose superior talents have captured the approbation and admiration of their fellow men."[55]

Buffon's brilliant *Epochs of Nature* popularized the view that a natural history could be written from the archives of nature and the laws of physics and astronomy. Combining the proofs furnished by the *Principia* that the earth was once a fluid and had hardened in the shape of an oblate spheroid, the experiments based on the rates of cooling in a globe the size of the earth suggested by Newton, the idea of a molten fluidity of the primitive earth borrowed by Leibniz, the evidence from fossils and strata formations of a long series of changes on the crust of the earth, Buffon unfolded, both in its life and structure, the cosmic evolution of the earth down to the present along an historical dimension of actual elapsed time. Though striving at all times to confine the series of natural operations within their smallest temporal scope, he could not come within 70,000 years of the five or six thousand allotted to the history of the world by Scripture, and an

[53] *Ibid.*, II, 318-19.
[54] J. B. L. Romé de l'Isle, *L'Action du feu central bannie de la surface du globe, et le soleil rétabli dans ses droits, contre les assertions de MM. le Comte de Buffon, Bailly, de Mairan, &c.* (Stockholm, 1779)
[55] *Ibid.*, p. 2.

honest appraisal of the necessary duration according to the evidences of nature would have required about a million years, he recognized.

He strongly emphasized that the natural processes and events should be proportioned to the time necessary for their completion, and that the time could be reconstructed by an application of the comparative method to the monuments of the processes.

> There is, then, the order of time indicated by facts and monuments; there are six epochs in the course of the first ages of nature; six spaces of duration whose limits, although indeterminate, are not the less real; because these epochs are not, like those of civil history, marked by fixed points, or limited by centuries and other portions of the time we are able to count and measure correctly. Nevertheless we can compare them to one another in evaluating their relative duration, and muster to each of these periods of duration other monuments and facts which will indicate contemporary dates, and perhaps intermediate and subsequent epochs as well.[56]

Buffon had not claimed that his *Epochs* presented more than an outline of the main epochs, and the duration of these he had foreshortened to appease the prejudice against a history of more than six thousand years. In a deleted passage of the manuscript copy of the *Epochs*, Buffon had written in a preamble to a digression on the duration of the ages that when he counted only 74,000 or 75,000 years for the time passed since the formation of the planets, he gave notice that he constrained himself in order to oppose received ideas as little as possible. To explain the phenomena satisfactorily, he continued, it was not some thousands of years, but a million, if not more, he would have to assign to the single epoch of cooling.[57] Picard observed, Buffon's "thought and imagination were not frightened of the horizons opened by modern science on the abyss of centuries and the immensity of time which, according to his own expression 'seems to flee and stretch out as we try to seize it.' "[58]

[56] *Oeuvres*, IX, 472.
[57] Picard, *Époques*, pp. liii-liv.   [58] *Ibid.*, p. liv.

THE EMBRYO-STATE UNIVERSE

David Hume brought three eighteenth-century world-views into juxtaposition through his interlocutors in the *Dialogues Concerning Natural Religion*, published posthumously in 1779. Demea represented traditional orthodoxy wherein a knowledge of God was given a priori and a knowledge of the world's origin was given by revelation. Cleanthes, the Lockean deist who denied all a priori knowledge, found an a posteriori proof of God in the evidences of design in nature. He eloquently praised the intricacies of the great machine of nature and all its infinite number of lesser machines as analagous, though on a vastly extended scale, to the productions of human contrivance. The sceptic Philo countered the mechanomorphic universe of Cleanthes with the idea of a universe which had simply grown out of an embryo-state through its own inherent principles of generation: "The world plainly resembles more an animal or vegetable, than it does a watch or a knitting-loom."[59] Philo suggested that the argument from analogy had been too much restricted to the mental faculties and that there were other analogies in nature which quite dispensed with the idea of God as the great Author and Artificer:

> Look round this universe. What an immense profusion of beings, animated and organized, sensible and active! You admire this prodigious variety and fecundity. But inspect a little more narrowly these living existences, the only beings worth regarding. How hostile and destructive to each other! How insufficient all of them for their own happiness! How contemptible or odious to the spectator! The whole presents nothing but the idea of a blind Nature, impregnated by a great vivifying principle, and pouring forth from her lap, without discernment or parental care, her maimed and abortive children.[60]

Philo represented an extreme *philosophe* view of nature, and although it was used by the *philosophes* to confound deism, it

[59] *Dialogues Concerning Natural Religion*, 2nd ed. (London, 1779), p. 131.
[60] *Ibid.*, pp. 219-20.

was more than an anticlerical instrumentality. It represented an increasing awareness of the power of organic nature as a dynamic force in cosmology from about mid-century on in eighteenth-century thought. The organic model of the universe was sometimes identified with Epicureanism—so it was with Hume's Philo—but it owed more to trends of biological thought than it did to the ancients. The organic view that the world is more like an animal than a knitting-loom had begun to contest the mechanism of deism about the time of La Mettrie's *L'Homme machine*, which was published in 1748, the same year in which Maillet's evolutionistic *Telliamed* was published. Aram Vartanian has indicated how the discovery by Abraham Trembley in 1740 that the polyp had the characteristics of both a plant and an animal and that it could regenerate its own parts created a great stir involving the nature of organic matter, the nature of species, and philosophical questions pertaining to the divisibility of the soul. Vartanian has also shown how it led to the forging of a new kind of materialism through the influence of La Mettrie's work, which had been inspired by the behaviour of the polyp.[61] Diderot had already exposed the inadequacies of the cosmology of Epicureanism to explain nature through the fortuitous concourse of atoms, and the new materialism of La Mettrie avoided this element of chance by attributing the emergence of an ordered universe out of vital principles in nature itself. On the basis of the reproductive powers of the polyp, La Mettrie asserted that matter has the ability to determine its own organic structure:

> We do not understand Nature: causes concealed within herself could have brought about everything. See . . . Trembley's polyp! Does it not contain within itself the causes which produce its regeneration? What absurdity would there be, consequently, in thinking that there are certain physical causes endowed with all that is necessary to them, and to which the

[61] "Trembley's Polyp, La Mettrie, and Eighteenth-Century French Materialism," in *Roots of Scientific Thought, A Cultural Perspective*, ed. Philip P. Wiener and Aaron Noland (New York, 1957), pp. 497-516.

whole chain of this vast universe is so necessarily bound and subjected that anything that occurs could not have not occurred? [62]

The determinist materialism of La Mettrie influenced a succession of works on an embryo-state universe, but *L'Homme machine* was only one of many forces in a shift of interest towards an organic view of the universe, an organic view which did not renounce mechanism, but extended it to the organic world. There was a considerable development of interest in biology by the 1740's and in it the influence of Leibniz was manifest, especially the emphasis he had given to the continuities in nature, the chain of being extending in a connected series from the bottom to the top of the scale of life, and his organic monad. Naturalists such as Bonnet saw in the polyp a connecting link between the vegetable and animal forms of life without being led into the deterministic materialism of La Mettrie.

The development of the organic model of nature went on at several different levels of cosmology, ranging from the received cosmology of Mosaic history to that of a generated universe progressing through a time process of eternity. Buffon, as we have seen, occupied a middle ground between the two extremes, and although he was not himself a Philo, he did aid the cause of the Philos indirectly through his efforts to replace the mechanomorphic universe of the deists with an organic view of nature. Indeed, Buffon occupies a central position in the extension of the scientific revolution to the area of biology, and when in his old age he had become a public idol, the subject of poetry and the object of pilgrimages to Montbard, the letter of Catherine II telling him that Newton had taken the first step forward in science, and he had taken the second step, was not an ill-founded observation. It was Buffon's ambition to extend the philosophical system of Newton from the world of dead matter to the world of living matter.

There is hardly an idea in Buffon's philosophy which cannot be

[62] Cited in *ibid.*, p. 508.

traced to someone else, but by such criteria the reputation of many a genius would tumble. More important, he framed and projected forward a new approach to nature with a clarity and forcefulness that was decisive. The first three volumes of his *Natural History* (1749) were published in a large edition, but they were sold out in six weeks. The work was translated into German, English, and Dutch in the same year, and new impressions were brought out the following year. In these first volumes he delivered a discourse on method in which he severely criticized the work of naturalists. Too much of the calculating and counting spirit had passed from physics to the study of nature, and this indiscriminate collecting of data would never lead to any new information about the functioning of the organic world. Likewise, the analytical method which had been so successful in physics was useless in living nature. All individuals in living nature were unique and must be studied empirically each for its own sake before abstractions and classifications of phenomena are attempted. The then current practice of imposing a classification system upon nature forced the data of organisms into an arbitrary, preconceived, value-laden structure which had little or no correspondence with the reality of nature. Furthermore the analytical method employed to fill out the classification scheme emphasized the discontinuities in nature. To Buffon, all nature was a *web*, not a chain, of being. The object of the naturalist should be to find in nature the principles which integrated and sustained it, not by trying to fit organic nature to the mechanics of dead matter, but by extending the methods of mechanical philosophy to organic nature, a new class of phenomena.

Buffon thought that the idea of carrying all phenomena to mechanical principles was one of the most ingenious discoveries in philosophy, for which Descartes should be given credit. But how was this discovery applied by Descartes? After a process of reflection, comparison, measurement, and experiment, general effects led to the assumption of a mechanical principle or a quality of matter. This principle or quality is an abstraction and its nature cannot be explained, but it is enough to know how it operates. Although mechanical philosophers were suspicious of any new quality or principle discovered, they have no reason to presume that their enumerated qualities represent the totality of nature. The trouble with the philosophy of Descartes was that he employed too small a number of general effects and then excluded the rest from his system. The situation was remedied to some extent by Newton, who discovered from general effects the operation of a new mechanical principle in nature. But still, Buffon thought, the study of general effects, out of which new mechanical principles are discovered, had not progressed beyond dead matter, and thus it left the whole world of living nature untouched.[63]

The mass of data in the organic world was overwhelming and it needed to be studied for those effects which would reveal integrating principles. Then, and only then, would be discovered the same kind of order which Newton and others had found in the chaos of phenomena pertaining to dead matter. Although the mechanical principle of gravitation could not be explained, we know from its effects that it penetrates all matter and furnishes the attractive forces which hold matter together. By analogy, Buffon said, there were other immaterial penetrating forces operating in organized bodies. From his study of nature Buffon concluded that such a Newtonian mechanical principle of attraction in living nature was: matter tends to organize itself. But how does this process take place? Again falling back on analogy, Buffon tried to formulate a kind of Newtonian atomic theory for living matter. Perhaps the monad of Leibniz was his model for the basic unit of his system, which was the *molécule organique*. These molecules could exist by themselves. They were finite in number, but innumerable. They were fixed in quantity, irreduci-

[63] *L'Histoire naturelle* (1749) in *Oeuvres philosophiques de Buffon*, ed. Jean Piveteau (Paris, 1954), p. 249.

ble, and immutable. They formed all the substance of organized matter. As a further explanation of how the organizing principle in nature functioned, Buffon brought forward his theory of *moules intérieurs*, about which his wellwishers prefer to say nothing. No one had seen one of these inner moulds, no one could, because we only know them from their effects. They had an active power, and as attraction penetrated matter and integrated it, so these moulds acted upon the *molécules organiques*. They governed the relationship of parts of an organism, its nutrition, development, and reproduction, utilizing the molecular building blocks of organic nature. The process of integrating went on unceasingly, and destruction was itself only a part of the endless process in which *molécules organiques* were freed and made available to the activity of integration by *moules*. These *moules* appear to be summed up in the general term of Nature as Buffon uses it, and he writes that for nature the work of organizing costs nothing and is stopped only by the limits and resistance of the materials in which the organic matter is incorporated. The sheer mass of this organizing activity is overwhelming, as Buffon shows at considerable length, and he carries his theory to the fossil strata to illustrate how much of the world is comprised of the *molécules organiques*.[64]

The theory of Buffon is fraught with difficulties, but it is not necessary here to do more than point out some of the ramifications of it. Aside from the general influence which he exerted on the study of nature, Buffon emphasized the process of living forces in nature with striking effect. He turned away from the Newtonian mechanical contrivances in nature and tried to impose a Newtonian system of operations, in which the whole was fixed, but all the parts were interchangeable. It was a balanced system following mechanical principles in which the processes of destruction were a necessary function for the continued activity of the organizing principle, since there was a fixed quantity of

[64] For example, in *Seconde Vue* (1765), *ibid.*, p. 37 ff.

organic matter to work with. Nature, not God creating *ex abrupto*, was the great worker in Buffon's system, and nature, though it had fixed limits, pressed its vivifying principles to the limit and in the process turned out great varieties of organisms.

The battle cry on method was taken up by Maupertuis and Diderot, as well as by Buffon, with Newton as the model. Who influenced whom is not easy to discern amongst men writing in the short span of years around the middle of the century, but there is a resemblance of ideas between La Mettrie, Buffon, Maupertuis, Diderot, and Holbach, to mention only a few. Diderot's *Pensées sur l'interprétation de la nature* (1754) was a brilliant restatement of much of what Buffon had said, including the idea that nature varies the same mechanism in an infinity of different ways. This same thought may be found also in the writings of Maupertuis, and it was developed in a more sensational way by the Baron de Holbach.

In his 1757 article in the *Encyclopédie* on *fossiles*, Holbach had expressed his sympathy with those ancients who believed that the sea had formerly stayed on our continents for a long course of ages. Any other system, he felt, was subject to insuperable difficulties in explaining the fossil strata of the earth. He developed his own views at greater length in the two sections of the article *"Terre"* (1765) on the strata of the earth and the revolutions of the earth. The alterations of the earth's axis had been responsible for revolutions of the earth's surface in ages long past, he conjectured, but there was also a continuing revolution being effected through the actions of winds, waters, volcanoes, and the constant changes in nature.

> We see all these causes, often combined, perpetually acting on our globe; it is not surprising then, that the earth shows us, almost at every step, a vast mass of debris and ruins. Nature is busy destroying in one part in order to produce new bodies in another . . . let us conclude then, that the earth has been and still is exposed to continual revolutions, which contribute with-

out cease, either suddenly, or little by little, to change its face.[65]

This thought on the constant changes in nature was expanded in Holbach's *Système de la nature* (1770), the "Bible of Atheism," to which Diderot may have added the notes and some pages of text.[66] Morley has said of the work, "No book has ever produced a more widespread shock. Everybody insisted on reading it, and almost everybody was terrified."[67] There were no final causes in the system, no external deity working on dead matter, no fixed species, no favored species, only endless trials, failures, and survivals in an eternal chain of cause and effect in the busy workshop of nature.

Matter was eternal, in Holbach's system, but all its forms were the products of time and change. Nature was always casting matter into new combinations, which could only survive if they met general laws and the particular circumstances and relationships of the environment, and what we call monsters are only productions inadequately organized or adapted for survival. All the individuals of a species are unique and vary from one another, however slightly, and the species have all undergone, and would continue to undergo, change in an infinity of successive developments as changing external conditions destroyed the suitability of some forms and made the survival of new variations possible. It is not clear, however, to what extent Holbach thought there was a genetic relationship between the species themselves.[68]

Holbach thought that the earth was a product of time, not an eternal form, and that all the organized beings on it were particular productions suitable to it alone. The earth had passed through many changes, however, and these were recorded in the earth

---

[65] *Encyclopédie*, XVI, 166 ff.

[66] See "Extrait de la correspondance de Grimm," in prefatory material of Paris edition, 1821. The title page also states that the new edition has notes and corrections by Diderot, and this is discussed in John Morley's *Diderot and the Encyclopaedists* (London, 1878), II, 173.

[67] Morley, *Diderot*, II, 174.

[68] *Système de la nature* (Paris, 1821), I, 97ff.

itself. Vast continents had been engulfed by the seas, whose sojourn on the very places we now inhabit is attested by shells, the remains of fish, and other marine productions, and the elements had long disputed the empire of our globe. The revolutions and overthrows of nature had left masses of debris and ruins which can be seen everywhere.[69] Confronted with this series of changing conditions, man must have changed his form many times, Holbach conjectured, or he would have perished ages ago.

The appearance of novity in man's civilization seemed to contradict a development through the long ages assumed by Holbach. Maillet had met this objection by suggesting that calamities, civil and natural, had periodically wiped out the gains made by man in the arts and sciences. Maupertuis had expressed a similar idea, referring to the fossil masses as an indication of great catastrophes which might have broken the continuity of civilization.[70] Holbach likewise supposed that the revolutions which convulsed nature in the past had periodically destroyed peoples, leaving only a few survivors who had to struggle against new conditions so desperately that only a lingering memory of previous progress in the arts and sciences was retained. Commenting on the terror which these revolutions must have struck in the heart of man, Holbach went on to trace the origin of nature worship, mythology, superstition, and finally religion, from primitive man's desire to protect himself against the ravages of nature by enlisting the aid of supernatural powers.[71]

The affinity of Holbach's system with Diderot's ideas on nature was so obvious that it was at first thought that Diderot had written the *Système de la nature*, and Diderot judiciously left Paris in case a warrant was issued against him. In his *Pensées sur l'interprétation de la nature*, Diderot had suggested the "embryo"

[69] *Ibid.*, I, 446-7.
[70] "Essai de cosmologie," *Oeuvres de M. de Maupertuis* (Lyon, 1756), I, 71-4.
[71] *Système*, I, 468ff.

theory of nature. "What we take for the history of nature," he wrote, "is only the very incomplete history of an instant." An individual is born, grows, exists, declines and perishes, he observed. Perhaps it is the same with entire species. Although faith teaches us that all the animals left the hands of the Creator as we now see them, would not the philosopher, left to his own thoughts, suspect,

> that from all eternity animal life has had its particular elements scattered throughout the mass of matter; that it finally came about that these elements united; that the embryo formed from these elements passed through an infinitude of organizations and developments; that it has had, in succession, movement, sensation, ideas, thought, reflection, conscience, sentiments, passions, signs, gestures, sounds, articulation, language, laws, sciences, and arts; that millions of years elapsed between each of these developments; that it will, perhaps, undergo still more development and extensions which are unknown to us; . . . that it could disappear forever from nature, or else, continue to exist under a form and with faculties completely different from those which characterize it at this instant of duration? [72]

In 1755, another work on cosmology appeared, though of a different order, the *Theory of the Heavens* by Immanuel Kant. The work was little read at the time and passed virtually unnoticed,[73]

[72] *Oeuvres complètes de Denis Diderot* (Paris, 1821), II, 217-8.

[73] This statement is often made, but I doubt that it suffered total obscurity. W. Hastie, for instance, in *Kant's Cosmogony as in his Essay on the Retardation of the Rotation of the Earth and his Natural History and Theory of the Heavens* (Glasgow, 1900), pp. xvii-xxviii, says that Arago, the French astronomer, first called the attention of scientists to Kant's cosmology in 1842, that Alexander von Humboldt again emphasized its importance in 1845, and that it was only after Kant's theory was made known in this fashion that Thomas Wright of Durham's theory of the universe was re-discovered. However, without making any effort to investigate the problem, I find in the catalogue of works in the well-known *Course of Lectures on Natural Philosophy and the Mechanical Arts* (London, 1807) by Thomas Young the following entries: "*Kant*, Allgemeine naturgeschichte. 8 Konigb. 1755," and "*Wright's* theory of the universe. 4 London, 1750." (II, 324-5) It is true that later editions of Young's *Course* omitted the

but its author was influenced by the currents of thought coming from France and England. There had been much talk of infinity in connection with the debates of Clarke and Leibniz, and in the Newtonian Age, poets such as Pope, Addison, and von Haller, had exercised their eloquence on the size of the universe. Kant quoted them on infinity—von Haller, for instance:

> Infinity! What measures thee?
> Before thee worlds as days, and man as moments flee!
> Mayhap the thousandth sun is rounding now;
> And thousands still remain behind!

There had also been some talk of eternity, as a natural concomitant of infinity, but great pains had been taken to ensure that this earth had been created. There were suggestions that the worlds of the universe might appear something like numbers in an infinite series, and Kant ingeniously saw the worlds appearing in an embryo-like universe which was doomed to grow, once generated, through all eternity. He made the process of growth commensurate with the size of the poet's infinite universe and the infinite series of mathematics.

Immanuel Kant had written a paper in 1754 on the question of

---

catalogue, but clearly the brilliant professor of physics, who took his doctor's degree in physics at Göttingen in 1796, deserves to take precedence over Arago in this matter. But earlier still, *The Edinburgh Review*, 1 (1803), 253-280, carried a review of Charles François Dominique de Villers, *Philosophie de Kant, ou, principes fondamentaux de la philosophie transcendentale* (Metz, 1801) which stated: "It is not merely as a metaphysician that he claims to be considered; for there is scarcely a science which he has not endeavoured to illustrate. 'He is a mathematician, an astronomer, a chymist: . . .' His commentator, zealous for his fame, contends that the planet *Herschell* ought rather to have been known to astronomers under another name; as, twenty-six years before the discovery of that portion of our system, its existence had been predicted by Kant, in some 'conjectures on the heavenly bodies which probably exist beyond the orbit of Saturn,' published in 1755, in a work entitled, 'The natural history of the world, and theory of the heavens, on the principles of the Newtonian philosophy.'" Could such a claim have passed before the eyes of Englishmen without investigation?

whether or not from a physical point of view, the earth aged but without pretending to answer the question in a rigorous scientific manner. The theme of his query was provided by the statement of Fontenelle about the roses trying to guess the age of their gardener. "Our gardener, they said, must be a very old man; within the memory of roses he is the same as he has always been; it is impossible he can ever die, or be other than he is."[74] To know if a thing is young, old, or older, instead of counting the number of years it has existed, Kant thought, its length of existence should be measured against the existence of other things. He concluded that if the parts of the system of creation were compared with one another the course of 5,000 or 6,000 years given to the duration of the earth would be only what a year is to the life of a man.[75] And despite the perennial complaints of old men that the earth is not what it used to be, even in a thousand years men might not be able to detect any more changes in the earth than the roses did in the gardener.

The answer to his question could not be found in living nature or even in recorded history, Kant explained, but must be sought in the whole succession of changing scenes of nature from beginning to end. The earth rose out of chaos and took on a spheroidal form while it was still fluid. As it hardened, large lumps of the atmospheric elements were caught inside the earth, and the action of these elastic particles under the hardened crust led to a bursting action on the surface, which flooded the lands with water and created mountains, valleys, and other topographical features. Seas were formed, and as waters cast upon the dry land tried to return to the seas they sculptured the land. The earth at this stage was young and fresh and only half formed, but the erosion of rains and floods brought about the maturation of the earth, while man, in Lucretian manner, was finally able to descend

[74] "Die Frage: Ob die Erde veralte? physikalisch erwogen," in *Immanuel Kant's Sämmtliche Werke in Chronologischer Reihenfolge*, ed. G. Hartenstein (Leipzig, 1867-9), I, 189.
[75] *Ibid.*

from the high mountains to newly made plains. Kant devoted some attention to the measurement of deposits by Manfredi, and others, and the time thus indicated for the resulting changes of land. The final end of the earth he thought might be brought about by the fiery material in the interior of the earth which fed volcanoes gradually eating away at the vault of the outer crust until the land collapsed into the fiery magma and was overflowed by it.

In the following year, 1755, Kant brought out his *Universal Natural History and Theory of the Heavens; or An Essay on the Constitution and Mechanical Origin of the Whole Universe Treated according to Newton's Principles.* He opened his Preface with a consideration of the relation of his system to religion. "I did not enter on the prosecution of this undertaking until I saw myself in security regarding the duties of religion," he wrote, and finding his efforts free from everything reprehensible, he was "ready to submit to the judicial severity of the orthodox Areopagus with a frankness which is the mark of an honest conviction."[76] That his system had a resemblance to those of Lucretius, Epicurus, Leucippus and Democritus, Kant would not deny, but he disavowed any sympathy for the blind chance of these authors. Kant found in the orderly processes and awesome intricacies of nature's machinery the highest manifestation of God. He wrote, *"there is a God, just because nature even in chaos cannot proceed otherwise than regularly and according to order."*[77] The greater the proportions of the system of creation, the more Kant found to admire in the power of God, and with this reverent attitude towards God's handicraft and intelligent purpose Kant made no effort to restrict his imagination to scriptural dogma.

The nebular theory unfolded in Kant's *Universal Natural History* was produced after Buffon's theories of the earth and planets and owed something to them, particularly the idea that the bodies of the planetary system had a common origin and that the scale

[76] Hastie, *op. cit.*, p. 18.
[77] *Ibid.*, p. 26.

of densities of the planets is in accordance with their distance from the sun.[78] Kant supposed that all the matter of the solar system had been broken up into its elementary particles at the beginning and was distributed throughout space. The forces of attraction and repulsion set the particles into a movement of vortices or whorls until they took on a uniform direction of movement in one plane. The matter aggregated first into rotating rings and then into globular bodies, the largest being the sun at the center. Before completely forming into their final global shape, however, the planets may have had rings about them like Saturn, Kant thought. "May it not be imagined that the Earth as well as Saturn once had a ring?"[79] This ring would maintain itself for a long time until the earth had reached its present rate of rotation through retarding forces. Kant could not resist an explanation of the Noachian deluge:

> A ring around the earth! What a beautiful sight for those who were created to inhabit the earth as a paradise! What a convenience for those on whom nature was designed to smile on all sides! But all this is still nothing compared with the confirmation which such an hypothesis may borrow from the record of the History of Creation, and which is no small recommendation of it for the approval of those who believe that they do not desecrate, but establish, the honour of revelation when they employ it to give confirmation to the revellings of their own understanding. The water of the firmament, which the Mosaic description mentions, has already caused not a little trouble to commentators. Might this ring not be used to help them out of this difficulty? This ring undoubtedly consisted of watery vapours. And besides the advantage which it might furnish to the first inhabitants of the earth, it had further this property of being able to be broken up on occasion, if need were, to punish the world which had made itself unworthy of such beauty, with a Deluge.[80]

[78] *Ibid.*, pp. 93-4.
[79] *Ibid.*, p. 129.
[80] *Ibid.*, p. 130.

The ring could have been destroyed either by the attraction of a passing comet on the regular movements of its particles, or by the cooling of the region in which it was situated. The condensation of the vapor particles and their precipitation would have resulted "in one of the most awful deluges upon the earth." The whole world would be submerged under water, while the poisonous vapors sucked into the rain would have brought all creatures near death and destruction. The figure of the pale light ring on the horizon would disappear from man's view, and he would associate the disappearance of that bow with the terror of Divine vengeance. The appearance of the rainbow after the tragic Deluge would be taken by man as an assurance from Heaven, a gracious sign and monument, of God's reconciliation and intention of preserving the now altered earth. This hypothesis of the rainbow as a memorial sign of the breakup of the ring may recommend itself, he thought, "to those who are devoted to the prevailing tendency to bring miracles of Revelation into a system along with the ordinary laws of nature."[81] For himself, he preferred to "sacrifice the transient approval which such harmonizings may awaken, entirely to the true pleasure which arises from the perception of the regular connection of things, when physical analogies support each other in demonstrating physical truths."[82]

Even if Kant had been serious about the Noachian Deluge, his conception of cosmic events was on such a grandiose scale that it would only appear as an incident in the universe. In describing the formation of the solar system Kant was merely using a particular instance of the cosmic process. He saw the sun as only one star among the myriads of the universe which had evolved out of the elementary particles of matter. Every star in the Milky Way possibly had a planetary system, and the Milky Way itself is only

[81] Burnet in his *Theory* (Bk. II, Ch. 5) thought that the rainbow was a postdiluvian phenomenon which first appeared as a sign, or promise, from God to Noah that the world should not be again destroyed by water.
[82] Hastie, *op. cit.*, p. 131.

a small part of the universe now and an infinitely smaller part of
the universe still in prospect.

In Kant's system the primary matter of the universe was not
distributed evenly throughout all space, nor did the stars all arise
at the same time. Leaning on the hypothesis of Thomas Wright
of Durham that the stars were spread out in the heavens in the
form of a gigantic grindstone, he supposed that the primary
matter congregated more densely in one area to form a nucleus
out of which the rest of the visible universe expanded in a flat
disc-like plane. The Milky Way was the center of this grindstone
and the other star-systems were spread out around it like a planetary system. The totality was governed by the laws of gravitation
as in our own system, and all the stars were members in a great
and connected chain of nature. From the center, the process of
creation continued to evolve systems out towards the remoter
regions, gradually filling up infinite space in the progress of eternity with numberless worlds and systems.

> . . . at the primary stirring of nature, formation will have begun
> nearest this centre; and in advancing succession of time the
> more distant regions of space will have gradually formed
> worlds and systems with a systematic constitution related to
> that centre. Every finite period, whose duration has a propor-
> tion to the greatness of the work to be accomplished, will al-
> ways bring only a finite sphere of its development from this
> centre; while the remaining infinite part will still be in conflict
> with the confusion and chaos, and will be the further from the
> state of completed formation the farther its distance is away
> from the sphere of the already developed part of nature.[83]

Within the larger framework of eternity itself there was also a
constant succession of finite periods of time in which worlds
arose out of chaos, reached completion, and then passed away.
The universe was constantly evolving and the process of creation
continued unceasingly.

[83] *Ibid.*, pp. 143-4.

There had mayhap flown past a series of millions of years and centuries, before the sphere of the formed nature in which we find ourselves, attained to the perfection which is now embodied in it; and perhaps as long a period will pass before Nature will take another step as far in chaos. But the sphere of developed nature is incessantly engaged in extending itself. Creation is not the work of a moment. When it has once made a beginning with the production of an infinity of substances and matter, it continues in operation through the whole succession of eternity with ever increasing degrees of fruitfulness. Millions and whole myriads of millions of centuries will flow on, during which always new worlds and systems of worlds will be formed after each other in the distant regions away from the centre of nature, . . . This infinity in the future succession of time, by which eternity is unexhausted, will entirely animate the whole range of space . . . But as, in fact, the remaining part of the succession of eternity is always infinite and that which has flowed is finite, the sphere of developed nature is aways but an infinitely small part of that totality which has the seed of future worlds in itself, and which strives to evolve itself out of the crude state of chaos through longer or shorter periods. The creation is never finished or complete. It has indeed once begun, but it will never cease.[84]

Buffon had repeatedly and eloquently extolled the activity of nature in organizing matter—organizing and destroying—through its own inherent powers. Maupertuis likewise became eloquent over the immense and unlimited fecundity of nature, wondering which honored nature the most, her precise economy or her prodigal superfluity of abundance.[85] Holbach asserted that the essence of nature is to act—all is movement in the universe, and this movement was produced, increased, and accelerated in matter without the aid of any exterior agent. This idea of a productive and organizing nature was so dominant a theme in the 1750's that it is not surprising to see it in the cosmology of Kant:

The whole portion of nature which we know, although it is

[84] *Ibid.*, pp. 145-6.
[85] *Venus physique*, in *Oeuvres*, II, 23ff.

only an atom in comparison with what remains concealed above or below the horizon, establishes at least this fruitfulness of nature, which is unlimited, because it is nothing else than the exercise of the Divine omnipotence. Innumerable animals and plants are daily destroyed and disappear as the victims of time; but not the less does nature by her unexhausted power of reproduction, bring forth others in other places to fill up the void. Considerable portions of the earth which we inhabit are being buried again in the sea, from which a favourable period had drawn them forth; but at other places nature repairs the loss and brings forth other regions which were hidden in the depths of being in order to spread over them the new wealth of her fertility. In the same way worlds and systems perish and are swallowed up in the abyss of eternity; but at the same time creation is always busy constructing new formations in the heavens, and advantageously making up for the loss.[86]

All that has had a beginning must at last perish, continued Kant, and though a world may appear stable and everlasting to our eyes, and though it may indeed have a duration of thousands or millions of centuries, it must decay and perish. We should not lament the loss of a world, however, for the prodigality of nature will make up for it in another place. In the universe the decay of heavenly bodies will first take place near the center where the productive process began, and from that region deterioration and destruction will spread to further distances till they come to bury all the world that has finished its period.[87] But on the boundaries of the developed world, nature is ever busy forming new worlds, so that while the universe grows old on one side near the center, it remains young and productive on the other. Could it be that Kant had in his mind the analogy of fossil beds—graphically portrayed by Buffon, Maillet, and Maupertuis as the remains of former worlds in the destructive part of the organic process—in his conception of the working of the cosmic process, an active process of generation on a surface ever-rising upon the remains of decayed worlds?

[86] Hastie, *op. cit.*, p. 149.   [87] *Ibid.*, pp. 150-6.

The Cleantheses of natural religion were pushing their pursuit of contrivance designs in nature down to the smallest gnat, while the Philos rejected the entire idea of a universe called into being as a completed knitting-loom. The organic view had by no means been eliminated by Descartes in seventeenth century thought, as Leibniz illustrated. Opposition to the mechanical world of Descartes was also offered by the Cambridge Platonists, who exerted their influence on the thinking of Newton. Cudworth, in 1678, criticized Descartes for rejecting Plastick Nature: *"For it is Manifest that the Operation of Nature is different from Mechanism, it doing not its Work by Trusion or Pulsion, by Knockings or Thrustings, as if it were without that which it wrought upon."*[88] There is in the generation of things a slow and gradual process, he had pointed out, "which would be Idle Pomp to an Omnipotent Agent who could dispatch his work in a moment." God had not been merely an outside artificer, claimed Cudworth, but had placed a "Manuary Opificer" in the form of "Nature" in the world to carry out His Work. There was then a vital energy, a plastic nature, at work—"there is a *Mixture* of *Life* or *Plastick Nature* together with *Mechanism*, which runs through the whole Corporeal Universe."[89] There was a plan, a design, a set of operating principles established by God in the working of the universe, but it was not fitting that God should set his own Hand to every work and do all the "Meanest and Triflingest things himself Drudgingly, without Making use of any Inferior and Subordinate Instruments."[90]

Descartes had set up a dualism between body and spirit and had excluded from mechanical philosophy that which pertained to spirit. The Cambridge Platonists could not accept the exclusion of spirit from the natural world, and Henry More, whose

[88] Ralph Cudworth, *The True Intellectual System of the Universe* (London, 1678), p. 156.
[89] *Ibid.*, p. 148.
[90] *Ibid.*, p. 149.

influence on Newton's philosophy has been made clear by E. A. Burtt and Alexandre Koyré, had insisted on the importance of spirit in the operation of nature—spirit as an immaterial power capable of penetrating matter and acting upon it, much as gravity was to function in Newton's framework of thought. Henry More defined the spirit of nature as

> *A Substance incorporeal but without sense or animadversion, pervading the whole matter of the Universe, and exercising a plastic power therein, according to the sundry predispositions and occasions of the parts it works upon, raising such Phenomena in the world, by directing the parts of the matter, and their motion, as cannot be resolved into mere mechanical power.*[91]

Newton had expressed his belief that the system of the world was the work of a divine creation, citing examples "contrived with so much Art." At the same time, he had only attempted to sketch a framework of principles in the operation of the system and reserved a place in the framework for the operation of immaterial agents. It was against these mysterious and unknown powers advanced by Newton to explain mechanical operations that the Cartesians aimed their shafts, thereby drawing out into the open this aspect of Newton's thought. As a result, we find that Newton was a source of influence in two different directions: The natural theology advocates were encouraged to go on pursuing the contrivances of the world, but Buffon was inspired to find other immaterial powers in nature, and for him nature itself became a Manuary Opificer, or secondary agent, working out the details of creation through an organic process of generation and destruction. In a system where the details were not given directly by God, it was pointless to seek designs of contrivance as a proof of deity; both Buffon and Maupertuis emphasized this.

Buffon, Maupertuis, and Kant stood with Newton on the

[91] Cited in Koyré, *From the Closed World to the Infinite Universe* (Baltimore, 1957), pp. 132-3.

existence of an external Creator who had established a framework of general principles in the universe,[92] although their concept of a creative process *in* nature was foreign to Newton, but the more extreme Philos moved farther in the direction of a trial-and-error world process, in which matter came together in a variety of combinations until organized beings capable of surviving resulted. Any organization with a defect would automatically perish in the restless universe, so that from an embryo-state of a few successful forms, gradually the trial-and-error process would develop a fully organized world with every appearance of design: "wherever matter is so poized, arranged, and adjusted, as to continue in perpetual motion, and yet preserve a constancy in the forms, its situation must, of necessity, have all the same appearance of art and contrivance which we observe at present."[93] Philo was bent on refuting the evidences of God from the analogy of design in nature, and he pointed out to Cleanthes:

> But were this world ever so perfect a production, it must still remain uncertain, whether all the excellencies of the work can justly be ascribed to the workman. If we survey a ship, what an exalted idea must we form of the ingenuity of the carpenter who framed so complicated, useful, and beautiful a machine? And what surprise must we feel, when we find him a stupid mechanic, who imitated others, and copied an art, which, through a long succession of ages, after multiplied trials, mistakes, corrections, deliberations, and controversies, had been

[92] H. Bentley Glass, in "Maupertuis, a Forgotten Genius," *Scientific American*, Vol. 193 (1955), p. 100, points out that Maupertuis was the first person on the continent to understand and appreciate Newton's laws of gravitation. Dr. Glass also points out that the idea of "a small number of laws, most wisely established, suffice for all movements" as developed by Maupertuis anticipated Claude Bernard's principle of the maintenance of the internal environment, Walter B. Cannon's principle of homeostasis, and Le Chatelier's law of chemical equilibrium. See also definitive chapters on Maupertuis by Dr. Glass in *Forerunners of Darwin*, ed. Bentley Glass, Owsei Temkin, and William L. Straus (Baltimore: Johns Hopkins Press, 1959).

[93] Hume, *Dialogues*, p. 149.

gradually improving? Many worlds might have been botched and bungled, throughout an eternity, ere this system was struck out; much labour lost; many fruitless trials made; and a slow, but continued improvement carried on during infinite ages in the art of world-making.[94]

The embryo-state theory of the universe passed by way of Buffon and Hume to Erasmus Darwin in England, directly through Buffon to Lamarck in France, and through the totality of Enlightenment philosophy to Herder, Lessing, and Goethe in Germany—not so much as a cosmic philosophy, but as an organic view of nature and history. The organic cosmic theories were a part of a total movement in the Enlightenment which began to find an interest in continuity, progression, and organic relationships, a movement marked by such diverse trends as the study of the growth of civilization, an increasing awareness among exegetes of historical development—even some appreciation for Spinoza, the sense of progress in history itself, and a heightened appreciation of the natural world, as seen in the growing Romantic movement.

Still, the whole trend of the speculation about a genetic cosmos became startlingly clear to the Demeas of the eighteenth century after the publication of Holbach's *System of Nature* and Hume's *Dialogues*. First a Cleanthes had put aside the a priori knowledge of God on the basis of the Lockean theory of knowledge, but with confident assurances that the analogies of design in nature were an adequate proof of the existence of God. Then a Philo came along and twisted the analogy argument into a proof of an open-ended creative process which destroyed the deists' proof of God. This organic cosmic process led straight towards eternalism and atheism, and the Demeas reacted violently against it. There was a renewed urgency to cut away the idea of an embryo-state universe and its process of becoming, and the simplest way to do it was to prove that the earth had been created *ex abrupto* so

[94] *Ibid.*, pp. 106-7.

recently, that is, about six thousand years ago, that there was no place in its history for the process of change and development.

Philosophe thought, by its brilliance and spirit of revolt, must naturally occupy the center of the stage in the Enlightenment period—it is the essence of enlightenment—but it rested on a broad base of solid orthodoxy in the eighteenth century which found expression in natural history through a rigid adherence to Mosaic History. Increasingly the pious naturalists attacked speculative cosmogony, appealed to the example of Newton and Bacon for a pure inductive empiricism in natural history, and sought proofs of the novity of the world and the reality of the Deluge. However, although they were a force of reaction against the genetic view, they helped to bring the time process of the speculationists into conjunction with the concrete evidence of stratigraphy.

THE RISE OF MOSAIC GEOLOGY

The philosophy of empiricism, whatever its shortcomings as a tool of received ideas, did stimulate field work. Fossils remained in the mineral classification, the third kingdom of nature, throughout the eighteenth century, and traveling naturalists added greatly to the store of knowledge about the identification and distribution of fossils. Linnaeus served as a model in field work, and he exerted an influence on the classification of fossils, although he was less successful here than in botany and biology. His travels around the Baltic Sea lands had familiarized him with many fossil deposits, and he remarked of the stone in one area, that it contained more fossils than porridge had grains. From his observations, he concluded that the fossil strata could not have been the work of one universal deluge, but were the work of time. In his last edition of the *Systema Naturae*, he wrote:

That all matter was primordially in a state of fluidity, and that the earth arose from the bosom of the waters, we have the testimony of Moses, Thales, and Seneca. And it is manifest, that the sea enveloping the chaotic nucleus, produced by slow and gradual means the continent, which by continually exhaling its dews into clouds, is regularly moistened by aetherial, rectified, deciduous showers. Genuine remains of the general deluge, as far as I have investigated, I have not found; much less the adamitic earth; but I have every where seen earths formed by the dereliction or deposition of waters, and in these the remains of a long and gradual lapse of ages.[95]

In line with his views on the succession of strata, Linnaeus put forth ideas which were later developed by Tobern Bergman and Abraham Gottlob Werner in connection with "formations," but his attempt to classify the materials of the earth by chemical and physical properties reflected the predominance of mineralogical aspects in the geological sciences. The practical interest in mining the natural resources of the earth had, of course, grown with the expansion of manufacturing and the utilization of the substances of the earth was of far more importance to mining engineers than cosmogony. Their primary concern was with the constitution of the earth's crust as it is, not as it was, and their pragmatic approach coincided neatly with the doctrinaire philosophy of empiricism. The remains of an organism in a stratum was only an empirical fact in the chemical analysis of minerals, but strata themselves were an important factor in mining because they grouped like kinds of material. Stratigraphy invariably led to cosmogony.

After his appointment to the Freiburg Mining Academy in 1775, Werner became the central figure in geology, raising it to a recognized science, and instilling in a generation of his students excellent observational techniques. But behind Werner's im-

[95] Charles Linné, *A General System of Nature*, ed. Gmelin, Fabricius, Willdenow, etc. (London, 1806), VII, 3. For the geological views of Linnaeus, see A. G. Nathorst, "Carl von Linné as a geologist," *Annual Report, 1908, Smithsonian Institution*, pp. 711-43.

pressive pragmatic science was an uncritical acceptance of the premise that water was the *prime* agency of geological action. He taught that all the substances of the earth were once dissolved in the universal, primordial waters, and that from time to time solid matter was precipitated or crystallized out of the waters to form the strata of the earth. He did envisage a succession in the deposition of materials, and he, like Linnaeus, became aware of a time process in the formation of the strata. In his *Allgemeine Betrachtungen über die festen Erdkörper*, delivered as a popular lecture in 1817, Werner remarked, "Our earth is a child of time and has been built up gradually."[96] However, in 1817 such a view had been fairly well established in geological thought, and Werner's most brilliant students, D'Aubuisson de Voisins, Leopold von Buch, and Alexander von Humboldt, had done much in establishing it after they abandoned the Neptunist teachings of their master. During the early, and most influential period of Werner's teaching, the lapse of time was susceptible to a great latitude of interpretation. There was no necessary time-cycle in precipitation, as there is in the growth span of an organism, and in a system of such precipitations, the whole process could have taken place very quickly, even within the forty days of the Deluge. The leading principle of Neptunism, that water was the prime agency in geological action, was also compatible with Mosaic cosmology, and had probably been derived from it, so it is not surprising that most of the Wernerians were also thoroughly convinced Diluvialists during the latter eighteenth century. That Neptunism had a strong theological bias was fully displayed by the violent attacks the Wernerians made on the Plutonists (or Vulcanists), who claimed that heat was an important geological agency, as well as water.

Evidences of volcanic action in the structure of the earth had often been mentioned in seventeenth and early eighteenth-century

[96] Cited in Frank Dawson Adams, *The Birth and Development of the Geological Sciences* (Baltimore, 1938), p. 221.

speculations on natural history and cosmogony, but after the middle of the eighteenth century a more systematic and objective examination of volcanic materials in the earth was undertaken by men such as Giovanni Arduino, Jean Etienne Guettard, Nicolas Desmarest, Lazarro Spallanzani, Rudolph Eric Raspe, Girard Soulavie, Peter Simon Pallas, Guy S. Tancrede de Dolomieu, and Faujas de Saint-Fond. Even the Neptunists would agree there had been some occasional volcanic activity in the past, but these Plutonists went further and gave an igneous origin to basalts, pointed out the extensive layers of lava in the strata of certain regions, particularly the Auvergne, and discovered the intrusion of once-molten material between sedimentary strata. When Desmarest, Soulavie, and Saint-Fond maintained that long periods of time must have occurred between the successive depositions of lava strata in Central France, empirically based Plutonism was brought into conflict with Mosaic history and its time scale, as well as the Neptunist doctrine of aqueous origins. This branch of Plutonism was leading in the same direction of atheism as that of the speculative systems of Plutonism, and the Wernerians took up the task of refuting all evidence which would give heat a prominent role in geological dynamics. Their horror of and their opposition to Plutonism was compounded when they were confronted with James Hutton's theory of the earth, which was first put forward in 1788 as an article in the *Transactions of the Royal Society of Edinburgh.*

In the development of cosmogonic thought, we have seen that catastrophes played an important explanatory function. The Mosaic cosmogonists utilized the idea of catastrophes to correlate natural events with the Days of Creation, the Deluge, and the divine creation of man. On the other hand, those who saw in the history of the earth a time process, were faced with the difficulty of explaining the extinction of species and the apparent novity of civilization, and they too fell back on the idea of revolutions and catastrophes. The analogy of earth history to civil history also carried with it the idea of revolutions, even catastrophes, in the course of history, and this feeling about the path of events was to be even further accentuated as Europe entered into its era of revolutions.

When Cleanthes set about refuting the eternalism in Philo's system, he appealed to the late origin of the arts and sciences and was forced to admit that human society was in a state of continual revolution, that it had often been threatened with extinction from barbarous nations, and that had these convulsions continued a little longer, learning might have been lost. However, if man had been on the earth for an eternity, was it not a certainty that other Columbuses would have discovered the new world and transplanted animals and plants. Yet we know that it has been less than three centuries since horses, cows, sheep, swine, dogs, and wheat were known in America. "Nothing less than a total convulsion of the elements will ever destroy all the EUROPEAN animals and vegetables which are now to be found in the Western world."[97] So it was that Hume set the stage for Philo:

> AND what argument have you against such convulsions, replied PHILO. Strong and almost incontestable proofs may be traced over the whole earth, that every part of this globe has continued for many ages entirely covered with water. . . . And were I obliged to defend any particular system of this nature . . . , I esteem none more plausible than that which ascribes an eternal inherent principle of order to the world; though attended with great and continual revolutions and alterations.[98]

A succession of catastrophes in a world with an inherent principle of order was somewhat incongruous, but no more so than a world machine from the hand of God so crude that its parts periodically shook violently and disrupted the works. At the beginning of the eighteenth century, when the "argument from design" began to sweep all before it, it was expected that the earth

[97] Hume, *op. cit.*, p. 123.
[98] *Ibid.*, pp. 123-4.

would turn out to be a smoothly functioning mechanism. In the *Spectator Paper* Number 543, November 22, 1712, for instance, we read that if the body of the whole earth, or indeed the whole universe, could be submitted to the examination of our senses, it would appear as well contrived a frame as that of the human body. "We should see the same concatenation and subservience, the same necessity and usefulness, the same beauty and harmony, in all and every of its parts, as what we discover in the body of every single animal." But with the increasing attention given to fossil beds, the idea of convulsions in the history of the earth became a commonplace, supported by the orthodox, admitted by the deists and determinists. It was the dubious glory of James Hutton to find in the operation of the earth the harmony sought by the deists and the order needed by the determinists.

Underlying the Huttonian system was the premise that the earth is a self-adjusting machine like an organism. "When we trace the parts of which this terrestrial system is composed, and when we view the general connection of those several parts, the whole presents a machine of a peculiar construction by which it is adapted to a certain end."[99] The end was to furnish a habitable world for living creatures, with man at the top of the hierarchy— "the globe of this earth is evidently made for man." The extent to which he believed in final causes in the design of the earth is exhibited by his remark that productions like diamonds which had a limited utility were scarce and confined to isolated localities, while a substance like iron, so universal in the operations of the globe and so necessary in a habitable world, "is found often in that profusion which equals its utility."[100]

Hutton believed that Mosaic history was correct in placing the beginning of man at no great distance in the past, since nothing

[99] James Hutton, "Theory of the Earth; or an investigation of the laws observable in the composition, dissolution, and restoration of land upon the globe," *Royal Society of Edinburgh Transactions*, 1 (1788), 209.
[100] *Ibid.*, p. 283.

had been found in written or natural monuments to alter such a view. But he took issue with the idea that the earth and other organic life had been recently created, for nine-tenths, perhaps ninety-nine hundredths, of the earth's surface was made up of the relics of sea animals. The natural histories of these animals indicated an inconceivably great period of time. Philosophers had concluded that the original constitution of the earth had been more regular and uniform than now, having been disturbed by some violent cause, and this was also the view of diluvialists. However, if the earth were considered as an organized body with a constitution that included a reproductive operation, Hutton thought, "we shall thus also be led to acknowledge an order, not unworthy of Divine wisdom, in a subject which, in another view, has appeared as the work of chance, or as absolute disorder and confusion."[101] However, "if no such reproductive power, or re-forming operation, after due enquiry, is to be found in the constitution of this world, we should have reason to conclude, that the system of this earth has either been intentionally made imperfect, or has not been the work of infinite power and wisdom."[102]

Hutton envisioned the processes of the earth in terms of the metabolism of an organic body. The whole was sustained through a constant activity of the delicately balanced forces of destruction and repair. In order to analyze these forces, however, it was necessary to consider them separately.

The present earth is sustained and nourished from the remains of a former one. A solid body of land would never answer the purpose of a habitable world, for a soil is necessary for the growth of plants. Weathering of the solid parts has slowly produced the substance of the soil, but while this process of degradation was taking place, the waters of the earth were busy carrying the soil to the sea. "If the vegetable soil is thus constantly removed from

101 *Ibid.*, p. 210.
102 *Ibid.*, p. 216.

the surface of the land, and if its place is thus to be supplied from the dissolution of the solid earth, as here represented, we may perceive an end to this beautiful machine; an end, arising from no error in its constitution as a world, but from that destructibility of its land which is so necessary in the system of the globe, in the oeconomy of life and vegetation."[103]

The total destruction of the land is an idea that is not easily grasped, Hutton pointed out, though we are the daily witness of its process. Every flood, every storm against our shores, every stream flowing down a mountainside is an attack on the bulwarks of our soil. "Thus, great things are not understood without the analyzing of many operations, and the *combination of time with many events happening in succession.*"[104] In the destruction of this ancient world "we are not to suppose, that there is any violent exertion of power, such as is required in order to produce a great event in little time; in nature, we find no deficiency in respect of time, nor any limitation with regard to power. . . . Nature does not destroy a continent from having wearied of a subject which had given pleasure, or changed her purpose, whether for a better or a worse; neither does she erect a continent of land among the clouds, to shew her power, or to amaze the vulgar man: Nature has contrived the productions of vegetable bodies, and the sustenance of animal life, to depend upon the gradual but sure destruction of a continent; that is to say, these two operations necessarily go hand in hand."[105]

An examination of the soil also shows that in it there is much decayed vegetable matter, and the hard parts of the earth, such as fossil strata, are comprised of the remains of sea animals and plants, so it is evident that organic life flourished in the former world.

The animals of the former world must have been sustained

[103] *Ibid.*, p. 215.
[104] *Ibid.*, p. 295. No italics in text.
[105] *Ibid.*, p. 294.

during indefinite successions of ages. The mean quantity of animal matter, therefore, must have been preserved by vegetable production, and the natural waste of inflammable substance repaired with continual addition; that is to say, the quantity of inflammable matter necessary to the animal consumption, must have been provided by means of vegetation. Hence we must conclude, that there had been a world of plants, as well as an ocean replenished with living animals.[106]

Since the present world is sustained by the remains of a former world, it is obvious that a process of renovation was involved in the destruction. The present world was being built even as the former one was being destroyed. As the remains of the ancient world were deposited on the floor of the seas, they were consolidated into strata by the pressure of the water above them and the heat coming up from the earth beneath them. After the strata had been formed, they were slowly elevated by the expansive force of this same central heat, and as they emerged from the seas, they repaired the losses of land taking place through degradation. These dual functions of heat in the operation and the balancing of the two processes of destruction and renovation were outside the realm of investigation and Hutton pressed them on grounds of necessity. It was impossible to determine the rate of renovation at the bottom of the sea, but since it was geared to the rate of destruction in the Huttonian system, ascertaining the one provided the answer to the other. We know that the process of destruction is going on, yet in several thousands of years we find its results to be hardly noticeable. A search of written records shows scarcely any change in the geographical features of the earth since the time of the Greeks. From this indication of the slowness of the process, Hutton concluded that our present continents would "require a time indefinite in length for its formation and destruction." We could not hope to find the actual elapsed time even for one cycle of destruction and renovation,

106 *Ibid.,* p. 291.

Hutton felt, yet we had enough data to see that there was wisdom, system, consistency, and an enormous time process in the system of the earth.

> For having, in the natural history of this earth, seen a succession of worlds, we may from this conclude that there is a system in nature; in like manner as, from seeing revolutions of the planets, it is concluded, that there is a system by which they are intended to continue those revolutions. But if the succession of worlds is established in the system of nature, it is in vain to look for any thing higher in the origin of the earth. *The result, therefore, of our present enquiry is, that we find no vestige of a beginning,—no prospect of an end.*[107]

"No vestige of a beginning—no prospect of an end," is one of the most often quoted phrases in geological writings. It brought against Hutton the full force of theological and diluvialist condemnation. Theologians expressed alarm at the direction the pretentious and fallacious new science of geology was taking, diluvialists singled out Hutton's disregard of Mosaic history, and Neptunists ridiculed his igneous principles of rock formation and uplift of strata. All were united in attacking Hutton's succession of worlds in an indefinite succession of ages, seeing in his system the same spirit of atheism that was being propagated by *philosophes* like Holbach. Ironically, had he been able to unfold his system of the globe as an organized body bearing all the qualities of a nicely adjusted piece of clockwork without crossing the threshold of Mosaic history, the supporters of natural theology could have acclaimed Hutton a genius. By taking haphazard chance out of the operations of nature and replacing it with design and purpose, he introduced a picture of the operations of the globe which was analagous to the Newtonian picture of the operations of the heavens in majesty of scope, harmony of functions, concatenation of parts, and organization for a purpose. In his hands the globe became a machine such as his compatriots had

[107] *Ibid.*, p. 304. No italics in text.

been extolling throughout the eighteenth century. Only on the one point did Hutton's system fail to meet all the qualifications for the perfect eighteenth-century conception of a mechanical system. He asked geologists to throw open the curtains of Biblical chronology and see the parts of the system functioning on a dimension of historical time whose ends disappeared over the horizon. The reaction to Hutton's theory cannot be understood from a geological point of view alone, for he brought to a head a latent contradiction in the development of the entire philosophical outlook of the eighteenth century. This contradiction rested in the tendency to mechanize Nature in the sciences of astronomy, physics, physiology, biology and psychology, while geology was set apart as a special sanctuary in which miracles had free play.

Richard Kirwan, President of the Royal Irish Academy, was a leader amongst the natural scientists opposing Hutton. He disputed Hutton's theory step by step. He saw no reason to suppose the solid body of land was subject to decay, that the stony parts were of any greater antiquity than the earthy parts, that heat under compression would fuse calcareous substances, or that heat had played any appreciable part in the formation of the materials of the earth. Kirwan could not conceive of a source of heat great enough to perform the role Hutton assigned to it, nor see how it could be sustained in the earth without fuel and air, nor, assuming such a heat, why it would be restrained from consuming all materials it came in contact with, instead of just fusing them to the proper degree to make new strata. The entire Huttonian system was to his mind a series of gratuitous assumptions, and he said categorically "that all the appearances of nature depose in favor of an aqueous solution or diffusion, and a crystallization, concretion or subsidence therefrom, and against an igneous solution or fusion."[108] Almost all his arguments were on points which made the endless succession of ages in Hutton's system

[108] "Examination of the supposed igneous origin of stony substances," *Transactions of the Royal Irish Academy*, v (1793), 66.

possible, for he asked, "Why should we suppose this habitable earth to arise from the ruins of another anterior to it, contrary to reason and the tenor of Mosaic history?"[109]

The reaction to Hutton's theory was generally so unfavorable that in 1795 he published a two-volume work entitled *Theory of the Earth, with Proofs and Illustrations,* in which he tried to meet some of the many objections to his system. Kirwan countered with an article in 1797 which was expanded into a book of *Geological Essays.* The mixture of moralism and geology was particularly strong in Kirwan's writings. In his 1797 article "On the Primitive State of the Globe and its Subsequent Catastrophe," he wrote:

> To those who may regard this inquiry as superfluous, and consider the actual state of the globe as alone intitled to philosophical attention, I shall beg leave to observe that its original state is so strictly connected with that which it at present exhibits, that the latter cannot be properly understood without retrospect to the former, as will amply be shown in the sequel. Moreover recent experience has shewn that the obscurity in which the philosophical knowledge of this state has hitherto been involved, has proved too favourable to the structure of various systems of atheism or infidelity, as these have been in their turn to turbulence and immorality, not to endeavour to dispel it by all the lights which modern geological researches have struck out. Thus it will be found that geology naturally ripens, or (to use a mineralogical expression) *graduates* into religion, as this does into morality.[110]

Kirwan, among other things, denied that calcareous strata were composed of the remains of shell-fish, one of the main points in Hutton's evidence for a great antiquity of the earth, and he asserted that the inclusion of occasional fossil specimens in the strata was the result of mixing when the whole material was in an aqueous state. After arguing away, sometimes with the aid of

[109] *Ibid.,* p. 63.
[110] *Transactions of the Royal Irish Academy,* vi (1797), 234.

miracles, most of the evidence of the opponents of diluvialism, Kirwan wrote: "I have been led into this detail by observing how fatal the suspicion of the high antiquity of the globe has been to the credit of the Mosaic history, and consequently to religion and morality; a suspicion grounded on no other foundation than those whose weakness I have here exposed."[111]

A few friends remained loyal to Hutton and defended his system in many of its essential parts.[112] John Playfair, an intimate companion of Hutton's, published a well-written and forceful summary of the system in *Illustrations of the Huttonian Theory of the Earth* (Edinburgh, 1802) with many additional notes of his own. Playfair's *Illustrations* gave to the Huttonian system a wide reading, and if the entire system was not wholeheartedly accepted, at least, an interest was expressed in its many facts gathered by investigation. In the *Edinburgh Review*, for instance, after a careful analysis of the work, the reviewer was left unconvinced on the bold postulates of a central fire fusing strata, then uplifting them, and the formation of new continents out of the old ones, but he still had praise for the work as a body of investigations which pointed out the inadequacies of the Neptunian hypothesis.[113]

On one point in particular Playfair took pains to relieve Hutton's system of some of the odium which had been attached to it. In discussing the vast duration of the globe's economy he said:

> To assert, therefore, that, in the economy of the world, we see no mark, either of a beginning or an end, is very different from affirming, that the world had no beginning, and will have no end. The first is a conclusion justified by common sense, as

[111] Ibid., p. 307. In his *Geological Essays* (London, 1799), pp. 65-6, Kirwan categorically states that Moses' account must be taken literally.

[112] Sir James Hall's experimental proofs of Hutton's theory, for instance, (*Trans. Roy. Soc. Edin.*, v (1799), 43-75; vi (1806), 71-185) but Hall remained a catastrophist ("On the Revolutions of the Earth's Surface," *Trans. Roy. Soc. Edin.*, vii (1815), 139-211.)

[113] *Edinburgh Review*, i (1803), 201-16.

well as sound philosophy; while the second is a presumptuous
and unwarrantable assertion, for which no reason from experience or analogy can ever be assigned. Dr. Hutton might, therefore, justly complain of the uncandid criticism, which, by sub-
stituting the one of these assertions for the other, endeavoured
to load his theory with the reproach of atheism and impiety.[114]

With regard to the objection that the high antiquity Hutton
ascribed to the earth was inconsistent with that system of chronology which rests on the authority of the sacred writings, Playfair distinguished between the history of the earth and the history
of mankind. "That the origin of mankind does not go back beyond six or seven thousand years, is a position so involved in the
narrative of the Mosaic books, that any thing inconsistent with it,
would no doubt stand in opposition to the testimony of those
ancient records." On this point Playfair thought geology was silent. The authority of the sacred books, on the other hand, seems
to be little interested in what regards the mere antiquity of the
earth itself; "nor does it appear that their language is to be understood literally concerning the *age* of that body, any more than
concerning its *figure* or its *motion*." Comparing Hutton's system
with that of Copernicus, he said

> It is but reasonable, therefore, that we should extend to the
> geologist the same liberty of speculation, which the astronomer
> and mathematician are already in possession of; and this may
> be done, by supposing that the chronology of MOSES relates
> only to the human race. This liberty is not more necessary to
> Dr. Hutton than to other theorists. No ingenuity has been able
> to reconcile the natural history of the globe with the opinion
> of its recent origin; and accordingly the cosmologies of Kir-
> wan and De Luc, though contrived with more mineralogical
> skill, are not less forced and unsatisfactory than those of Bur-
> net and Whiston.[115]

The eternalism in the Huttonian system was too evident to be

[114] Playfair, *Illustrations*, p. 120.
[115] *Ibid.*, pp. 126-7.

disguised. The progress of things on the globe gives to time its existence, Hutton had said, but to nature time is endless and as nothing. The operations of the globe had been going on indefinitely, and they were so carefully adjusted that there was no reason why they should not continue to do so. As Playfair said of Hutton's theory, when comparing it with Buffon's, in it "no latent seed of evil threatens final destruction to the whole; and where the movements are so perfect, . . . they can never terminate themselves. This is surely a view of the world more suited to the dignity of NATURE, and the wisdom of its *Author*, than has yet been offered by any other system of cosmology." [116]

Mosaic geologists were spurred to greater effort to find in the earth evidences of the novity of the earth, and the work of the Neptunists in stratigraphy proved to be as essential as the uniformitarianism of Hutton in discovering the antiquity of the earth, for the key to geo-chronology lay in correlating fossil species with particular strata.

The first significant recognition that fossil species could be used as a label for strata appears to have been made by the Abbé Sauvages de la Croix, Professor of Medicine and later Professor of Botany at the University of Montpellier, in a "Mémoire contenant des observations de lithologie, pour servir à l'histoire naturelle du Languedoc, & à la théorie de la terre," read before the French Academy in 1749 and 1750, and published in the *Mémoires* of 1746 (1751). In Holbach's article on fossils in the *Encyclopédie*, mention was made of the plan of Guillaume-François Rouelle to study fossils by groups in a district so that similar groups anywhere could be ascertained by means of a few characteristic species. Although Rouelle, known mostly as a chemist, apparently did not undertake the project, he did exert a great influence as a teacher. [117] The relationship of particular fossil spe-

[116] *Ibid.*, pp. 485-6.
[117] For a contemporary appreciation of Rouelle, and his influence on Lavoisier, see Nicolas Desmarest's four-volume article on "Geographie physique" (1794-1811) in the *Encyclopédie méthodique*, esp. I, 416.

cies to certain strata was also pointed out by the Abbé Giraud-Soulavie in his seven-volume *Histoire naturelle de la France méridionale* (1780-84), and on the basis of this relationship, he ascertained five successive ages in the calcareous strata of Vivarais. But William Smith, because of the comprehensiveness of his work, is generally credited with establishing the identification of strata by particular fossil species. Although his work was not published in a completed form until 1815, Smith had made many of his ideas available to a few friends as early as 1799. Some of his conclusions were, as a result, presented to the public by his friend, the Reverend Joseph Townsend, in a work entitled, *The Character of Moses Established for Veracity as an Historian, Recording Events from the Creation to the Deluge* (Bath, 1813, 1815). Neither Smith, nor Townsend grasped the idea that time was involved in laying down the successive strata, and both thought they had contributed support to Mosaic cosmogony. Townsend attacked Hutton for holding and spreading infidel opinions by giving the earth millions of years antiquity and by dismissing supernatural agents in explaining the disorder of the solid parts of the earth.

At the same time that Smith was outlining the strata of Britain, a similar task was being carried out in the Paris Basin, though with a different emphasis. Smith was a practical engineer who had hit upon a useful system for tracing coal measures and ascertaining the direction of strata in connection with draining marshland. Zoology was the paramount interest of the investigators of the Paris Basin, Lamarck, Cuvier, and Brongniart, who, along with Blumenbach in Germany, founded the modern science of paleontology. (Baron von Schlotheim was raising paleobotany to a science in Germany about the same time.) They studied the individual fossils, as well as their position in the strata, and recognized the succession of species forms as well as a chronological order in the strata. A realization of the time involved in the succession of life histories represented in the fossil species also made evident to them the long time process in the formation of the strata, and consequently, they called for a revolution in the conception of the earth's age.

Lamarck was in the direct line of succession, especially through Buffon with whom he had worked, of eighteenth-century speculation about an organic world. In the grand manner of Buffon, he saw nature as an integrated whole and ridiculed the triflings of the empiricists who only wanted to accumulate facts instead of seeking out the general principles behind the chaos of data. He acquired the advantage over the speculationists of a concrete knowledge of invertebrate fossils and was thereby able to merge the ideas of cosmic evolution with those of biological evolution on the basis of stratigraphy.

Early in his career, Lamarck outlined a program for the investigation of terrestrial physics, and the pattern of his work closely followed this program. First, the atmosphere must be comprehended, second, the external crust of the earth, and third, living bodies. Lamarck studied chemistry, physics, and meteorology, and in 1798 he published a collection of his writings on these subjects in *Mémoires de physique de l'histoire naturelle*, which did not enhance his reputation. Lamarck then turned to the study of the earth's crust. In 1802, he brought out his main work on the subject, *Hydrogéologie*, an integration of his theories about meteorology, hydrogeology, and the action of living bodies on the formation of the earth's crust. After 1802, Lamarck devoted his attention primarily to biology and zoology. Nevertheless, it was in his *Hydrogeology* that he began to make the transition from eighteenth-century cosmic evolution to nineteenth-century biological evolution.

Lamarck projected a theory of the earth and the operations of nature to explain the origin of fossil strata. Physical and mechanical forces were given a major role in shaping the crust of the earth in his system, and as his title *Hydrogeology* suggests, water was a prime agency, but it was not diluvial water, for he was a thoroughgoing uniformitarian. The cosmogonic part of his system bore some resemblance to that of Maillet, but it was still more like that of Leonardo da Vinci, even to such details as the shifting of the earth's center of gravity through endless ages.[118]

In all mechanical changes taking place in the system of Lamarck there were no forces in action other than those visible in the present, or rather forces almost invisible in the present because they were acting so slowly and with effects almost imperceptible within the lifetime of a man. These mechanical changes were all working towards the degradation of the earth and its matter—all the compounds and organic products without the vital force of life were slowly, but irresistibly, breaking down under the action of the physical agencies. However, Lamarck thought that life was the great counterbalance to the tendency of destruction. It compounded matter as the other forces of nature broke it down. In line with the tradition we have already examined, he portrayed the enormous influence of organic beings in the constitution and transformation of the earth's surface, but he carried it too far, and supposed that even granite and minerals were composed of the remains of organic bodies or their secretions. He thought *all* compounds in nature owed their origin to the action of living bodies, for he saw in life the process of integration. Thus, in the system of changes on the surface of the earth, marine organisms were constantly adding to the formation

[118] Leonardo had no monopoly on this conception. Bertrand, *Recueil de divers traités sur l'histoire naturelle de la terre et des fossiles* (Avignon, 1766), p. 43, writes: "Il en est d'abord qui ont supposé que le centre de gravité n'étoit pas fixe, mais mobile, & qu'il se mouvoit effectivement d'un mouvement très-lent, en s'approchant successivement & uniformément de tous les points de la surface du Globe. BERNIER [François, 1625-1688, French traveler?] a adopté cette singulière supposition." Nevertheless, it was possible that Lamarck knew of Leonardo's speculations. Napoleon had confiscated the Leonardo da Vinci manuscripts in the Ambrosian Library at Milan in 1796 and deposited them at the Bibliothéque Nationale and the library of the National Institute. G. B. Venturi went through them carefully and marked them with the lettering they now retain. Venturi's *Essai sur les ouvrages physico-mathématiques de Leonardo da Vinci* (Paris, 1797) could very well have been known by Lamarck.

of strata under water, while vegetation and animals added to the increase of soil on the exposed parts of the earth.

In contrast to the pre-established harmony between the forces of destruction and renovation in Hutton's system, Lamarck thought the life principle constantly expanded along lines of indefinite progression.[119] He was convinced that this was indicated by the fossil record. He ridiculed the idea that fossils were authentic monuments of the Deluge or of some great catastrophe in nature.[120] Not only did many strata show successive generations of animal remains quietly deposited throughout great expanses of time, but the juxtaposition in certain places of pelagic with littoral shells showed that the sea and land areas had existed contemporaneously. The delicacy of some of the fossil shells also ruled out their having survived a catastrophe. Changes, yes, but catastrophes, no. Everything in nature is undergoing changes and mutation, and as for the time necessary to accumulate great changes through small ones, Lamarck wrote: "For Nature time is nothing, and is never a difficulty; she always has it at her disposal, and it is for her a power without limits with which she does the greatest things like the smallest."[121]

Throughout his *Hydrogeology* Lamarck kept driving home the necessity of seeing the vast periods of time employed by nature to carry out the changes now preserved in the crust of the earth.

> Oh! how great is the antiquity of the terrestrial globe! and how little the ideas of those who attribute to the globe an existence of six thousand and a few hundred years duration from its origin to the present!

The natural philosopher and the geologist see things much

---

[119] See D. R. Newth, "Lamarck in 1800. A Lecture on the Invertebrate Animals and a Note on Fossils Taken from the *Système des Animaux sans Vertèbres* by J. B. Lamarck," *Annals of Science*, VIII (1952), 229-54.

[120] *Hydrogéologie, ou recherches sur l'influence générale des eaux sur la surface du globe terrestre* . . . (Paris, 1802), pp. 22, 66, 74, 76, 83.

[121] *Ibid.*, p. 67.

differently in this respect; because, if they consider ever so little, first, the nature of fossils spread in such great numbers in all the parts of the exposed globe, either at heights, or at considerable depths; second, the number and disposition of the beds, as well as the nature and order of the materials composing the external crust of the globe, studied in a great part of its thickness and in the mass of the mountains,—how many occasions they have to be convinced that the antiquity of this same globe is so great that it is absolutely outside the power of man to appreciate it in any manner! [122]

Our chronologies do not go back very far, he added, but this is quite natural considering that everything changes, including languages, so that man's knowledge cannot be expected to reach very far back into the past.

How much this antiquity of the terrestrial globe will still grow in the eyes of man, when he has formed a just idea of the origin of living bodies, as well as the causes of the development and gradual perfecting of the organization of these bodies, and especially when he has conceived that, time and circumstances having been necessary to bring into existence all the living species such as we see them, he is himself the latest result and the present *maximum* of this perfecting, whose end, if there is one, cannot be known! [123]

Lamarck believed that the sea basins were slowly rotating around the earth and he calculated that some nine million centuries were necessary for one complete revolution while the evidence in the crust of the earth indicated that the circuit had been completed at least several times. "As we put all duration in comparison with that of our ephemeral existence, how must our imagination be astonished in thinking of a space of time so enormous! But for Nature, these durations which overwhelm our thought are only instants." [124]

The ideas of Lamarck had already been sufficiently ridiculed

[122] *Ibid.,* p. 88.
[123] *Ibid.,* pp. 89-90.
[124] *Ibid.,* pp. 266-7, note 1.

by the time he wrote his *Hydrogeology* to remove any illusion an author might reasonably expect of finding a receptive audience. He knew the temper of the times, with its slavish Wernerian empiricism and the domination of Mosaic history in geology. "Posterity," he shrewdly observed, "will very probably someday regard as a kind of puerility this eagerness that prevails in this century to give a particular name to every variation of a mineral substance to be met with and to regard it as constantly existing in Nature," instead of seeking out the unifying principles underlying them.[125] In a memoir published in 1805 which restated the principles of his *Hydrogeology* Lamarck sounded a note of despair, apparently feeling that his conception of a vast antiquity of the earth was a major objection to the acceptance of his ideas:

> These considerations, I know, having never been presented elsewhere than in my Hydrogeology, and not having obtained the serious examination that I believe they deserve, can only appear extraordinary even to the most enlightened persons.
> Indeed, man, who judges the greatness of duration only relative to himself and not to nature, will undoubtedly never actually find the slow mutations which I have just presented and consequently he will believe it necessary to reject without examination my opinion on these great objects.[126]

Undaunted, Lamarck continued throughout his life, even under the handicap of blindness in later years, to develop his ideas and researches, so that even those, like Cuvier, who found his evolutionary theories ridiculous could not fail to pay him homage for his careful studies of invertebrate fossils.

At about the same time that French readers were being exposed to Lamarck's views on the time process in nature, English readers were confronted with somewhat similar ideas from Erasmus

---

[125] *Ibid.*, p. 95.
[126] "Considerations sur quelques faits applicables à la théorie du globe, observé par M. Péron dans son voyage aux Terres australes, et sur quelques questions géologiques qui naissent de la connaissance de ces faits," *Annales du Muséum d'Histoire Naturelle*, vi (1805), 26-52, p. 50.

Darwin's *Zoonomia; or, the Laws of Organic Life* (1794-96).
Darwin was well informed on the literature about fossils and was
familiar with the works of Buffon and Hutton. He accepted the
idea of a central heat in the earth, but his cosmic view was that of
the sceptic Philo advocating an embryo-state universe. Would it
be too bold to imagine, Darwin wrote, that in the great length of
time since the earth began to exist, perhaps millions of ages before the commencement of the history of mankind, that all warm-
blooded animals arose from one living filament, which the Great
First Cause endued with animality, with the power of acquiring
new parts, and of delivering down these improvements by generation to its posterity, world without end? [127]

Like all those who understood the life principle to be an integrating force in nature, an organizing principle, Darwin had an
exaggerated conception of the extent of organic remains in the
earth, as is indicated in the following passage, which also shows
his own filiation with the views of Philo:

> The late Mr. David Hume, in his posthumous works, places
> the powers of generation much above those of our boasted
> reason; and adds, that reason can only make a machine, as
> a clock or a ship, but the power of generation makes the maker
> of the machine; and probably from having observed, that the
> greatest part of the earth has been formed out of organic recre-
> ments; as the immense beds of limestone, chalk, marble, from
> the shells of fish; and the extensive provinces of clay, sandstone,
> ironstone, coals, from decomposed vegetables; all which have
> been first produced by generation, or by the secretions of or-
> ganic life; he concludes that the world itself might have been
> generated, rather than created; that is, it might have been grad-
> ually produced from very small beginnings, increasing by the
> activity of its inherent principles, rather than by a sudden evo-
> lution of the whole by the Almighty fiat. What a magnificent
> idea of the infinite power of the Great Architect! [128]

[127] *Zoonomia*, 3rd ed. (London, 1801), II, 240. This statement does not
appear in the first edition.
[128] *Ibid.*, p. 247.

The *Zoonomia* had reached a third edition by 1801, and in it the theory of a generated world was sharpened, but this view was vigorously countered the next year by the publication of William Paley's *Natural Theology*, the grand synthesis of the argument for the existence of God from the evidences of design in nature. The alternative to design, Paley warned, was chance, and he underscored the threat of atheism in the philosophy of chance, adding,

> There is another answer, which has the same effect as the resolving of things into chance; which answer would persuade us to believe, that the eye, the animal to which it belongs, every other animal, every plant, indeed every organized body which we see, are only so many of the possible varieties and combinations of being, which the lapse of infinite ages has brought into existence; that the present world is the relic of that variety; millions of other bodily forms and other species having perished, being by the defect of their constitutions incapable of preservation, or of the continuance by generation.[129]

The works of Darwin and Lamarck were read, but the French Revolution brought a change of climate in European thought. The liberal intellectuals amused themselves with the theories of Darwin and Lamarck, the narrowly orthodox, as an exercise against satanic influences, attacked them. Empirical geologists dismissed them as lingering survivals of the old speculative school. But Hutton was too good a geologist to be easily dismissed and the Plutonist-Neptunist debate grew violent. Charles C. Gillispie has noted that in the debate, it was the antiquity of the earth issue "that transformed a discussion among scientists into a dispute between zealots, even though the ostensible difference between the two schools centered around the primacy of heat as opposed to water in the formation of the crust of the earth."[130] It was the same issue of the antiquity of the earth that lay behind the debate

[129] *Natural Theology*, Ch. v, par. 4. The previous paragraph contains remarks on fossil shells.
[130] *Genesis and Geology* (Cambridge, Mass., 1951), p. 43.

between catastrophists and uniformitarians. Popular works continued to provide the generality of the public with the history of
the earth in terms of Mosaic history, in which the fossil strata
were cited as an indisputable proof of the reality and universality
of the Flood, works such as Goldsmith's *History of the Earth and
Animated Nature* and Bernardin de Saint Pierre's *Studies of Nature*. But there was now a new class of works springing up written by experts in geology which tried to interpret the science of
geology in the framework of Mosaic history, and to do this,
against the increasing evidence of the antiquity of the earth, it
was imperative to fall back on more and greater catastrophes to
foreshorten the time process portrayed by a Lamarck. The em-
bryo-organic-developmental cosmology was eclipsed before the
advancing successes of Mosaic geologists, but it was a temporary
eclipse. Even the Newtonian machine in astronomy paid its obei-
sance to diluvialism and catastrophism at the end of the century
through the guiding hands of Laplace, who was engaged upon
showing its flawless performance throughout endless ages, and
upon bringing the support of astronomy to the Plutonists.

In the nebular hypothesis of Pierre Simon, Marquis de Laplace
(1749-1827), set forth in his *Exposition du Système du Monde*
(1796),[131] the solar system was assumed to have been originally
a nucleus surrounded by an atmosphere of gases somewhat like
the nebulae of the stellar regions. In contrast to Buffon's theory
of a comet striking the sun, Laplace pictured the sun, planets, and
satellites evolving out of this nebulous mass, but the principal
agent of evolution was the same as Buffon's—the dissipation of
heat, or progressive refrigeration, to which he added the principle
of the conservation of rotational momentum.

As the nebular mass cooled, it contracted and condensed,
thereby increasing the velocity of rotation, and this in turn in-

[131] The theory was given in Note VII. The translation used here, Henry
H. Harte, *The System of the World* (Dublin, 1830) has many errors, and
my citations have been checked against the original French edition.

creased the centrifugal force of the rotating mass. Successive parts fell outside the controlling limits of gravitation which kept the mass together, and these parts formed the satellites of our planetary system, while the remaining nucleus became the sun. As the planetary globes cooled and condensed, they passed from a gaseous state to a liquid state, then to a solid state, and this conclusion, Laplace thought, was borne out by evidences drawn from natural history. The figure of the earth, for instance, indicated a once-fluid state, and so, too, did the variety of mixed substances in the earth, a mixture which could only have come about prior to solidification. And,

> it is necessary likewise to consider the wonderful changes which this depression ought to cause in the interior and at the surface of the earth, in all its productions, in the constitution and pressure of the atmosphere, in the ocean, and in all substances which it held in a state of solution. Finally, we should take into account the sudden changes, such as great volcanic eruptions, which must at different epochs have deranged the regularity of these changes. Geology, thus studied under the point of view which connects it with astronomy, may, with respect to several objects, acquire both precision and certainty.[132]

The cooling of the earth would continue, according to Laplace, until its temperature reached that of its ambient atmosphere. There was an abundance of evidence that the earth still contained within its interior a heat in excess of the regions of the upper mountains, or as the balloon ascents of the 1780's demonstrated, the upper atmosphere. As long as it cools, the earth must condense, and as long as it condenses, its rate of rotation must accelerate.

A clue to the age of the earth could be found in the relationship of the temperature of the space surrounding the earth and the consequent increase in the rate of rotation of the earth as it cooled from a molten condition. Laplace did not attempt the

[132] *Ibid.*, II, 365.

calculation, but he did point out that from astronomical evidence dating back about 2,300 years there had not been more than 1/100 of a second's alteration in the length of the day. From this fact it was clear that the acceleration of rotation, and the consequent shortening of the duration of a day, must be progressing at an infinitesimally small rate. The implication which Laplace did not draw out, but which was obvious, is that if this process had run through a series of changes extending from a gaseous nebula to the present state of the globe, it must have required myriads upon myriads of ages for its accomplishment. Laplace, sincerely or not, seemed anxious to placate the Mosaic geologists. He mentioned that the perigee of the sun coincided with the vernal equinox about 4,089 years before our epoch, and "it is remarkable that this astronomical epoch is nearly that at which chronologists have fixed the creation of the world."[133]

Besides the inference that some catastrophe through an unusually strong conjunction of forces may have been the point in the earth's history at which creation was thought to have taken place, Laplace discussed the remote probability of a comet striking the earth.

> Nevertheless, the small probability of this circumstance may, by accumulating during the long succession of ages, become very great. It is easy to represent the effect of such a shock upon the earth: the axis and motion of rotation would be changed, the waters abandoning their antient position, would precipitate themselves towards the new equator; the greater part of men and animals drowned in a universal deluge, or destroyed by the violence of the shock given to the terrestrial globe; whole species destroyed; all the monuments of human industry reversed: such are the disasters which the shock of a comet ought to produce, if its mass was comparable to the mass of the earth.
>
> We see then why the ocean has covered the highest mountains, on which it has left incontestible marks of its former abode: we see why the animals and plants of the south may

[133] *Ibid.*, II, 24.

have existed in the climates of the north, where their relics and impressions are still to be found: *lastly*, this explains the short period of the existence of the moral world, whose earliest monuments do not go much farther back than five thousand years. The human race reduced to a small number of individuals, in the most deplorable state, occupied only with the immediate care for their subsistence, must necessarily have lost the remembrance of all sciences and of every art; and when the progress of civilization had created new wants, every thing was to be invented again, as if mankind had been just placed upon the earth.[134]

This statement that a comet might have displaced the axis of rotation is a remarkable inclusion in Laplace's *System*, for a few pages later he wrote:

Every hypothesis founded on a considerable displacement of the poles on the surface of the earth, must be rejected as incompatible with the property of which I have been speaking [i. e., great continents could emerge from the ocean without affecting the figure of the terrestrial spheroid]. Such a displacement has been suggested, in order to explain the existence of elephants, of which fossil remains are found in such great abundance in northern climates, where living elephants cannot exist. But an elephant, which is with great probability supposed to be cotemporaneous with the last flood, was found in a mass of ice well preserved with its skin, and as the hide was covered with a great quantity of hair, this species of elephant was guaranteed by this means, from the cold of the northern climates, which it might inhabit and even select as a place of residence. The discovery of this animal has therefore confirmed what the mathematical theory of the earth had shewn us, namely, that in the revolutions which have changed the surface of the globe and destroyed several species of animals and vegetables, the figure of the terrestrial spheroid, and the position of its axis of rotation on its surface, have undergone only slight alterations.[135]

The latter position is more consistent with the character of

[134] *Ibid.*, II, 49-50.
[135] *Ibid.*, II, 117-8.

Laplace's work, for he above all demonstrated the stability of the solar system. One of the particular proofs of its stability was his demonstration that the secular inequalities in the axis of the earth's rotation were cyclical and never exceeded a total change of three degrees. Within the solar system he allowed for only one factor making for a progressive change in the otherwise stable motions of the planetary spheres, and that was the dissipation of heat, but even this did not mean that the system was running down, for once the temperatures of the planets reached that of space they might run on forever. Until that point was reached, however, the system had been and was still undergoing a cosmic evolution on a vast scale of duration.

The reputation of Laplace as an astronomer served to give his nebular hypothesis a wide and respectful reading, and he added astronomy to those forces in geology supporting long lapses of time in the earth's history. Investigation on the nature of heat itself continued and the process of dissipation was reduced to mathematical laws by Fourier, Carnot, and others. The works of Fourier in 1820 and of Poisson in 1835 were especially important in renewing and strengthening the nebular hypothesis of Laplace with its principles of refrigeration and a once-molten earth. Ampère, the celebrated French physicist, lent his support to the theory in 1833, and Henry de la Beche gave it a clear and convincing presentation in his *Researches in Theoretical Geology* (1834). During the 1830's the nebular hypothesis became a commonplace of cosmogony and the pioneer efforts of Buffon, Leibniz, and Descartes were renovated and praised for their penetrating insight; but by this time the first concessions on the antiquity of the earth had already been made by Mosaic geologists.

IV
THE BIBLICAL AGE OF
THE EARTH SURRENDERED

THE FLOOD TRIUMPHANT

As the French Revolution ran its course, spreading terror, shocking the sensibilities of the civilized world, and converting Europe into an armed camp, conservatism settled over the intellectual world. There was an increased respect for the role of tradition, custom, and ancient institutions in providing social stability. The guardians of religious institutions were quick to profit from the conservative mood and vigorously pressed the orthodox position forward. Even in France, orthodoxy, like the legendary phoenix, rose from the ashes of the *ancien régime*, heralded by the *Génie du christianisme, ou beautés de la religion chrétienne* of Chateaubriand which was published in 1802 on the eve of Napoleon's re-establishment of the Catholic religion in France.

Chateaubriand fell back on all the old dogmas of traditional Christianity, but he wove around them a fabric of sentiment, and with his brilliant eloquence, appealed to the emotions, rather than the reason, of his readers. More than this, he set about showing that Christianity, which the *philosophes* had treated as a monument of Gothic superstition blocking the path of enlightenment and progress, was in reality the very cradle of enlightenment and progress. Turning to the long history of Christianity, he pointed out how the Church had preserved the torch of learning after the fall of Rome, and how it had fostered the growth of education, the literary tradition, oratory, music, sculpture, painting, and architecture. He also indicated how the Church had worked steadily for the amelioration of man's social condition through opposing slavery, encouraging charity, instituting hospitals, and trying to civilize man's passions.

In unfolding "the beauties of the Christian religion," Chateaubriand treated the Bible as a work of literature, as well as a source of doctrine and revelation. He also expressed an appreciation of the aesthetic significance of medieval churches, the mystery of the sacraments, and the elaborate church rituals, all of which were extolled as symbolic of the drama of life. Christianity was portrayed as being in perfect harmony with Nature, and in Chateaubriand's treatment, Christianity and its institutions were rendered "natural," in contrast to the revolutionary view of them as comprising an unnatural monster foisted on man by priestcraft.

The *Génie du christianisme* struck a responsive chord in a public weary of sophistries and rational blueprints for social reform. The work was also tailored to the interests of Romanticism. Its success was immediate and it enjoyed an immense popularity. The author was promptly rewarded by Napoleon for the influence of his work in preparing the way for the re-establishment of the Roman Catholic Church in France, but the influence of Chateaubriand's work was no less important for its part in making the espousal of orthodoxy popular in sophisticated circles and in stimulating a dynamic view of institutionalized Christianity without turning to evangelical or pietist methods—a view which became a source of strength when the hollow literalism, upon which the orthodox were willing to stake Christianity, came under fire in the succeeding decades. Nevertheless, the first impact of Chateaubriand's work was to bring a powerful support to the most dogmatic literalism.

Among the main propositions which Chateaubriand felt that

he had established beyond all doubt was: "All the pretended proofs of the antiquity of the earth can be refuted."[1] In the first part of Chateaubriand's work, on dogmas and doctrines, a book was given over to the refutation of those savants who maintained that the world bears the marks of an antiquity greater than the origins given in the Bible. The accuracy and sufficiency of Biblical chronology were defended in a chapter on chronology, the arguments for long ages based upon ancient ruins in Egypt and the traditions of a great antiquity in the dynasties of Egypt and Hindu philosophy were disposed of with stock arguments in a chapter on logography, and the suggestion that Egyptian, Chaldean, and Indian astronomy carried evidence of long ages was countered with "incontestable facts" in a chapter on astronomy. Turning to the Deluge, Chateaubriand began: "Astronomy then being incapable of destroying the chronology of Scripture, we return to the attack by natural history. . . ."[2] He had Buffon in mind, and in the contest between Buffon and Moses, there was no doubt about the outcome. Chateaubriand embellished upon the words in Genesis and gave a frightening picture of the destruction visited upon the world of sinful man. And it was this violent catastrophe which left the elephants of India in the cold regions of Siberia and whole banks of marine bodies near the summits of the Alps, the Taurus, and the Cordilleras. Indeed, these very mountains were "monuments that God left in the three countries to mark his triumph over the impious, as a monarch plants a trophy in the field where he has defeated his enemies."[3] In the next chapter, on the age of the earth, Chateaubriand, still ranging Buffon against Moses, took up the question of innumerable years indicated by fossils, marbles, granites, and lavas, and put forward an argument which was taken up by others later in the century when geology had made its case stronger. "*God could create, and*

[1] *Oeuvres complètes de Chateaubriand* (Paris, n. d.), II, 523.
[2] *Ibid.*, p. 80.
[3] *Ibid.*, p. 82.

*without doubt did create, the world with all the marks that we
see of old age and completion."* [4]

The amount of attention given by Chateaubriand to the age of
the earth is an indication that the question had become serious to
the defenders of orthodoxy, but there was a tone of easy confidence in Chateaubriand's marshalling of religious arguments
against the scientific insurgents. In the glow of conservatism
around 1800, the orthodox did not distinguish natural evidence
from sentiment in the heretical writings of the *philosophes,* but
the naturalistic basis of heresy in the arguments of a Buffon,
Laplace, Hutton, or Lamarck were in a different class than the
philosophical arguments of a Voltaire, Hume, or Holbach. Slowly
at first, and then with a rush, it dawned on the orthodox that on
the age of the earth they were pitted, not against rhetorical free-
thought, but natural science.[5]

If the turn towards orthodoxy was strong in France, it was

[4] *Ibid.,* p. 83.

[5] An excellent example of this trend can be seen in connection with
Teyler's Stichting (institution) of Haarlem. This institution was founded
for the study of theology, natural science, and art, and in 1787 it offered a
prize for the best answer to the following question: "Jusqu'à où peut-on
conclure, de ce que l'on connoît, de la Nature des Fossiles, de leurs situations, et de ce qu'on sait d'ailleurs relativement aux formes ancienne et
nouvelle de la surface du globe, d'après des fondemens incontestables, quels
changemens ou révolutions générales a subis la surface de la terre, et com-
bien il doit s'être écoulé de siècles depuis lors?" The prize was won by
François Xavier Burtin, author of *Oryctographie de Bruxelles, ou description des fossiles tant naturels qu'accidentels, découverts jusqu'à ce jour dans
les environs de cette ville* (Bruxelles, 1784), who decided that the Deluge
explained nothing about fossils. The extinct fossils were of inestimable
antiquity, he concluded, and so were the coal beds and fossil banks which
contained them. His scientific work was detailed, enlightened, and on the
whole, sound. It was possible that the fossils were the result of revolutions
during the period of the chaos prior to the days of the creation, he conceded, but the scriptural chronology of the world and its fifty-eight centuries was totally inadequate for the time necessary for the production of
the enormous fossil masses. *Verhandelingen, uitegeeven door Teyler's Twee
de Genootschap.* Achtste stuk. (Haarlem, 1790) (A French translation is
included. Available at Yale University Library).

perhaps even stronger in Great Britain, where orthodoxy was patriotically mustered into war service against the French. The government's political policies set the pace for reaction, but the nation had already gone a long way towards religious conservatism in the late eighteenth century through the Methodist evangelical movement. By the early nineteenth century, bibliolatrous zeal was bubbling up everywhere in the religious institutions. The voices of evangelicals within the Nonconformist sects and the Low Church Party were ringing in unison on literalism, however much discord there was over party, and by the 1830's the Tractarian movement led by Newman, Keble, and Pusey carried literal dogmatism to even greater extremes. The middle-of-the-road Liberal Protestants were hemmed in by a militant orthodoxy, against which they were cautious and timid, and the rigid literalism remained enthroned over the British mind past mid-century. Thomas Henry Huxley in the Prologue of his *Essays Upon Some Controverted Questions* has given a picture of its absolute empire in the 1840's, drawn from his own youthful experience:

> My memory, unfortunately, carries me back to the fourth decade of the nineteenth century, when the evangelical flood had a little abated and the tops of certain mountains were soon to appear, chiefly in the neighbourhood of Oxford; but when nevertheless, bibliolatry was rampant; when church and chapel alike proclaimed, as the oracles of God, the crude assumptions of the worst informed and, in natural sequence, the most presumptuously bigoted, of all theological schools.
>
> In accordance with promises made on my behalf, but certainly without my authorisation, I was very early taken to hear "sermons in the vulgar tongue." And vulgar enough often was the tongue in which some preacher, ignorant alike of literature, of history, of science, and even of theology, outside that patronised by his own narrow school, poured forth, from the safe entrenchment of the pulpit, invectives against those who deviated from his notion of orthodoxy. From dark allusions to "sceptics" and "infidels," I became aware of the existence of people who trusted in carnal reason; who audaciously doubted

that the world was made in six natural days, or that the deluge
was universal; perhaps even went so far as to question the literal
accuracy of the story of Eve's temptation, or of Balaam's ass;
and, from the horror of the tones in which they were mentioned, I should have been justified in drawing the conclusion
that these rash men belonged to the criminal classes. At the
same time, those who were more directly responsible for providing me with the knowledge essential to the right guidance of
life (and who sincerely desired to do so), imagined they were
discharging the most sacred duty by impressing upon my child-
ish mind the necessity, on pain of reprobation in this world and
damnation in the next, of accepting, in the strict and literal
sense, every statement contained in the Protestant Bible. I was
told to believe, and I did believe, that doubt about any of them
was a sin, not less reprehensible than a moral delict. I suppose
that, out of a thousand of my contemporaries, nine hundred, at
least, had their minds systematically warped and poisoned, in
the name of the God of truth, by like discipline. I am sure that,
even a score of years later, those who ventured to question the
exact historical accuracy of any part of the Old Testament and
a fortiori of the Gospels, had to expect a pitiless shower of
verbal missiles, to say nothing of the other disagreeable con-
sequences which visit those who, in any way, run counter to
that chaos of prejudices called public opinion.

Against this wall of prejudice, geologists had to make their
way. Yet, the early nineteenth century was the glorious Heroic
Age of Geology, and the systematic investigation of the earth
brought to light such an abundance of evidence supporting the
idea of a long succession of time in the history of the earth, that
it was no longer possible for the sincere geologist, however orthodox, to avoid considering the question of the age of the earth.
Even the orthodox reader of geological works had the question
forced upon his attention. Here and there a doubt was planted
about the adequacy of Scripture as a work on natural history.
Philip Howard was representative of such a tendency, and his
popular *Scriptural History of the Earth and of Mankind* (London,
1797) probably infected others. The book was comprised of a

series of letters addressed to a Frenchman who had embraced Buffon's view of a cooling earth. Point by point, Howard countered Buffon's natural evidence with scriptural facts, tradition, population statistics, and Neptunist geology in his effort to establish that the earth could not be more than five or six thousand years old. As he was writing his refutation of Buffon, the theory of Hutton came to his attention. This, too, he dissected to show its fallacies, but the clouds of doubt hung heavily over his head, and when he could not dispel them, Howard took refuge in the "extended days of creation" theory already suggested by Buffon. Moses had not given a definite duration to the first day of creation, he suggested, nor to the preceding period of darkness. "Why not," he asked, "refer the combination and aggregation of various substances, for whose confection philosophers are so much in pain to find time, to this absolutely and necessarily undetermined space?"[6]

The first three days of creation might belong to the universe and all its systems, Howard thought, while only on the fourth day, when the sun took its position in the heavens, did the Mosaic narrative refer specifically to events on the earth. He consoled himself that a different order of events had prevailed in these supernatural times in any case, and by tucking the long ages demanded by the philosophers out of the reach of investigation in the supernatural days of creation, Howard added the final touch to his aim of showing "that it is not impossible to conciliate the present formation and apparent changes which have happened to this globe with the short duration generally allotted to it."[7]

Howard's approach to what became known as Mosaic geology was that of a poorly informed naturalist working out of the corpus of theology to explain a contradiction raised by geology. His type of approach accounted for a flood of literature attempting to reconcile geology and Genesis in the early nineteenth

[6] *Scriptural History*, p. 515.
[7] *Ibid.*, p. 597.

century. It was a scholastic approach which still treated natural science as a handmaid to theology, but there was another type of Mosaic geology in which the writers were primarily geologists and secondarily expositors of concordances between Scripture and their science. Their piety, by and large, cannot be doubted, but their quest for harmony between the Word of God and the Works of God was an attempt to make room in the traditional outlook for the new science. In retrospect, we can see that this was accomplished by the geologists, with the unwitting help of some of the orthodox, by drawing through the gate of Biblical chronology a Trojan horse, thought to be laden with glorious scientific proofs of the universal Noachian Deluge and the history of nature given in Genesis. Accidentally perhaps, the chief architect of the stratagem was Baron Cuvier, contemporary of Chateaubriand in the new orthodox France. He was himself guided by suggestions and ideas formulated by Buffon and Deluc.

Prominent in the life work of Jean André Deluc (1727-1817), which included some fifty years of geological field work, was the ambition to corroborate Mosaic history by natural proofs and to stamp out theories, such as Buffon's, which contested the Biblical age of the earth and the actuality of the Flood. After the appearance of Hutton's work, Deluc intensified his search for *facts* to prove that "our continents are of such small antiquity, that the memory of the revolution which gave them birth must still be preserved among men; and thus we are led to seek in the book of Genesis the record of the history of the human race from its origin."[8] However, he could not overcome the many data pointing to long lapses of time in natural history, so he solved the prob-

---

[8] *An Elementary Treatise on Geology* (London, 1809), p. 82. Deluc considered the antiquity of the earth to be the foremost question of his day— "It is thus that all geological questions concentre in a single point, the decision of which embraces them all. . . ." (*Geological Travels* [London, 1810-11], I, 8.)—and not only for geologists, but for everyone because of the "intimate connexion between the history of *man* and that of *continents*." (*Ibid.*, III, 2.)

lem by drawing a cut-off line at the Deluge for the empire of natural knowledge. Beyond this line, Deluc maintained, supernatural forces were acting because the earth was in a state of gestation preparatory to the birth of the present continents, and the stages of the pregnancy were narrated in the first verses of Genesis. Each of the days may have involved long periods of time, as the fossil memorials suggested, but since the earth was still in the shaping hands of the Creator, and subject to the supernatural forces He was likely to employ, this period was not amenable to scientific deductions based on the analogy of natural laws. Knowledge of the postdiluvial world could be derived from scientific investigation, but man could not hope to know more of the antediluvian world than was revealed to him in the writings of Moses.

The empirical work of Deluc was not without value for geology, but his reputation rested primarily on his efforts to support Mosaic geology. His extensive publications, particularly between 1798 and 1813, won for him many plaudits and some dissent from other Mosaic geologists. He was especially influential in popularizing the idea that the Deluge was a dividing point between man's history and the history of the earth,[9] an idea earlier expressed by Buffon and subsequently elaborated by Cuvier.

Of those eighteenth-century advocates of a generated universe, the only one who brought a sound knowledge of fossil species to the support of his evolutionary theories was Lamarck, but his reputation was greatly overshadowed by that of his countryman and rival, Cuvier. Taking for his field the little-known fossil quadrupeds, and applying to them the principles of comparative anatomy, Cuvier astonished the world by reconstructing prehis-

---

[9] He claimed for his system that "it completely breaks the thread of those pretended operations of the *running waters* on our *continents*, in consequence of which the birth of the latter has been referred to an incalculable *antiquity.* . . ." *Ibid.*, 1, 63.

toric forms of animal life whose existence had never been suspected. As he examined the contents of fossil strata, he could not fail to see that the age of the earth was more than six thousand years. Like so many of his predecessors who had closely studied the beds of fossils, he recognized that extensive changes had taken place on the surface of the earth in ages past.

> We are therefore forcibly led to believe, not only that the sea has at one period or another covered all our plains, but that it must have remained there for a long time, and in a state of tranquility; which circumstance was necessary for the formation of deposits so extensive, so thick, in part so solid, and containing exuviae so perfectly preserved.[10]

It is to fossils, he observed, that we owe the very commencement of a sound theory of cosmogony, and without them we could not have even suspected that there had existed epochs in the formation of the earth. The influence of Buffon's *Époques* was evident in Cuvier's conception of epochs in the history of the earth. He pointed out that the deposition of fossil strata required long periods of time, and the strata were like "so many fixed points, answering as rules, for directing our inquiries respecting this ancient chronology of the earth." The naturalist who tried to unravel the epochs of this ancient chronology, he pictured "as an antiquary of a new order" learning the "art of deciphering and restoring."

Cuvier's cosmogony was unfolded in a brilliant "Introduction" to his *Recherches sur les ossemens fossiles* (1812) republished separately many times as a *Discours sur les révolutions de la surface du globe*. In it he reiterated Lamarck's plea for more time in the geological process:

> Genius and science have burst the limits of space; and a few observations, explained by just reasoning, have unveiled the mechanism of the universe. Would it not also be glorious for

[10] *Essay on the Theory of the Earth*, tr. Robert Jameson (Edinburgh, 1822), p. 8.

man to burst the limits of time, and by a few observations, to ascertain the history of this world, and the series of events which preceded the birth of the human race.[11]

It was a noble proclamation, but Cuvier could not, or would not, rise fully to the occasion. He had no feeling of sympathy for the views of Hutton or Lamarck, who had burst the limits of time, and after he had cracked open Biblical chronology enough to let in the epochs of those fossil formations in which he was interested, he undertook the strengthening of Mosaic history.

A substantial part of Cuvier's *Discours* was taken up with an attempt to prove that the Deluge was real and that the history of man on earth was short. He reviewed the traditions of a deluge among the various nations and asserted that such a confluence of traditions in support of a deluge could not be mere chance. Chronologies and ancient astronomical systems with pretensions of a greater antiquity than that given by Biblical chronology were examined by Cuvier with all the tedious pedantry of the most learned scriptural apologists, and with the same sterile result. Antediluvian history was connected with post-diluvian history in one uninterrupted series, he reasoned, but supernatural operations took place in the world prior to the Deluge. Like Deluc, he thus made the Deluge a watershed between the supernatural and natural in earth history.

It so happened that the formations in the Paris Basin which Cuvier studied had alternate strata of marine fossils, fresh-water fossils, and strata without a fossil content. The separation between them was sharply marked and Cuvier promptly decided that the changes in the constitution of the strata were the result of great supernatural catastrophes which had changed the position of the seas. "These repeated irruptions and retreats of the sea have neither been slow nor gradual; most of the catastrophes which have occasioned them have been sudden," he wrote.[12] As to explaining

[11] *Ibid.*, pp. 3-4.
[12] *Ibid.*, p. 15.

these ancient revolutions by now-existing causes, he said, "unfortunately this is not the case in physical history; the thread of operation is here broken, the march of nature is changed, and none of the agents that she now employs were sufficient for the production of her ancient works." [13] Cuvier thought that to search among natural forces still in existence for an explanation of the revolutions memorialized in the earth would be vain, and that such futile searches were the reason why so many conflicting theories had plagued geology. Supernatural causes alone were sufficient to effect the revolutions.

The deposits made between revolutions, however, were regarded by Cuvier as the product of natural forces and time. By breaking the "thread of operations" through catastrophes, Cuvier defended the existence of supernaturalism in the antediluvian world, and his theory had the added merit of breaking those threads of biological continuity in the past which evolutionists had taken for granted. When, as the greatest authority on comparative anatomy, he "proved" that each species had only a limited ability to vary, he further vouchsafed the divine origin of species and the recent origin of man. Lest these conclusions should not be manifest to the English reading public, Cuvier's English translator, Robert Jameson, founder of the Wernerian Natural History Society and a thoroughgoing catastrophist, spelled them out, with the approval of Cuvier, in the introduction:

> The subject of the *deluge* forms a principal object of this elegant discourse. After describing the principal results at which the theory of the earth, in his opinion, has arrived, he next mentions the various relations which connect the history of the fossil bones of land animals with these results; explains the principles on which is founded the art of ascertaining these bones, or in other words, of discovering a genus, and of distinguishing a species, by a single fragment of bone; and gives a rapid sketch of the results to which his researches lead, of the new genera and species which these have been the means of

[13] *Ibid.*, p. 24.

discovering, and of the different formations in which they are contained. Some naturalists, as Lamarck, having maintained that the present existing races of quadrupeds are mere modifications or varieties of those ancient races which we now find in a fossil state, modifications which may have been produced by change of climate, and other local circumstances, and since brought to the present great difference by the operation of similar causes during a long succession of ages,—Cuvier shews that the difference between the fossil species and those which now exist, is bounded by certain limits; that these limits are a great deal more extensive than those which now distinguish the varieties of the same species, and consequently, that the extinct species of quadrupeds are not varieties of the presently existing species. This very interesting discussion naturally leads our author to state the proofs of the recent population of the world; of the comparatively modern origin of its present surface; of the deluge, and the subsequent renewal of human society.[14]

Cuvier's vigorous espousal of the Deluge as an actual geological event mollified some of the orthodox into thinking it was now safe to interpret Biblical chronology as applying to man only. Thus Cuvier provided a safety valve between the irrefutable proofs of an ancient earth and Mosaic history, between the push of geology and the drag of theology.

The nature of the days of creation in Genesis had given the Church Fathers some difficulty, and their arguments that the word "Day" might mean a long period of time were re-examined with new interest after Cuvier's entrance onto the chronological scene. One of the early attempts in England to integrate the Cuvierian system with that of Moses was James Parkinson's *Organic Remains of a Former World.* The first volumes, published in 1804 and 1808, were written with the usual deference to Mosaic chronology, but the third volume, published in 1811, acknowledged the work of Lamarck and Cuvier on extinct species and admitted that the formation of the globe's crust and

[14] *Ibid.,* pp. ix-xi.

the creation of its inhabitants "must have been the work of a vast length of time, and must have been effected at several distant periods."[15] Parkinson expressed a pleasant surprise at how well the days of creation could be expanded to take care of this apparent contradiction to Biblical chronology, while the study of fossil remains produced an unexpected additional proof of the order of creation as given in Genesis. How convincing this new view seemed!

> From the whole of this examination a pleasing, and perhaps unexpected accordance appears between the order in which, according to the scriptural account, creation was accomplished, and the order in which the fossil remains of creation are found deposited in the superficial layers of the earth. So close indeed is this agreement, that the Mosaic account is thereby confirmed in every respect, except as to the age of the world, and the distance of time between the completion of different parts of the creation. These, in consequence of the literal acceptation of the word *day*, in that account, are reckoned to be much less than what every examination of the earth's structure authorizes their being supposed. If we are constrained to receive this word as descriptive of that length of time in which this planet now performs its diurnal revolution; and are to consider the words morning and evening, applied to a time when the sun is said not to have been formed, as bearing the same meaning which they now convey, it must be acknowledged that the stumbling-block is immovable. But if, on the other hand, the word day be admitted as figuratively designating certain indefinite periods, in which particular parts of the great work of creation were accomplished, no difficulty will then remain. The age of the world, according to the scriptural account, will then agree with that which is manifested by the phenomena of its stratification.[16]

Extending the length of the days of creation formed one means of reconciling the narrative of Moses with the demand of geology

[15] *Organic Remains of a Former World*, III, 449.
[16] *Ibid.*, III, 451-2. Parkinson was one of the original members of the Geological Society of London (1807).

for a great antiquity for the earth. Another means was found in an old interpretation of the first verses of Genesis, and it was revived by Thomas Chalmers. In 1804, as a young clergyman in the Scottish Church, Chalmers startled his audience during a lecture by stating:

> There is a prejudice against the speculation of the geologist which I am anxious to remove. It has been said that they nurture infidel propensities. By referring the origin of the globe to a higher antiquity than is assigned to it by the writings of Moses, it has been said that geology undermines our faith in the inspiration of the Bible, and in all the animating prospects of immortality which it unfolds. This is a false alarm. *The writings of Moses do not fix the antiquity of the globe. If they fix anything at all, it is only the antiquity of the species.*[17]

As the resort to the metaphorical interpretation of the days of creation gained in popularity through the writings of Cuvier and Parkinson, Chalmers became critical of it. When in 1813 Jameson published his English edition of Cuvier's *Essay on the Theory of the Earth*, Chalmers took occasion in a review of the work to express his opinion on the relation of geology to Genesis. He wrote, "it is high time to confront the theory of our geologist with the sacred history—with a view both to lay down the points of accordancy, and to show in how far we are compelled to modify the speculation, or to disown it altogether."[18] His position in brief was that the recorded testimony of a witness, such as Moses, to an event was more reliable than any reconstruction of the event at a later date from fragmentary remains, as was being done in geology, no matter how ingenious the latter might be. Yet there was something to be said for that evidence which Cuvier had gathered from geology indicating that the hand of God was apparent in the past operations of nature. The organic world

[17] William Hanna, *Memoirs of the Life and Writings of Thomas Chalmers* (1849-52), I, 81.
[18] *The Works of Thomas Chalmers* (Glasgow, 1836-42), XII, 362. The review first appeared in the *Christian Instructor* (1814).

must have had a beginning, for instance, because there were no
fossil remains in the oldest strata, and the occurrence of supernatural catastrophes was confirmed in earth history by the sharp
breaks in the order of the strata, breaks which marked the elimi-
nation of old species and the creation of new ones. Chalmers did
not question the soundness of Cuvier's geology, but he refused to
abandon the literal history of Moses, stating firmly, "We cannot
consent to the stretching out of the days, spoken of in the first
chapter of Genesis, into indefinite periods of time."[19] Once
liberties were taken with the text of Scripture there was no telling where they would end. But there was a way out of the difficulty, he thought, which would be satisfactory to both geologists
and theologians.

> We conclude with adverting to the unanimity of geologists
> in one point,—the far superior antiquity of this globe to the
> commonly received date of it, as taken from the writings of
> Moses. What shall we make of this? We may feel a security
> as to those points in which they differ, and, confronting them
> with one another, may remain safe and untouched between
> them. But when they agree, this security fails. There is no
> neutralization of authority among them as to the age of this
> world; and Cuvier, with his catastrophes and his epochs, leaves
> the popular opinion nearly as far behind him, as they who trace
> our present continent upward through an indefinite series of
> ancestors, and assign many millions of years to the existence of
> each generation.
> Should the phenomena compel us to assign a greater antiquity
> to the globe than to that work of days detailed in the book of
> Genesis, there is still one way of saving the credit of the literal
> history. The first creation of the earth and the heavens may
> have formed no part of that work. This took place at the
> *beginning*, and is described in the first verse of Genesis. It is
> not said when this *beginning* was.[20]

The first verse of Genesis described a primary act of creation,

[19] *Ibid.*, p. 366.
[20] *Ibid.*, pp. 369-70.

Chalmers thought, and we are at liberty to place it as far back as we wish. The first half of the second verse, "And the earth was without form, and void," may have described a state of the earth after it had already existed for ages and had been the seat of geological revolutions, while the second half of this verse, "And the Spirit of God moved upon the face of the waters," marked the beginning point of the detailed operations leading to the present earth, for "Moses may be supposed to give us not a history of the first formation of things, but of the formation of the present system."

This interpretation of the first verses of Genesis had been suggested by the Church Fathers,[21] but the basic idea that many great changes had taken place in the interim between the "beginning" and the actual creation of the world was best known through Milton's *Paradise Lost*. In Books V and VI, Milton has Raphael narrate to Adam the battle between Michael and Satan, with the resultant Fall of the rebel angels, in a graphic presentation which owed little to scriptural authority. Hitchcock, writing in 1851, observed in regard to this section on the Fall of the angels:

> The great English poet, in his Paradise Lost, has clothed this hypothesis in a most graphic and philosophical dress; and probably his descriptions have done more than the Bible to give it currency. Indeed, could the truth be known, I fancy that, on many points of secondary importance, the current theology of the day has been shaped quite as much by the ingenious machinery of Paradise Lost as by the Scriptures; the theologians having so mixed up the ideas of Milton with those derived from inspiration, that they find it difficult to distinguish between them.[22]

It will be recalled that in Book VII of *Paradise Lost*, Raphael relates how God, after expelling Satan and the rebel angels from

[21] A selection of relevant quotations from the Church Fathers is given in Gerald Molloy, *Geology and Revelation, or the Ancient History of the Earth* (London, 1870), Chapters 19-20, and Appendix.

[22] Edward Hitchcock, *The Religion of Geology* (Boston, 1851), p. 80.

Heaven, decided to create another world and other creatures to inhabit it, and in the work of six days brought forth this earth and man. The theory of Chalmers that an immense period of time occurred prior to the days of creation was adopted by other Mosaic geologists and was later blended with the Miltonic hypothesis in what became known as the "restitution" theory, the theory that the present earth was restituted out of a previous one destroyed when Satan was banished to the bottomless pit.

The movement to establish harmony between geological science and Genesis was well under way by 1815, but it was met with contempt by the unbending literalists, and cries of heresy filled the air. Huxley's description of bibliolatry would have been drawn as even more oppressive had he grown up in the England of 1815. Huxley would have seen geological science and the advancement of scientific truth being pilloried and stoned by the ignorant literalists, and in an age which has been orientated to the adulation of the heroic warriors in the army of science, it is easy to accept Huxley's point of view. To do so, however, is not entirely fair to a generation whose intellectual and emotional life centered around the drama of salvation. Bigotry, stupidity, hypocrisy, and time-serving, there certainly was, but there was also a rich and loving devotion to the intimate Biblical world of history centered around man. William Hazlitt's description of his father in the essay, "My First Acquaintance with Poets," which appeared in the *Liberal*, April, 1823, captures something of the world in which so many of the orthodox lived.

> After being tossed about from congregation to congregation in the heats of the Unitarian controversy, and squabbles about the American war, he had been relegated to an obscure village, where he was to spend the last thirty years of his life, far from the only converse that he loved, the talk about disputed texts of Scripture and the cause of civil and religious liberty. Here he passed his days, repining but resigned, in the study of the Bible, and the perusal of the Commentators,—huge folios, not easily got through, one of which would outlast a winter! Why

did he pore on these from morn to night . . . ? Here were "no figures nor no fantasies"—neither poetry nor philosophy— nothing to dazzle, nothing to excite modern curiosity; but to his lack-lustre eyes there appeared, within the pages of the ponderous, unwieldy, neglected tomes, the sacred name of JEHOVAH in Hebrew capitals: pressed down by the weight of the style, worn to the last fading thinness of the understanding, there were glimpses, glimmering notions of the patriarchal wanderings, with palm-trees hovering in the horizon, and processions of camels at the distance of three thousand years; there was Moses with the Burning Bush, . . . there were out- lines, rude guesses at the shape of Noah's Ark and of the riches of Solomon's Temple; questions as to the date of the creation, predictions of the end of all things; the great lapses of time . . . ; and though the soul might slumber with an hieroglyphic veil of inscrutable mysteries drawn over it, yet it was in a slumber ill-exchanged for all the sharpened realities of sense, wit, fancy, or reason. My father's life was comparatively a dream; but it was a dream of infinity and eternity, of death, the resurrection, and a judgment to come!

It is indeed understandable that men as learned in the lore of the Bible as Hazlitt's father, or less learned but as deeply im- mersed in it, would resent the imputation that theirs was a world of superstition and error. Their resistance to the inroads of geol- ogy into the Mosaic creation was seated deeply in their emotions and sense of otherworldly values. They did not comprehend the equally strong faith of those curious fellows with picks and hammers who felt compelled to chisel away at Genesis, and it was all too easy to see only evil motivations in the actions of such per- sons. However, there were among the orthodox those schooled in integrity and great personal courage, men like Chalmers, and later John Pye Smith, who, seeing the force of the geological evidence, stood up before their congregations and fearlessly rammed their convictions into the hostile audiences.

The situation was explosive, and "it was a mooted question whether geology and orthodox Christianity were compatible";

but open warfare was avoided in spite of the noisy controversy that developed. The Cuvierian compromise must be given a large amount of credit in smoothing the troubled waters. The harmonists seized upon it to establish a middle ground between Genesis and geology and thereby diffuse the tension between theology and science.

The sensational revelations made by Cuvier of prehistoric monsters, his dramatic "succession of former worlds," each perishing in a mighty holocaust, his magnificent prose style, and his propensity for publicity, brought Cuvier to the attention of the world at large. The cataclysmic revolutions of his earth history struck a sympathetic chord in an age familiar with revolutions in civil history,[23] while his attention to the great catastrophe of the Flood heightened its importance in the traditional Mosaic history. Traces of Cuvier's influence can be found in a diversity of writings around the second decade of the nineteenth century, including German historical works and romantic literature in general.[24] For a time, it heightened the sense of supernaturalism and divine intervention in history. The existence of the prehistoric monsters and a succession of former worlds focussed attention on the enormity of death and destruction which had stalked the earth and the power of the God who had wreaked such a vengeance on the antediluvian worlds. But even this emphasis was car-

[23] The association of the ideas of revolutions in civil and in natural history was drawn to my attention by Dr. Owsei Temkin in the work of J. G. G. Ballenstedt, *Die Urwelt oder Beweis von dem Daseyn und Untergange von mehr als einer Vorwelt*, 3rd ed. (Quedlinburg & Leipzig, 1818-19), Abt. I, iii, 205.

[24] *The Philosophy of History* (1828) of Frederick von Schlegel is an interesting example of how the Cuvierian cosmogony, though apparently derived through a German popularizer, Schubert, was elaborated in the philosophy of one of the numerous converts to Catholicism early in the century among the German intellectuals. His close friend, Count Friedrich Stolberg, companion of Goethe to Italy and another convert to the Roman Catholic Church, had in turn been strongly influenced by the geological ideas of Deluc, while Goethe was a Neptunist.

ried too far and fostered doubts about Mosaic history through making the punishment for Adam's sin seem disproportionately great. It was the mischievous Lord Byron who managed to draw out this effect. In his *Don Juan*, Byron caricatured and sported with the Cuvierian worlds. Juan, in Canto IX, forgot what he was about to say, and continued:

XXXVII

But let it go:—it will one day be found
   With other relics of "a former World,"
When this World shall be *former*, underground,
   Thrown topsy-turvy, twisted, crisped, and curled,
Baked, fried, or burnt, turned inside-out, or drowned,
   Like all the worlds before, which have been hurled
First out of, and then back again to chaos—
The superstratum which will overlay us.

XXXVIII

So Cuvier says:—and then shall come again
   Unto the new creation, rising out
From our old crash, some mystic, ancient strain
   Of things destroyed and left in airy doubt;
Like to the notions we now entertain
   Of Titans, giants, fellows of about
Some hundred feet in height, *not* to say *miles*,
And mammoths, and your winged crocodiles.

XXXIX

Think if then George the Fourth should be dug up!
   How the new worldlings of the then new East
Will wonder where such animals could sup!
   (For they themselves will be but of the least:
Even worlds miscarry, when too oft they pup,
   And every new creation hath decreased
In size, from overworking the material—
Men are but maggots of some huge Earth's burial.)

These paragraphs were written between 1822 and 1823, but in 1819, Byron had treated the Cuvierian worlds more seriously. In the preface to *Cain: A Mystery*, he noted:

> The reader will perceive that the author has partly adopted in this poem the notion of Cuvier, that the world had been destroyed several times before the creation of man. This speculation, derived from the different strata and the bones of enormous and unknown animals found in them, is not contrary to the Mosaic account, but rather confirms it; as no human bones have yet been discovered in those strata, although those of many known animals are found near the remains of the unknown. The assertion of Lucifer, that the pre-Adamite world was also peopled by rational beings much more intelligent than man, and proportionably powerful to the mammoth, etc. etc., is, of course, a poetical fiction to help him make out his case.

Whatever else *Cain* may be, it is certainly a dramatization of Death.[25] As Lucifer took Cain on a tour of Hades and unfolded the vision of the former worlds inhabited by enormous creatures, lying by myriads underneath the surface of the earth, the scale of death was oppressive. When Cain wanted to know why all this destruction of life had taken place, Lucifer reminded Cain that the animals were all made for man, and asked, "You would not have their doom Superior to your own? Had Adam not Fallen, all had stood." Cain sadly replied, "Alas, the hopeless wretches!"

Byron ended *Cain* in such a way that the moral had a semblance of accordance with orthodoxy, but he left the impression that the punishment imposed on the world hardly fit the crime of Adam and Eve. The work was actually a fine portrayal of the majesty of man caught in the grip of fate, and transcended orthodoxy completely, but the author rightly suspected that he would be accused of Manichaeism. *Cain* raised a furore amongst the

---

[25] Ernest Hartley Coleridge in his edition of *The Works of Lord Byron* 2nd ed. (London, 1905) says that the key-note of *Cain* is " 'Man walketh in a vain shadow'—a shadow which he can never overtake, the shadow of an eternally postponed fruition" (v, 200).

English and there was talk of a trial for blasphemy, although it is a little difficult to see what it would be based upon, except outraged feelings.[26]

The theme of death was further elaborated by Byron in *Heaven and Earth: A Mystery*, written in 1821, but here the Deluge was the only catastrophe invoked and it was treated in accord with the conventional diluvial theory which explained the fossil shells in the mountains as having been left there by the inundation experienced by Noah.[27] The liberties Byron was wont to take with British decorum and propriety made it improbable that he would be regarded as a spokesman for the religious point of view, and, for our purposes, his handling of Mosaic history had the effect of so enlarging the scale of the creation that man appeared only as an insignificant mite in it—"men are but maggots of some huge Earth's burial." With unerring intuition the poet had struck the tender nerve of the orthodox reluctance to extend the age of the earth. As the seventeenth-century doctrine of a plurality of worlds had raised doubts about an anthropocentric spatial universe, so now the doctrine of a plurality of *former* worlds must inevitably make the anthropocentric view of history seem improbable. As long as the scale of time was brief and the events few, Mosaic history could carry conviction, but how could epoch after epoch, creation after creation, be fitted to the teleology of man's redemption? Geological discoveries were puffing up a mammoth camel to be squeezed through the eye of the Christian needle of eschatology.

Byron's influence on attitudes towards Sacred history is not easy to determine, but considering how widely his works were read, it is not difficult to imagine that he contributed to the conditioning of the minds of the militant rationalists of the following generation. His orthodox contemporaries shuddered at the poetry of the young genius in their midst, but they apparently closed

[26] See *ibid.*, v, 202-4.
[27] *Ibid.*, v, 301, lines 238-40.

their minds to his novel handling of Genesis.

In spite of the heretical tendencies in Byron's adaptation of Cuvier's theory and orthodox resistence in general, the work of harmonizing geology and Mosaic history proceeded rapidly along the paths marked by Cuvier and Chalmers. It was given a tremendous boost by the support of the Reverend William Buckland, for whom a readership in geology was established at Oxford in 1819. He became the "Dean" of English geology, as well as Dean of Westminster (in 1845 by appointment of Sir Robert Peel).

In his *Inaugural Address* at Oxford in 1819, Buckland wrote, "The grand fact of an universal deluge at no very remote period is proved on grounds so decisive and incontrovertible, that had we never heard of such an event from Scripture or any other Authority, Geology of itself must have called in the assistance of some such catastrophe to explain the phenomena of diluvial action which are universally presented to us, and which are unintelligible without recourse to a deluge exerting its ravages at a period not more ancient than that announced in the Book of Genesis."[28] Deluc, in his support of Mosaic geology, had leaned heavily on the inference that large erratic boulders found far from their parent strata had been scattered about by the Deluge. Saussure had also used this evidence in support of the Deluge, and, about the same time, it was noticed that many rock surfaces had large areas with grooves running in the same direction, apparently made by the erratic boulders moving over their surface. These purported evidences of the Deluge had forced Sir James Hall to abandon the Huttonian system, in spite of the fact that he had helped Hutton with experimental confirmation of the system. Hall offered the suggestion that the boulders had been attached to large floating pieces of ice during the Deluge.[29] The carrying

[28] *Vindiciae Geologicae, or the Connexion of Geology with Religion Explained* (Oxford, 1820), p. 24.

[29] "On the Revolutions of the Earth's Surface," *Transactions of the Royal Society of Edinburgh*, VII (1815), 139-211.

power of icebergs was confirmed by Playfair in 1816,[30] and it was not until 1840, when Agassiz published his *Études sur les glaciers*, that the true explanation of the boulders and their scratches was forthcoming. In the meantime, glacial effects took their place as proofs of a Deluge. To these proofs, Buckland added the marks of the Deluge to be found, as he thought, in the detritus of ancient caves.

Utilizing the method of comparative anatomy developed by Cuvier for the study of fossil remains, Buckland brilliantly reconstructed from the successive layers of bones on cave floors, most notably in that of the Kirkdale cave in Yorkshire, the history of animal life occupying the caves for hundreds of centuries. Between the fossils of extinct hyena species and other still extant animal species he thought he had found an extensive deposit of alluvium left by the Deluge, and this was advanced as a decisive confirmation of the narrative of Moses. To account for the fact that Moses had not mentioned "antediluvian" species, Buckland pointed out that Moses was giving a moral, not a natural history in the Book of Genesis. Therefore, aside from mentioning that there had been a beginning and briefly giving an outline of the creation to satisfy man's curiosity, Moses passed over detailed history until man entered upon the scene. Thereafter, particulars were given by Moses, because moral purposes were involved, and among the particulars was the account of the Deluge. Buckland, however, went into much more detail than Moses in explaining the Deluge, in *Reliquiae Diluvianae: or Observations on the Organic Remains contained in Caves, Fissures, and Diluvian Gravel, and on other Geological Phenomena, attesting the Action of an Universal Deluge*, a two-volume work published in 1823. The treatise was of such a high scientific calibre, in spite of its fallacious premises, that it firmly implanted the actuality of the Deluge in the minds of geologists, as well as non-geologists, not only in Britain, but throughout Europe and America. Buckland's influ-

[30] As expanded by Lyell and others, the transport of "erratic blocks" by floating icebergs became known as the "drift theory."

ence in Britain was especially strong, however, for, as Gillispie
has stated, "Almost all of Buckland's professional colleagues in
the 1820's, including Lyell, regarded themselves as his pupils."[31]
Theologians who were prepared to make concessions for geology
regarded the *Reliquiae Diluvianae* as a great victory for the testimony of Moses and were less reluctant to let Biblical chronology
apply only to the period after the creation of man.

The literalists were far from being silenced, however. A typical
example of literalist opposition to the extension of the antiquity
of the earth was George Bugg's *Scriptural Geology*, written in
1826 to overthrow the antediluvian theories of Cuvier and Buckland. Modern geologists had based their conclusions on two
gratuitous assumptions, Bugg argued. They took for granted
that the strata were *regularly* and *successively* superimposed upon
each other in a time sequence. They then proceeded to use the
strata as "chronometers" to compute their thousands and thousands of years. However, no one had seen fossil strata taking
shape, and geologists were merely basing their reasoning on the
analogy of forces now operating in nature. The induction of
principles through human reason was fallible, whereas Scripture
was not, and in Mosaic history there were only two periods in
which the changes in the constitution of the earth could have
taken place—the days of creation and the Deluge. The duration
of these events was explicitly given in Genesis:

> If then the Scriptures are *positive and decisive*, and therefore
> *correct* in what they assert respecting the "low antiquity of the
> human race," they are equally decisive and correct in asserting
> the *low antiquity* of animals and fishes of "every race." And,
> therefore, the vast *antiquity* of the objects of *Geology* are fabu-
> lous and visionary.[32]

The geologists had mistakenly assumed a succession in time from

[31] Charles Coulston Gillispie, *Genesis and Geology* (Cambridge, Mass.,
1951), p. 103.

[32] *Scriptural Geology: or, Geological Phenomena Consistent Only with
the Literal Interpretation of the Sacred Scriptures* (London, 1826), I, 157.
See also p. 321.

the position of the strata, but there was no reason why the position of the strata might not have been given in the instantaneous act of creation. To attempt to raise a time scale from the accident of one piece of the earth's crust being on top of another was to Bugg the height of folly. He urged geologists to confine their research to the gratification of curiosity and the advancement of the practical arts, instead of disturbing the morals of youth by casting doubt on the testimony of Moses.

The central point upon which Bugg, Granville Penn, and numerous others based their resistance to geology was the earth's age. In the popular and authoritative *Outlines of the Geology of England and Wales* (1822) by W. D. Conybeare and William Phillips, the observation was made about the bearing of geology upon the physical facts recorded in the inspired writings: "Two points only can be in any manner implicated in the discussions of Geology: I. The Noachian Deluge. II. The Antiquity of the Earth."[33] The general agreement among geologists in the 1820's about the Noachian Deluge left only one point of controversy. Conybeare and Phillips quoted Cuvier at length to show that geology brought strong collateral testimony in support of Moses, but on the second point they merely pointed out some of the alternatives for geologists. The 1600 years between the Creation and Deluge could be made to suffice for the explanation of great changes by resorting to violent convulsions of supernatural force; each "day" of creation could be extended to a long interval of time; or a long period could be interpolated between the "beginning" of the first verse of Genesis and the creation subsequently given. The authors were inclined to agree with John Bird Sumner, who stated in his *Treatise on the Records of Creation* (1816) that

[33] *Outlines*, p. lvi. William Whewell, *History of the Inductive Sciences*, 3rd ed. (New York, 1897), II, 525, says of this work that "it enabled a very wide class of readers to understand and verify the classifications which geology had then very recently established. . . . The vast impulse which it gave to the study of sound descriptive geology was felt and acknowledged in other countries, as well as in Britain."

there was nothing in geology hostile to the Mosaic account of Creation and that we are not called upon to deny the possible existence of previous worlds from whose remains our own was organized. They were not prepared to take a stand on which of the above alternatives should be followed, but they cautioned against scepticism such as that appearing in Lamarck's *Hydrogéologie*, on the one hand, and against the overzealous attempts to mold geology to the words of Scripture, on the other hand. They also expressed the growing sentiment that it was too much to expect Revelation to include a detailed and orderly physical description of the universe.

The chronological outlook during the 1820's may be summed up by saying that the traditional Biblical view prevailed for the most part, but among geologists and harmonists a division was made between antediluvian and postdiluvian times, supernatural forces prevailing in the former and only natural forces in the latter. By confining Biblical chronology to man's history alone, they claimed a measure of freedom in the antediluvian period to fill out segments of geochronology on the basis of observed evidence, but the approach was piecemeal and without any over-all estimate of the duration of the earth, except that it was "vast." The attacks on geologists by literalists, who called them infidels, atheists, heretics, and the corrupters of the morals of youth, made the geologists wary of extensive generalizations upon the age of the earth, while their silence, if not agreement, on the historical outline of Mosaic history gave the doctrine of the Noachian Deluge a firm place in geological thought. One stupendous, supernatural cataclysm easily led to another in the geological record, and this in turn gave aid and comfort to the parallel theory in biology of a series of miraculous special creations of species. This parallelism was later indicated by Lyell when he said of the system of an influential geologist,

> De Beaumont's system was properly selected by him as directly opposed to my fundamental principles. It was well selected,

because it not only assumed returning periods of intense activity, or, as Sedgwick termed them, "feverish spasmodic energy," which tore asunder the framework of the globe, but also violent and concomitant transitions from one set of species to another.[34]

THE LYELLIAN REVOLUTION

The spell of the Cuvier-Buckland compromise between geology and theology was broken in 1830 by the publication of Sir Charles Lyell's *Principles of Geology*, and another stage commenced in the controversy over the age of the earth. Lyell "was taught by Buckland the catastrophical or paroxysmal theory," and in 1823, he was defending Buckland's notions on diluvial formations with vigor against Ferussac, who was "not orthodox." About this time, however, he became familiar with the uniformitarian views of Constant Prevost and George J. Poulett Scrope, and after considerable observation and continued reading, he came around to the theory of uniformitarianism himself.[35] Prominent in his reading, was the work of Lamarck, which he "devoured" with pleasure. Lyell was attracted to Lamarck's concept of geological process, but not to his theory of the transformation of species. Writing to his friend George Mantell, March 2, 1827, Lyell confided both his reaction to Lamarck and his own plans:

> His theories delighted me more than any novel I ever read, and much in the same way, for they address themselves to the imagination, at least of geologists who know the mighty inferences which would be deducible were they established by observations. But though I admire even his flights, and feel none of the *odium theologicum* which some modern writers

[34] *Life, Letters and Journals of Sir Charles Lyell*, Bart. (London, 1881), II, 3-4.

[35] *Ibid.*, II, 6-7.

in this country have visited him with, I confess I read him
rather as I hear an advocate on the wrong side, to know what
can be made of the case in good hands. . . . That the earth is
quite as old as he supposes, has long been my creed, and I will
try before six months are over to convert the readers of the
Quarterly to that heterodox opinion.[36]

Later in the year, Lyell forcefully presented in the *Quarterly
Review* the thesis that geological monuments were the result of
natural forces acting in the ordinary course of nature over a
long period of time.[37] The occasion for his defending the uniformitarian view of geological process was a review of Scrope's
Geology of Central France, which also contained compelling
arguments for uniformitarianism. Subsequent geological tours in
France, Italy, and Great Britain convinced Lyell that uniformitarianism was irrefutable, and he brought his arguments together
in the next few years, laying the foundations for his *Principles
of Geology*. In January, 1829, he told Murchison that his work
was all planned and partly written, and that in it he would attempt only to establish the principle of uniformitarianism, using
his facts as illustrations of that principle.[38] In the meantime, he
and Murchison were pushing their uniformitarian views before the
Geological Society, where they met ridicule and great opposition.[39] However, they pressed the Diluvialists hard, and after one
stormy meeting Lyell wrote, "Murchison and I fought stoutly, and
Buckland was very piano. Conybeare's memoir is not strong by
any means. He admits three deluges before the Noachian! and
Buckland adds God knows how many *catastrophes* besides, so we
have driven them out of the Mosaic record fairly."[40]

Under some kind of a *quid pro quo* arrangement, when the
Principles went to press, Scrope was designated to review it for

[36] *Ibid.*, I, 168.
[37] *Quarterly Review*, XXXVI (1827), 437-83.
[38] Lyell's *Life*, I, 234.
[39] *Ibid.*, I, 252 ff.
[40] *Ibid.*, I, 252-3.

the *Quarterly*. Lyell promptly got a letter off to him with instructions on how to handle it.[41] "I am sure," he wrote, "you may get into Q. R. what will free the science from Moses, for if treated seriously, the party are quite prepared for it." Lyell was convinced that the church party had at last begun to see the mischief and scandal which had been brought on theology by Mosaic systems. Taking up the question of a "beginning," he told Scrope that he supposed there was one, but that he preferred Hutton's doctrine of no signs of a beginning and no prospect of an end, adding, "but there is no harm in your attacking me, provided you point out that it is the proof I deny, not the probability of a beginning." He had carefully avoided drawing the moral of his work relative to Moses, he continued, for he thought it a wise policy not to irritate the age. Also, everything pertaining to modern writers had been left out of his introductory sketch of geological thought, because it would then be easier for them to overcome their prejudice for deluge systems without embarrassment. The sketch itself was to be a gentle means of discrediting their physico-theological views without attacking them personally. "I conceived the idea five or six years ago, that if ever the Mosaic geology could be set down without giving offence, it would be in an historical sketch, and you must abstract mine, in order to have as little to say as possible yourself. Let them feel it, and point the moral."

In the historical sketch, Lyell gave to "prepossessions in regard to the duration of past time" first place among those prejudices which had most retarded the progress of geology.[42] Undervaluing the quantity of past time had created an apparent coincidence of events which were in fact widely separated in time, and it made it difficult for men to perceive the aggregate effects of natural causes operating with no greater intensity than in the

---

[41] *Ibid.*, I, 268-71.
[42] *Principles of Geology*, 9th ed. (New York, 1857), p. 63. See also *Life*, II, 6.

present. "Now the reader may easily satisfy himself, that, however undeviating the course of nature may have been from the earliest epochs, it was impossible for the first cultivators to come to such a conclusion, so long as they were under the delusion as to the age of the world, and the date of the first creation of animate beings."[43] Seeing disconnected geological monuments in close contact with each other, without the intermediate events, made the passage from one state of things to another appear so violent that the idea of revolutions naturally suggested itself. It was as if, in human history, thousands of years were reduced to hundreds. A crowd of incidents would then follow one another so rapidly that the course of history would take on the appearance of superhuman magnitude and paroxysmal violence.

The geologists had been working under the fallacy that the data in a formation presented a fairly complete historical record, unaware that an enormous quantity of intermediate data were missing in the succession of strata, and as a result, they assumed that the gaps in the fossil record were gaps in the processes of nature itself. When Lyell interpolated time and continuous process into the gaps, all supernatural cataclysms, including the Deluge, and therewith the "broken thread of operations" which had been a proof of the sudden appearance of new species, were rendered superfluous. However, such an interpolation was necessarily based on inference rather than actual observation, and was therefore open to the charge of being "merely hypothetical."

When the first volume of the *Principles of Geology* was published in January, 1830, it was met with praise for its content of practical geology and condemnation for its principle of uniformitarianism. It was immediately apparent that much of Mosaic geology had been swept away by Lyell, but his judicious handling of the subject did help his cause. Lyell has recorded the reaction of a Mr. Smith whom he met at a club dinner shortly after the publication of the *Principles*, "who poured out, 'I am in the mid-

[43] *Principles*, p. 63.

dle, and full of astonishment and admiration at your having, among other things, been the first to take the bull by the horns, about the antiquity of the Earth, and contrived to do it in so inoffensive a way,' &c."[44] The offspring of Genesis and geology had become more unnatural with every new geological discovery, and in some quarters, at least, there was probably a feeling of relief in finding geology so extensively freed from the influence of Moses. Among the leading geologists, Biblical chronology and Diluvialism were soon dropped out of prehistory.

It must be emphasized, however, that Lyell's assault on Mosaic history pertained only to prehistory, and even there it was not entirely consistent. Man was not included in the geological scheme of things. Lyell was unequivocal on this point: "The comparatively modern introduction of the human race is proved by the absence of the remains of man and his works, not only from all strata containing a certain proportion of fossil shells of extinct species, but even from a large part of the newest strata, in which all the fossil individuals are referable to species still living."[45] Nor did Lyell abandon the idea of a supernatural special creation of each species, an idea which had been so strongly associated with the breaks in the fossil record. His deep religious convictions and his habitual attacks on the transformist views of Lamarck were carried over into his geological thinking without being subjected to a rigid examination at this time.

Although no work was more decisive on the course of geological thought than Lyell's *Principles of Geology*, its assimilation and acceptance took time. Harmonists were spurred to renewed efforts to find a common ground between Mosaic history and geology, while the new concessions they were forced to make on literalism aroused greater hostility amongst the narrowly orthodox to both geologists and the harmonists.

F. Henri Reusch observed in 1867 that in the attempt to solve

[44] Lyell's *Life*, 1, 326.
[45] *Principles*, p. 182. See also pp. 147, 687, and 764.

the difficulties between Mosaic history and natural evidence, a series of works had been given birth, particularly in his century, which form a literature entirely apart.[46] This literature is much too extensive to review in detail, nor is it of sufficient interest to warrant such an undertaking. Since it is largely repetitive of a few main arguments, a representative sampling will suffice to show the direction of thought in connection with the transformation of ideas about the age of the earth in the contest between Mosaic history and geology.

After having done so much to establish the Deluge in geology, attention naturally centered on Buckland to see how he would react to his pupil's work on uniformitarianism. He was commissioned to write the sixth Bridgewater Treatise, one of a series endowed "to demonstrate the Power, Wisdom, and Goodness of God, as manifested in the Creation." An announcement of the work appeared, and then a review of it in the Quarterly, some time before publication. There was much speculation as to the cause of the delay. "Was Buckland having trouble making up his mind?" Robert Bakewell, an eminent geologist, thought that the clergy were delaying it because the review indicated Buckland had yielded too much on Mosaic history, and he remarked to Benjamin Silliman: "Geology is in a rather strange state in England at present; the rich clergy begin to tremble for their incomes, and seek to avert their fate by a revived zeal for orthodoxy, and are making a great clamor against geology as opposed to Genesis."[47] Parliament had appointed an ecclesiastical commission to review the financial and administrative affairs, among other things, of the Church of England. Although incomes were hardly in jeopardy, some of the clergy, led by Tractarians, had shown a renewed zeal for orthodoxy.

When Buckland's *Geology and Mineralogy Considered with*

---

[46] *La Bible et la Nature* (Paris, 1867), p. 1.

[47] John F. Fulton and Elizabeth H. Thomson, *Benjamin Silliman, 1779-1864, Pathfinder in American Science* (New York, 1947), p. 135.

Reference to Natural Theology was published in 1836, it was evident that he had reversed himself on Diluvialism and had completely abandoned Biblical chronology in prehistory, but he had by no means given up the attempt to bring revelation and geology into harmony. On the consistency of geological discoveries with sacred history, he observed:

> It may seem just matter of surprise, that many learned and religious men should regard with jealousy and suspicion the study of any natural phenomena, which abound with proofs of some of the highest attributes of the Deity; and should receive with distrust, or total incredulity, the announcement of conclusions, which the geologist deduces from careful and patient investigation of the facts which it is his province to explore. These doubts and difficulties result from the disclosures made by geology, respecting the lapse of very long periods of time, before the creation of man. Minds which have been long accustomed to date the origin of the universe, as well as that of the human race, from an era of about six thousand years ago, receive reluctantly any information, which if true, demands some new modification of their present ideas of cosmogony; and, as in this respect, Geology has shared the fate of other infant sciences, in being for a while considered hostile to revealed religion; so, like them, when fully understood, it will be found a potent and consistent auxiliary to it, exalting our conviction of the Power, and Wisdom, and Goodness of the Creator.[48]

All observers were now agreed, Buckland continued, that the geological phenomena required a lapse of very long periods of time as an essential condition of their production. This did not mean that revelation was in error, and in fact, he thought, the first verse of Genesis seemed to assert that the creation of the universe and the earth had preceded the operations of the six days described in Genesis, "nor is any limit fixed to the time during which these intermediate events may have been going on: millions of millions of years may have occupied the indefinite

[48] *Geology and Mineralogy Considered with Reference to Natural Theology* (London, 1836), 1, 8-9.

interval, between the beginning in which God created the heaven and the earth, and the evening or commencement of the first day of the Mosaic narrative."[49] Moses records the history of the earth in its present state only, he said, and no matter how much time we allow for the previous history of the earth, it still remains an earth created in finite time.

Buckland had supported the extended "days of creation" interpretation of Mosaic history, but useful as it was in opening up the time scale for geological epochs, the continued progress of paleontology failed to confirm in the fossil record the order of appearance of plants and animals given in Genesis. He now turned to the "restitution" hypothesis. The period of chaos was sufficiently vague that geologists could move more freely in raising their epochs in it. Buckland did not give his support to the story of the fall of bad angels, an elaboration which he credited to Simon Episcopius (1583-1643), but he thought it was a significant confirmation of the validity of the restitution interpretation to find Biblical scholars prior to the rise of geology allowing an indefinite interval of time between the "beginning" and the "days."

Although the High Church Party, whose dominant leadership was looking kindly towards the Roman Catholic Church, undertook zealous opposition to all inroads on literal dogmatism, the Roman Catholics had at least one eminent spokesman, the English Cardinal Nicholas Wiseman, who viewed geology without alarm and tried to place his religion above controversy with science. His two-volume *Twelve Lectures on the Connexion between Science and Revealed Religion* (1836), first delivered before the English College in Rome in 1835, reviewed the history of geology and indicated how deeply concerned most of its cultivators had been with confirming the truths of Christianity. The tendency of the science had been towards religion, not away from it, he noted, and geologists had taken great care to advance proofs

[49] *Ibid.,* I, 21-2.

of the occurrence of the Deluge and the recent creation of man in accordance with Biblical chronology. However, the well-meaning geologists had allowed their religious enthusiasm to carry exegesis too far along the road of physical proofs, he warned. Detailed parallels in physical science should not be relied upon to support religious truths, for in a science advancing as rapidly as geology, principles changed with new evidence from decade to decade. The geologists were to be congratulated for finding so many corroborative proofs of Genesis, but their proofs were in no way essential to the truths of Scripture. Even on the matter of the Deluge and the recent appearance of man, he wrote, geological proofs were incidental, adding:

> Should it be possible to discover an accurate system of geological chronology, and should any of these appearances be shown to belong to a remoter epoch, I would resign them without a struggle; perfectly sure, in the first place, that nothing could be proved, hostile to the sacred record; and in the second, that such a destruction of the proofs which we have here seen, would only be preliminary to the substitution of others much more decisive.[50]

The English had continued since the Revolution to harbor the caricature of the French as a nation of atheists. Wiseman also tried to reassure his countrymen of the pious inclinations of French geologists during the post-Revolution era.

Anti-clericalism had survived amongst the Republicans in France, but the monarchist reaction, the romantic orthodoxy stimulated by Chateaubriand, and the aggressive policy of the conservative clergy, among other forces, left France in the grip of a narrow orthodoxy throughout most of the early nineteenth century. The movement towards harmonizing geology and Genesis had its proponents in France, however. Cuvier was a prophet who reveled in the honor given him by his country, and it is not surprising that he should have a large following. One of the more

[50] *Twelve Lectures*, I, 353-4.

successful popular harmonizing works was the *Revolutions of the Globe* of Alexander Bertrand, which gave a history of geological speculations and advocated a theory combining Buffon's concept of a cooling earth with the Cuvierian catastrophical system. The work passed through many editions in France and England, and was used extensively in the French schools.[51]

An outstanding French harmonist after the period of Lyell's *Principles* was Marcel de Serres. In his *De la cosmogonie de Moïse comparée aux faits géologiques* (1841) credit was given to Lyell for his illustrious work, although it played no part in de Serres' cosmogony. He adopted the thesis that there were two periods of time indicated in Genesis, an indefinite period of primitive creation followed by the period of the seven days. The cosmogony of Moses, he asserted, nowhere admits that the formation of the earth was spontaneous. On the contrary, it teaches us that life has progressed from the simple to the complex, and this was a process which required long spaces of time and numerous generations in the ancient world. The days of creation were epochs of indeterminate duration in which these stages of complexity were finally evolved. Genesis does not give us precise notions about the progression until the two principal epochs of human history are reached, man's arrival on the earth and his renewal after the Deluge. Man's creation could not have taken place more than 7,000 years ago, nor the Deluge more than 5,000 years ago, and scriptural chronology is borne out on these points by the traditions and monuments of all nations.[52]

[51] Bertrand, *The Revolutions of the Globe Familiarly Described*, 5th ed., tr. with notes and appendix by S. C. Horry (London, 1835), presents contemporary scientific data to vindicate the theories of Descartes, Leibniz, Buffon, and Laplace on the igneous origin of the earth. He cites, for instance, Cuvier as saying in an 1826 *Discourse* that the success of the German chemist M. Mitcherlich in forming artificial mica was a rigorous demonstration of the igneous theory (p. 44).

[52] *De la Cosmogonie de Moïse comparée aux faits géologiques,* 2nd ed. (Paris, 1841), II, 179.

Since the mantle of Lamarck's transformism had been taken on by Geoffroy St. Hilaire, de Serres vigorously refuted the ideas of Geoffroy and his supporters because by the gratuitous assumption of a transformation of species they wished "to admit a greater antiquity to human species."[53] Within the memory of man there had been no appreciable change in species, and to introduce such changes it was necessary to extend human history far beyond the six or seven thousand years Moses had given it. "The circle of Biblical chronology which seems so short for system makers is still vast enough for historians."[54]

Although he denounced attempts to extend human history, de Serres crusaded for an extension of prehistoric time. He thought it was necessary to adopt the hypothesis of a central heat in the earth, as suggested by Descartes, Leibniz, and Buffon. The latter was given credit for being the first to recognize the long duration involved in the process of cooling, but de Serres thought Buffon's weakness was in not fully appreciating how enormously long it was. Proof of the existence of a central heat had been provided by Fourier, and Laplace had shown how slowly the heat is dissipated. De Serres thought that the rise of life in ever-increasing complexity was closely correlated with the cooling of the globe, but that the evolution had taken place through a special creation of a species when a new stage of the environment was ready for it.

Objections met de Serres' attempt to extend the antiquity of the earth, and in 1843, he brought out another work on the subject of Mosaic cosmology, this time bringing in arguments drawn from astronomy as well as geology.[55] A new proof of the antiquity of the earth was advanced from the length of time it takes for the light from stars to reach the earth. An estimate of the finite velocity of light had been reached as early as 1676 by Ole

[53] *Ibid.*, II, Ch. 2.

[54] *Ibid.*, II, 90.

[55] *De la création de la terre et des corps célestes, ou examen de cette question: l'oeuvre de la création est-elle aussi complète pour l'universe qu'elle paraît l'être pour la terre?* (Paris, 1843).

Roemer through a comparison of the observed and computed times of the eclipses of the moons of Jupiter.[56] The discovery of "aberration of light" by James Bradley in 1728 led to further refinements in the measurement of the velocity, and, although a precise determination of the velocity was not possible until new techniques were worked out by Armand H. L. Fizeau in 1849 and Jean B. L. Foucault about 1862, the velocity was known to be great. De Serres spoke of the velocity, "as all the world knows," as being 80,000 leagues per second.[57] This is unquestionably the velocity of 192,000 miles per second determined by Bradley and used by Sir John Herschel, upon whom de Serres relied heavily for his astronomical information.[58]

In order for the velocity of light to have a bearing on chronology, some conception of the distance it traveled was imperative. One of the glories of the seventeenth-century scientific revolution had been the infinitization of the universe and the break-up of the conception of the universe as an enclosing sphere of the fixed stars. Nevertheless, there was a real difficulty in the measurement of stellar distances. The parallax of stars was inadequate for it, and the apparent magnitude was unreliable, since it was recognized that the brightness was not necessarily an indication of distance. William Whiston, for instance, came to the conclusion that three stars he had studied were the same distance from the earth, in spite of their varying magnitudes, "contrary to the general Opinion hitherto; which has suppos'd the fix'd Stars of all manner of various distances from us, and those which appear'd the smallest to have therefore been at the most remote, and the largest at the nearest places."[59] If his conclusions were borne out,

[56] "Demonstration touchant le mouvement de la lumière trouvé par M. Roemer," *Académie Royale des Sciences Mémoires*, x, 575-77. See I. Bernard Cohen, "The First Determination of the Velocity of Light," *Isis*, xxxi (1940), 327-79.

[57] *De la création*, p. 12.

[58] See John Herschel, *Astronomy* (London, 1833), p. 297.

[59] *A New Theory of the Earth*, 2nd ed. (London, 1708).

he added, "we must be forc'd to alter our Opinion, and to believe that they are all pretty nearly in a Spherical surface from us, and that our Sun with its System is, as it were, plac'd in the Center of the rest of the Systems and of the visible World." The advanced views of Thomas Wright and Immanuel Kant did not everywhere prevail in eighteenth-century astronomy. On the contrary, they were hardly known, and the more theologically satisfying theory of Whiston seems to have had a wide following among the run of the mill astronomers.

The elder Herschel, William, who devoted himself to the question of the dimensions of stellar space wrote in 1784:

> Hitherto the sidereal heavens have, not inadequately for the purpose designed, been represented by the concave surface of a sphere, in the center of which the eye of the observer might be supposed to be placed. It is true, the various magnitudes of the fixed stars . . . would have better suited the idea of an expanded firmament of three dimensions; but the observations upon which I am now going to enter still farther illustrate and enforce the necessity of considering the heavens in this point of view. In future, therefore, we shall look upon those regions into which we may now penetrate by means of such large telescopes, as a naturalist regards a rich extent of ground or chain of mountains, containing strata variously inclined and directed, as well as consisting of different materials. A surface of a globe or map, therefore, will but ill delineate the interior parts of the heavens.[60]

Sir William hoped that in the near future new and larger telescopes would reveal more details on the "various *nebulous and sidereal strata* (to borrow a term from the natural historian)." The telescopes revealed, as it turned out, that what had been regarded as nebulae were mere clusters of stars at a vast distance, further confirming the variable distances of parts of the universe.[61]

[60] "Account of some Observations tending to investigate the Construction of the Heavens," *Royal Society of London Transactions*, LXXIV (1784), Pt. II, 438.

[61] "On Nebulous Stars, properly so called," *Ibid.*, LXXXI (1791), Part I, 71-88.

For a time this gave pause to the acceptance of Laplace's nebular hypothesis, and Herschel's suspicion that the little asteroids between Mars and Jupiter had once been parts of a planet also raised doubts about Laplace's assumption on the stability of the planetary system. Later observations confirmed the existence of nebulous formations, but in the meantime Herschel's researches on the relative brightness of stars and the distance traveled by light reinforced Laplace's conception of the Universe as vast in space and duration.

The effect of Herschel's view on a contemporary, about the extent of the universe, has been recorded by Thomas Campbell, after a visit with the astronomer in 1813:

> In talking of some inconceivably distant bodies, he introduced the mention of this plain theorem, to remind me that the progress of light could be measured in the one case as well as the other. Then, speaking of himself, he said, with a modesty of manner which quite overcame me, when taken together with the greatness of the assertion: "I have looked *further into space than ever human being did before me*. I have observed stars, of which the light, it can be proved, must take two millions of years to reach the earth." I really and unfeignedly felt at this moment as if I had been conversing with a supernatural intelligence. "Nay, more," said he, "if those distant bodies had ceased to exist two millions of years ago, we should still see them, as the light would travel after the body was gone."[62]

The proofs upon which Herschel based the distances of celestial bodies were to a large extent only well-informed convictions, for he had no way of ascertaining the relationship of the intensity of light coming from a body and its apparent magnitude. The solution of this problem was made by F. W. Bessel in the years 1837-1840 by determining the stellar parallax of the binary star 61 Cygni, which is fairly close to us, through the use of Frauenhofer's excellent heliometer. It was upon the results of Bessel's

[62] William Beattie, *Life and Letters of Thomas Campbell* (London, 1849), II, 234.

observations that de Serres relied for the calculation of the time it takes for light to reach us from various stellar formations. Some of the light from visible stars had been in transit for 100,000 to 230,000 years, he noted. If, then, there had been only a single creation at the time given by traditional Biblical chronology, Adam would not have seen most of the stars. Some would have successively come into view with the passage of time, but many could still not be seen for many thousands of years to come. This was manifestly absurd and de Serres concluded that the creation of the stars must have taken place a great many centuries prior to the creation of man.[63]

The task of Bible-geologists was complicated by the time of the third decade of the nineteenth century from the Higher Criticism, which, flourishing in Germany, threatened to take away the divine character of revelation. Briefly, the founding of Old Testament criticism is attributed to J. G. Eichhorn, despite earlier efforts in this direction by Hobbes, Spinoza, Astruc, Bishop Lowth, and others. Eichhorn's *Introduction to the Old Testament* (1780-1783) treated Scripture as a literature and applied to the Old Testament the canons of criticism which had been developing in the areas of the secular writings of antiquity. Alexander Geddes, a Scot and a Roman Catholic priest, applied somewhat the same method to a revision of the Bible, though he progressed only from Genesis to Chronicles in *The Holy Bible or the Books accounted Sacred by Jews and Christians, otherwise called the Books of the Old and New Covenants* . . . (London, 1792, 1797). Geddes held that the Pentateuch was not written by Moses, and he absolutely denied the doctrine of divine inspiration of the sacred writings. Instead, he believed that the Pentateuch had been compiled out of fragments of ancient documents which had

[63] De Serres, *De la création*, pp. 8-19. This argument is also developed at length by John Pye Smith in *The Relation between the Holy Scriptures and some parts of Geological Science*, 5th ed. (London, 1854), Note B, pp. 329-34.

existed before the days of Moses. He suggested that the Hebrew historiographer *invented* his Hexaemeron to enforce more strongly the observance of the Sabbath. Likewise, the history of the Fall was an excellent *mythologue* to account for the origin of human evil and man's antipathy to the reptile race.[64] This was the last contribution from the British Isles for several decades to the cause of Higher Criticism, and even after it had been fully developed in Germany the English resisted its introduction into their theology.

On the Continent, de Wette subjected the sacred writings to the same criticism of historical validity as other early documents in his *Beiträge zur Einleitung in das Alte Testament* (1806-1807). Gesenius in a *Geschichte der hebräischen Sprache und Schrift* (1815) and other works, helped to free Semitic philology from many of the religious trammels which had prevented a scientific study of it. The entire rationalistic approach to Scripture attempted to explain away superstitions and miracles which were not consistent with experience in order to isolate the mythic elements.

How much the movement of Higher Criticism was influenced by developments in geology, I cannot say. Its direct evolution goes back through the entire course of Biblical exegesis; its methods and techniques are indigenous to literary and philological fields; and the logical discrepancies in Scripture cried out for the same treatment as those in any other field of literature. Also, the growing awareness of historical development was an important conditioning factor. However, the grip of conviction on matters of religious faith had repeatedly snuffed out rational approaches to Scripture. Chronologically the rise of Higher Criticism closely paralleled the challenges which fossils and geology made to Genesis, and this may very well have encouraged a critical examination of the divine revelations. John Hamilton

[64] See the *British Critic*, IV (1794), 1-2, 147-58, for a reaction of the British to Gedde's *Bible*.

Davies expressed this view when the Rationalist approach was being introduced to England, writing:

> It is probable that Gesenius—of whom how much it is to be lamented, that his humble reverence for the word of God was not equal to his gigantic scholarship and hermeneutical skill—was influenced, by the unhappy use which some of the continental philosophers had made of the revelations of geology, to cast discredit on the scriptural narrative of Creation, when he wrote: "The book of Genesis, veiled, in a significant expressive *mythus*, a problem which no philosophy has satisfactorily solved."[65]

Similar accusations, correct or not, are made elsewhere against the Rationalists, and it would be strange, if they had not been influenced by the breakdown of the literal accuracy of Genesis through science.[66] A determination of the extent of geological influence on Higher Criticism would require extensive research outside the subject of the present work. The influence of Higher Criticism on Mosaic geology, however, was pervasive.

Attacks on the divine nature of Scripture through Higher Criticism renewed the urgency of the harmonists to find in science proofs of the divine character of the Pentateuch. The hermeneutical results coming from the studies of the rationalist scholars in Germany could not be ignored, much as they were abhorred, by conventional Biblical scholars. Dr. John Pye Smith, divinity tutor of nonconformist Homerton College, early tried to introduce to English theologians the exegetical additions accumulating

[65] John Pye Smith, *op. cit.*, p. xlii.

[66] F. M. Powicke in *Modern Historians and the Study of History, Essays and Papers* (London, 1955) writes: "Sometimes people talk as though the 'higher criticism' of texts in recent times has had more influence upon the human mind than the higher criticism of nature. This seems to me to be nonsense. The higher criticism has been simply an application of an awakened critical faculty to a particular kind of material, and was encouraged by the achievement of this faculty to form its bold conclusions. If the biologists, the geologists, the astronomers, the anthropologists had not been at work, I venture to think that the higher critics would have been either non-existent or a tiny minority in a world of fundamentalists" (p. 228).

in Germany and at the same time to combat their irreligious effects. His skill at the task gained him renown in theological circles, and in 1839 the Committee of the Congregational Lecture, thinking, no doubt, of slaying another dragon, requested Smith to deliver a course of lectures for the purpose of showing the "Relation between the Holy Scriptures and some parts of Geological Science." With a limited knowledge of geology, Smith immediately sought out the best works on the subject and concentrated on assimilating their contents.

In the words of his biographer, "Dr. Pye Smith found that he had no ordinary difficulties to encounter, in treating a subject which was regarded with dislike or distrust by a great number of the orthodox. On the one hand, he had to refute the arguments and to unveil the sophistry of infidelity; on the other, to remove the fears and anxieties of those who did homage only to Divine Truth."[67] From his studies Smith concluded that the diluvial hypothesis was untenable and that the Noachian Deluge was not, and could not have been, universal. "Pursuing his scientific investigations," added his biographer, "he found it necessary to show the erroneousness of the popular chronology, which is calculated from the Hebrew text of the Scriptures."

Smith declared that getting some thousands of species on one man-made ark was too incredulous to be supported—so too was the gathering of plants and animals from all over the world, preserving on one small ark species as diverse as those from the tropics and the arctic, and then redistributing them again, all in the short space of time given in Genesis. Against the traditions of a Deluge so prevalent among various peoples of the world, he countered with the proposition that each people had a local deluge which became the basis of their traditions, since there was no evidence that they all occurred in the precise years given in Hebrew chronology. He added a novel consideration based on the tree-ring method of dating. The technique of counting the annual

[67] Smith, *op. cit.*, p. lii.

rings of growth to obtain the age of a tree (now developed into the science of dendrology) was brought to the attention of botanists by the work of John Stevens Henslow and John Eddowes Bowman in 1835 and 1837. The method of making deep borings in living trees had not been developed, nor had the frequency of periods of growth in tropical climates been accurately determined, but through the use of sections taken out of a tree and estimates for the remainder, it was suggested that some trees in the world, such as the baobab (*Adansonia digitata*) and the cypress (*Cypressus disticha*), were from 4,000 to 6,000 years old. In the light of subsequent knowledge the estimates were not improbable. Smith pointed out that if these estimates were correct, trees now living had been standing undisturbed since before the Deluge was supposed to have flooded the earth. Indeed, they went back to the origin of the earth itself, according to the Hebrew chronology.[68]

Smith's main arguments against the universal Deluge were drawn from Lyell's *Principles*, however, and from the same source came his recognition of the time necessary for the operation of geological forces:

> If from the discoveries of Astronomy and Geology we infer that the created universe, including our own globe, has existed through an unknown but unspeakably long period of time past; and IF, from the records of revelation, *we draw the conclusion* that the work of creation, or at least so far as respects our planet, took place not quite six thousand years ago; it is evident that the two positions cannot stand: one destroys the other. One of them must be an error; both may be wrong; only one can be right.[69]

His sympathies were plainly with the geologists on the antiquity of the earth, so much so that at one point Smith remarked, "I seem to be taking the part of an enemy, adducing materials for

[68] *Ibid.*, pp. 149, 267, and Note L, 408-15.
[69] *Ibid.*, p. 15.

scepticism, and doing nothing to remove them."[70] He went straight down the geological line, arguing forcibly the Lyellian position, and in effect conceding all the points that his theological partners had expected him to refute. Instead of defending traditional theology, Smith called for a new interpretation of it. Along with some of the proponents of the Higher Criticism, he suggested that Genesis was not the work of one man, but had been compiled out of the archives of the Hebrew nation and the traditions handed down from the prophets. The revelations themselves, successively given to the prophets of the Israelite nation at various times, "were conveyed in *representations to the senses,* chiefly that of *sight,* and in *words descriptive* of those representations."[71]

The hypothesis that a long period of time was indicated in the separation of the "beginning" passage from the others in Genesis was supported by Smith, but in general he objected to the attempts being made to torture the text of Scripture to fit the needs of geology. On the other hand, he was not prepared to go the length of the *mythic* hypothesis of the German rationalists. The revelations themselves he thought were authentic, but if they were to be intelligible to the Hebrew prophets, they had to be presented in graphic terms which in their primitive stage of simple culture those seers could understand. Genesis did not attempt to give a knowledge of natural history, for the accurate details would have been completely lost on the understandings of these first people.

> It is a further evidence that the style of this primitive document was framed in conformity to the phraseology of simple men in unpolished times, that the successive processes are described in a child-like-conversation form. "God said, Let there be light; —let there be a firmament;—let the earth bring forth;—let us make man:" the author using in each instance the same formula, first, an introduction of the matter, and then narrating the effect.[72]

[70] *Ibid.,* p. 148.   [71] *Ibid.,* p. 219.   [72] *Ibid.,* p. 257.

Instead of talking in terms of modern chemical elements, which these people could not have comprehended, God spoke of "dust" and used other homely expressions to convey His thoughts. Reaching the point at which he had been aiming, Smith said, "I speak my own conviction, and I trust I have brought forward sufficient evidence to support that conviction, that the alleged discrepance between the Holy Scriptures and the discoveries of scientific investigation, is not in reality, but in semblance only. . . ." He sought the basis of a conciliation between science and Scripture, not by distorting the language of Scripture to give it the appearance of teaching science, but by showing that the Author of revelation merely spoke to mankind in such language as primitive man was accustomed to use.[73]

The reaction to Smith's commissioned work by the British public was vigorous, but hardly favorable, according to his biographer:

It would be difficult, at this distance of time [1854], to give an adequate idea of the outcry which, in some quarters, was raised, on the publication of these Lectures, against their accomplished Author. The public, who, usually, in their knowledge of scientific matters, are at least a generation behind the discoveries of the philosophers of their own age, could not, in many instances, understand how a Theologian, so eminent and revered, could throw discredit on the usually-received interpretation of any portion of the Sacred Scriptures. Geology had not been a favourite science with the greater number of intelligent Englishmen, and the few who had directed their attention to an investigation of its facts, and who had written in its defence, were held in considerable suspicion. But, when a divine could unhesitatingly proclaim his disbelief in the popular theories of Creation, the Deluge, and the antiquity of the world; and when he could interpret Scripture in any other than in its literal and "common sense meaning;" astonishment was expressed by many, and fears were entertained by a few for the "orthodoxy" of the Lecturer. Letters of remonstrance

[73] *Ibid.*, p. 282.

poured in upon him from many parts of the country. Not a few persons, in their zeal for the maintenance of their narrow interpretations, forgot the courtesies and proprieties of life; and, as so often unhappily occurs in theological disputations, evil motives were imputed to him by those who had neither the ability nor the inclination to test the soundness of his argumentations and the truth of his conclusions. By some he was charged with infidelity, or with having been for years a disguised enemy to evangelical opinions.[74]

By the time Smith took pen in hand to harmonize geological history with Mosaic history, the advances in knowledge about the earth's crust and its organic remains were becoming sufficiently complex so that it was no longer possible to correlate the two histories by simply picking out illustrations from geology to support scriptural texts. Perhaps it would be better to say it was possible to attempt it, for in fact it continued to be done, but it could not be executed convincingly by those in full possession of the facts of natural history. Smith's work was representative of a change of emphasis in the harmonizing movement: to generalize the Mosaic history of creation and avoid exact parallels between the two records.

In the harmonizing movement ideas flowed rapidly and freely between writers in Great Britain, France, Germany, and America, and in Germany the idea of a pictorial revelation crudely expressed was popular as the "Mosaic vision of creation." Dr. J. H. Kurtz, Professor of Theology at Dorpat, in his *Bibel und Astronomie* (2nd ed., 1849), was representative of this school. The pre-Adamic past was as unknown to primitive man as the future, he held, and the Mosaic narrative was simply prophecy aimed backwards. "Before the eye of the seer," he says, "scene after scene is unfolded, until at length, in the seven of them, the course of creation, in its main *momenta*, has been fully represented."[75] Thus

[74] *Ibid.*, p. lv.

[75] Cited in Hugh Miller, *The Testimony of the Rocks* (Boston, 1859), p. 182.

the revelation of Genesis was like other prophecies of vision which a seer experiences. The actual phenomena are presented to the mind's eye of the prophet and are then retold by him in the simple language of his time.

In Britain again, two anonymous works, *"The Mosaic Record in Harmony with Geology"* and *"The Genesis of the Earth and Man"* (about 1850), presented the same interpretation, but the most famous of all exponents of this theory in English was the self-educated stone-mason and geologist Hugh Miller. In *"The Mosaic Vision of Creation"*[76] he called to mind those sections in the history of creation given in *Paradise Lost* where Adam is carried by Michael to the top of a mountain and coming events are described as rising up in vision before him. This, Miller thought, was the manner in which Moses had the Creation revealed to him, or as Kurtz had said, he was an eye-witness to the vision instead of a recipient of words. Moses then retold what he had seen in his own words. This being so, the same principle of interpretation should be applied to this prophecy of the past as is applied to prophecies of the future. The event which is foretold is the only key to a prophecy of the future. In the light of history, when the term of the prophecy has been fulfilled it can then be understood, and the same is true of the Mosaic prophecy of the past. Scientific discovery, he maintained, was the key to the revealed prophecy looking backward.

> In what light, or on what principle, shall we most correctly read the prophetic drama of creation? In the light, I reply, of scientific discovery,—on the principle that the clear and certain must be accepted, when attainable, as the proper exponents of the doubtful and obscure. What fully developed history is to the prophecy which of old looked forwards, fully developed science is to the prophecy which of old looked backwards.[77]

[76] *Ibid.*, pp. 179-210.
[77] *Ibid.*, p. 194.

On this principle the meaning of the days of creation became clear through science. The first was the Azoic day, the second the Silurian, the third the Carboniferous, the fourth the Permian, the fifth the Oolitic, and the sixth the Tertiary, all successively revealed as a series of visions to Moses, and each of which included distinctive advances in the history of the earth.

In his Preface, Miller remarked that a critic had twitted him for changing his views about the days of creation. He frankly admitted that he had once believed with Chalmers and Buckland that the six days were natural days of twenty-four hours each— that they had comprised the entire work of the existing creation, —and that the latest of geologic ages was separated by a great chaotic gap from our own. "All I found necessary at the time to the work of reconciliation was some scheme that would permit me to assign to the earth a high antiquity, and to regard it as the scene of many succeeding creations."[78] After nine years more of exploration into the deposits, he was compelled to conclude that no blank chaotic gap separated man from the rest of creation, and before man was ushered into being, familiar animals had lived side by side with extinct ones for perhaps thousands of centuries.

Miller observed that new evidence of the continuity of life in the fossil record—the filling in of the breaks between the previous and the existing creations—made a new scheme of reconciliation necessary. The "restitution" hypothesis, put forward by Chalmers fifty years earlier, still remained "the most popular of the various existing schemes,"[79] especially as refined by J. Pye Smith in 1839. However, Miller felt that Smith had let too much Mosaic history slip out of the history of creation, including the universality of the Deluge, which Smith regarded as a local event. The chaos had replaced the rest of Mosaic history in the interpretations of the "restitutionists," and unnecessarily so, thought

[78] *Ibid.*, p. viii.
[79] *Ibid.*, p. 143.

Miller. By applying the concept of a "Mosaic vision" to the extended "days of creation" theory, Genesis would be preserved as a majestic account of all creation. The days were the salient epochs of the past, described by Moses much as a visitor to the British Museum who was unversed in science might explain from memory the reconstructed remains he had seen there. Such an interpretation, Miller believed, brought geology into close harmony with Genesis and saved the reputations of both.

Miller's theory won supporters, but in general, the Mosaic vision theory was applied to both the "chaos" period and the "days of creation." The "restitution" hypothesis continued to enjoy great popularity amongst the harmonists, particularly in Germany, where it formed a part of Biblical exegesis. A leading harmonist in Germany, Andreas Wagner, was a professor of zoology and paleontology at Munich, but most of the outstanding Germanic harmonists were theologians. Franz Delitzsch was Professor of Theology at Erland, C. F. Keil and J. Henri Kurtz, Professors of Theology at Dorpat, P. W. Schultz, Professor of Theology at Breslau, Otto Zoeckler, Professor of Theology at Giessen, Antoine Westermayer, Pastor of the City of Munich, and Philippe-Frederic Keerl, Pastor at Lauterhausen, to mention a few.

Andreas Wagner did much to establish the true "restitution" theory which added the embellishment of a restituted earth after the fall of the bad angels to Chalmer's concept of an undefined period of time between the Beginning and the Days. This Miltonic drama became an integral part of the history of creation among the Continental harmonists who adopted the restitution theory. The Kurtz-Miller-Wagner synthesis that resulted was somewhat as follows: the earth at the beginning supported the life which can be found in the fossil record, but at this time it was also the abode of Lucifer and his legions; when Lucifer revolted the earth was destroyed, and a period of chaos and darkness ensued; then God decided to create man and a new earth, and out of the chaos he constructed the present scheme of things, as narrated in Genesis; and finally, Moses was shown the view of past events, but seeing things from his station on a mountain top according to the laws of perspective, that which lay at the greatest temporal distance was the most indistinct. A further modification was added by Frederic Rougement, a pupil of Louis Agassiz, to reconcile the scheme with the results of the Higher Criticism. He shifted the vision from Moses to Adam, and suggested that Moses had only been the editor of surviving fragments of Adam's narrative of the prophecy.[80]

The theory of restitution enjoyed an extensive vogue well into the sixties, even after the publication of Darwin's *Origin of Species* had become a subject of widespread attention. The many arguments and shadings of this school are ably presented by Franz Heinrich Reusch in *La Bible et la Nature*, which was published from his lectures at the University of Bonn, where he was Professor of Theology. The only end of the Bible is to teach religious and moral truths, said Reusch, but that God created the world is such a truth. Whether or not the "restitution" hypothesis could be demonstrated, he subscribed to it along with many others of the Protestant and Catholic faiths. He held that the revelation that the earth was made in six days was not made to give us chronological data, nor to direct us in our geological researches. It makes no difference whether the "day" of creation is understood to be a number of minutes and hours, years, or millenia. It is the number of days which is important, for the week of creation is the divine original from which our week with its Divine Sabbath is the terrestrial copy.[81] To the geologist and astronomer Reusch conceded as much time as they desired in the early periods of the earth's history. Genesis was limited to telling of the last formation of the earth's productions and the species of plants

[80] *Histoire de la terre d'après la Bible et la géologie* (Geneva & Paris, 1856), p. 254.
[81] *La Bible et la nature*, p. 153.

and animals still living. The partisans of the "restitution" theory, he suggested, had no need to enter into an examination of the lessons of paleontology, and the paleontologists were free to teach what they wished.

> Paleontology is then, after this theory, in possession of a vast domain on which the Bible raises no pretensions; all the mass of transition and sedimentary terrains, as well as all the series of formations of the paleozoic and mesozoic periods, are in its province. In these domains it is absolute master. It is only in the superior beds, belonging to the tertiary or neozoic period, that limits to its domination are found. The paleontologists and theologians would, it is true, have to agree on a precise determination of these limits, but we shall return to this later.[82]

Reusch represents the attempt of theologians to rid themselves of geological considerations in Biblical exegesis. On the principal point of chronological controversy he was willing to concede everything to geology except the principle that man was of recent origin, and on this he expected even the scientists to agree. An even stronger movement had been under way among scientists to remove theological considerations from their work in the areas of geology and paleontology. One approach was to ignore theology, and this was increasingly done after the publication of Lyell's *Principles*, but another method lay in the complete separation of natural theology from revealed theology. The argument from design which portrayed the majesty of God through the excellence of His workmanship, though highly developed in other fields, had not progressed in geology during the reign of catastrophic principles. Even after Huttonianism had been accepted in regard to the operation of heat, the concept of orderly design in the dynamics of geology and meteorology had not prevailed, for the simple reason that the Deluge was an act of supernatural power which disrupted the entire machinery of nature. It was

[82] *Ibid.*, p. 294.

only after the Deluge and chaotic demiurgic processes had been subtracted from these sciences by the principle of uniformitarianism that the mechanistic view of natural theology could be applied to the earth sciences.

The full application of natural theology to the sciences, and the resultant divorce of natural from supernatural theology, was brilliantly executed by the Reverend Baden Powell, Savilian Professor of Geometry of the University of Oxford. Severely critical of the mixing of revelation and science, he wrote, "The evidences of the Divine operation seem to me manifested precisely in proportion as *we can* trace material laws and physical laws."[83] If the evidences of physical truth and natural theology are not sought for separately from revelation, it is an argument in a circle, he emphasized, and to expect to find truths of science enforced by revelation was as unreasonable as to expect to find theorems of Euclid enforced by an Act of Parliament. "Scriptural geology is as preposterous in principle as statutable geometry."[84]

Geology, like other inductive sciences, was subject to uniformly acting laws: "whatever may have been the magnitude of some of the operations in remote epochs, yet we find no deviation from the continuation of action of the same kind; no real suspension of regular laws, no simultaneous universal destruction and reconstruction of the globe."[85] Instead, we have evidence that the same system of gradual changes existed through all these periods and the present state of things was, "by slow degrees, evolved out of previous orders of existence."[86] Erroneous first principles had been especially prevalent in geology.

From ill-informed, or, too often, prejudiced persons, we hear frequent remarks disparaging the inquiries and conclusions of

[83] *The Connexion of Natural and Divine Truth; or, the Study of the Inductive Philosophy Considered as Subservient to Theology* (London, 1838), p. 168.
[84] *Ibid.*, p. 240.
[85] *Ibid.*, p. 58.
[86] *Ibid.*

the geologist, while they allow and applaud the inferences of the astronomer and the chemist; they condemn as visionary and presumptuous the results of the one as to the antiquity of strata, and the successive aeras of animal organization, the monuments of which are before their eyes, while they revere as unquestionable truths the most marvelous and paradoxical inferences of the other: which refer to subjects utterly beyond the scope of the senses, to periods and distances which transcend our arithmetical powers to conceive, and to processes of nature which exceed our faculties to apprehend.[87]

The mathematician puts down some figures on paper, he continued, and announces that the matter on Jupiter weighs somewhat more than one-fifth the average materials on the earth, or the chemist asserts that a bell glass which appears empty is in fact filled with an invisible compound of indestructible atoms aggregated by perfectly regular laws with particular weights for these molecules which no microscope has ever seen. This is accepted. "Yet when the geologist contends that the crust of the earth, with its organized productions, has been gradually brought into its present conditions by a series of creative changes, going on through millions of ages, his conclusion is condemned as chimerical and dangerous."[88]

There is a singular partiality shown to some sciences, concluded Powell, when the most inconceivable assertions of the astronomer are admitted without hesitation while the geologist is accused of arrogance for pretending that millions of years ago the earth was going on, governed by the same laws as today. But, if the foundations of one science are to be assailed, all others are involved. Inductive evidence must stand or fall on its own merits, he warned, and not according to the area in which it is applied. "If the conclusions of the geologist are in principle and method fallacious, those of the astronomer and the chemist must be re-

[87] *Ibid.*, pp. 67-8.
[88] *Ibid.*, p. 68.

jected on the same ground."[89] There was no reason why great
changes and sudden interpositions by Divine interference should
take place in one sphere of nature and not the others, so far as
Powell could see.

To the Professor of Geometry a world enveloped in entire
obscurity as to physical causes would be a world without evidence of a Deity. A universe without appreciable laws would be
a chaos, not a creation. "Yet so powerful has been the prejudice
to the contrary, that not only have the unexplained obscurities
of nature been religiously venerated as the penetralia of natural
worship, but it has been held dangerous to indulge in the most
philosophical *conjectures. . . .*"[90] Theologians had resisted one of
the strongest proofs that the world had been the work of an intelligent Creator, Powell believed, by their resort to miracles instead of natural laws. The evidences of design were as much
present in geology as astronomy, if men's minds could only be
opened to them. Powell was not gentle in his own attempt to
break the spell of Scriptural geology.

"Although words of Scripture can be made to fit geologic facts,
was this the sense *actually intended by the author*. If not, what is
the coincidence worth?" It could hardly be imagined, said Powell,
that in the delivery of Judaical law it was intended to embrace
the doctrines of geology, and this with expressions directly contradictory to those doctrines.[91] If such were the case, we would
be driven to suppose a design was used of revealing truths by
concealing them, since we know the hidden sense was not disclosed from the time of Moses to the present, and when disclosed
no instruction resulted, since the expressions could not be understood until the facts were learned from geology, at which time
the scriptural instruction would be superfluous. By trying to construct systems of philosophy and science out of the Bible or by

[89] *Ibid.,* p. 72.
[90] *Ibid.,* p. 168.
[91] *Ibid.,* p. 249.

forcing the language of Scripture into accordance with scientific results, both science and theology were brought into ridicule and the integrity of each was endangered. Geological interpreters of the Bible, he explained, had taxed the utmost powers of philology in trying to convert the six days into periods of millions of years and to make the order of creation fit geological epochs, but this scheme was at length found to answer the views of neither party. The then currently popular view of an indefinite period of chaos after the "beginning" was likewise destined to be equally unsatisfactory, because geology showed that there never has been any trace of an elemental change or a temporary chaos, followed by a restitution of things.[92] But much as he deplored these systems of revelation and science, Powell was forced to admit that they had served a useful purpose:

> . . . some of those expositions which have recently obtained most popularity, have not been without their use in exploding the more gross errors of those which preceded them, and in some measure preparing the way for truth. Thus men's minds were formerly startled at the bare notion of long continued periods and successive dynasties of organized life before the creation of man. The theory of the "days" interpreted as periods of "indefinite" length, had, at least, the recommendation that it got over one main part of the novelty and difficulty, and some notion of the immense duration of the globe became, in a certain degree, familiarized to men's minds as associated with the scripture terms "day" and "year."
>
> They were consequently now less incapable of listening to the disclosures of geological research, and less shocked at the boldness with which induction cleared its own way, to the utter disregard of extraneous authority, and followed up its conclusions, without respect to received opinions, precisely as the clear evidence of facts illumined the path to truth.[93]

The critical attacks that Powell made in 1838 were followed up in 1859 by *The Order of Nature considered in reference to the*

[92] *Ibid.*, pp. 250-1.
[93] *Ibid.*, pp. 262-3.

claims of Revelation, in which he further decried the fact that the greater body of English writers on geology cultivated the science on principles founded on *faith.* However, he shrewdly observed that while many professed harmonizing Scripture and geology, they in fact made complete concessions on all substantial points; "so manifest the evasions and subterfuges they exhibit, that we can only regard them as disguised allies, merely offering a nominal homage to the prejudices of a religious party. . . ."[94]

Enlightened advocates of natural theology, such as Powell and Babbage, undoubtedly influenced many to abandon narrower views of geological science, but to others their work only represented the heretical tendencies of the new science. Conservative-minded people remained unmoved and continued to think of the world as only about 6,000 years old. Robert Maxwell Macbriar, for instance, delivered a blistering attack on geologists in 1843, and maintained a strict literal interpretation of Genesis. Neptunists, Plutonists, Nebularists, Harmonists, Rationalists, and Uniformitarians all came in for ridicule at his hands, with special denunciations reserved for Herschel, Lyell, Babbage, Whewell, and J. Pye Smith. "There is nothing for which cosmogonists ask with more incessant importunity, than for a great quantity of time. If this requisite be granted, they can account for every thing; without it, they are perfectly helpless."[95] On this point, however, Scripture was explicit.

One of the more ingenious attempts at resolving the dilemma between the evidences of geology and Mosaic chronology was the *Omphalos* of Philip Henry Gosse, written in 1857. The work was not gauged to oppose geologists, Gosse assured his readers, but to find the truth all were seeking behind the flat contradiction which the Works seemed to present to the Words of God. For the efforts of the Bible-geology school of reconciliation he felt

[94] *Order of Nature,* p. 222.
[95] *Geology and Geologists, or Visions of Philosophers in the Nineteenth Century* (London, 1843), p. 43.

sympathy, but thought its approach was futile. The inference from geology of "an antiquity mensurable not by years or centuries, but by *secula seculorum*" could in no way be reconciled to the literal sense of Scripture by devious metaphorical interpretations of "days of creation" nor by placing a long interval between the "beginning" and the days of creation. The efforts were well meaning. "What else could good men do?" he asked. Even geologists were reluctant to oppose the testimony of Scripture, but the evidence had left them no alternative. The good intentions of geologists and theologians he did not impugn, but the dilemma he attributed to a failure to recognize heretofore the existence of the law or principle of *prochronism*. Gosse hoped "that the thousands of thinking persons, who are scarcely satisfied with the extant reconciliations of Scriptural statements and Geological deductions,—who are silenced but not convinced,—may find, in the principle set forth in this volume, a stable resting-place."[96]

Gosse held that the course of nature is a circle tending to repeat itself throughout all eternity. Every plant or animal is part of an endless cycle of seed-growth-maturity-seed. "This, then, is the order of all organic nature. When once we are in any portion of the course, we find ourselves running in a circular groove, as endless as the course of a blind horse in a mill. It is evident that there is no one point in the history of any single creature, which is a legitimate beginning of existence."[97]

Omphalos, the Greek word for navel, is a throwback to seventeenth-century rational exegesis, when it was earnestly debated whether or not portraits of Adam should show him with a navel. Created as he was by God, Adam did not need one, but then, would he have the appearance of a man? The reasonable answer seemed to be that God had created him with a navel, just *as*

[96] *Omphalos: an Attempt to Untie the Geological Knot* (London, 1857), p. viii.
[97] *Ibid.*, p. 122.

though he had been born of woman. This concept had already been applied to cosmogony by Chateaubriand, but Gosse tried to extend it and compound the idea of a created world with an eternal one so as to avoid all possibility of evolution.

> Creation, the sovereign fiat of Almighty Power, gives us the commencing point, which we in vain seek in nature. But what is creation? It is *the sudden bursting into a circle*. Since there is no one stage in the course of existence, which more than any other affords a natural commencing point, whatever stage is selected by the arbitrary will of God, must be an un-natural, or rather preter-natural, commencing point.[98]

Wherever God broke the circle to initiate the existence of an organism it would have all the appearances of having been in prior existence. When He created a plant, for instance, He might have started its existence in the real world as a seed, a young plant, or a mature plant, but at any point the plant would bear all the marks of having gone through the previous part of its life cycle. Gosse devoted the major part of his book to illustrations of this concept such as that of Adam, who was created an adult in full possession of speech and other functions, even though his navel connects him with a life cycle of an unborn infant in the womb of a parent. His body presupposes the growth of bones, skin, hair, nails, blood, and lungs—all evidence of a process of time in their formation. Had these results of growth in the life cycle of a man not been present, Adam would not have been a man. By analogy then, when God created a species, the first representatives bore all the marks of having gone through the full cycle of development. Those appearances of development in the organism at the moment of its creation Gosse called *prochronic*, because time was not an element in them. Those developments which have had an actual existence since the organism was created he distinguished as *diachronic*, that is, occurring in time.[99]

[98] *Ibid.*, p. 123.
[99] *Ibid.*, p. 125.

Extending the principle of prochronism to the life history of the globe, Gosse wrote:

> Admit for a moment, as a hypothesis, that the Creator had before his mind a projection of the whole life-history of the globe, commencing with any point which the geologist may imagine to have been a fit commencing point, and ending with some unimaginable acme in the indefinitely distant future. He determines to call this idea into actual existence, not at the supposed commencing point, but at some stage or other of its course. It is clear, then, that at the selected stage it appears, exactly as it would have appeared at that moment of its history, if all the preceding eras of its history had been real.[100]

He admitted that he could not prove that the life history of the globe was a cycle, but since it was important to his eternalism to confine all changes to circular repetition and not to admit the prospect of evolution, he spent some time in showing that the economy of the globe, its winds, tides, and movements, were of a recurring cyclical nature, while all the universe obeyed the law of circularity in its movements. There was no doubt in his own mind that the earth embodied the prochronic principle, and Gosse left the burden of proof against the theory to his opponents.

In the absence of a witness there was absolutely no way of telling at what point in the life cycle of the earth creation had commenced, and if it had begun at a recent date God would have included in the earth all the fossils and strata as though the earth had had a real existence prior to the point where the cycle had been broken. Under the pretence of complete dispassion, Gosse refrained from claiming that Moses was such a witness, but the possibility was suggested. Although his system was designed to sustain the literal character of Scriptural chronology, Gosse encouraged the work of geologists. On the latter he wrote:

> Finally, the acceptance of the principles presented in this volume, even in their fullest extent, would not, in the least

[100] *Ibid.*, p. 351.

degree, affect the study of scientific geology. The character and order of the strata; their disruptions and displacements and injections; the successive floras and faunas; and all the other phenomena, would be *facts* still. They would still be, as now, legitimate subjects of examination and inquiry. I do not know that a single conclusion, now accepted, would need to be given up, except that of actual chronology. And even in respect of this, it would be rather a modification than a relinquishment of what is at present held; we might still speak of the inconceivably long duration of the processes in question, provided we understand *ideal* instead of *actual* time;—that the duration was projected in the mind of God, and not really existent.[101]

Outside the fact that he failed to explain satisfactorily how fossil species became extinct if their life cycles were eternal, Gosse made a compelling case for those who accepted his major premises. Prochronism was the most brilliant and logically satisfactory system of reconciling Biblical and geological time, and Gosse expected to take the world by storm with it. The silence which met *Omphalos* left its author bewildered. It has had a small following down to the present,[102] but by 1857 it could only appear quixotic in the face of the solid advances of geological science.

MOSAIC GEOLOGY IN AMERICA

Americans remained dependent on Europeans for guidance in natural history well into the nineteenth century, but interest in theories of the earth and in American varieties of plants, animals, minerals, and fossils was not lacking in this country, even during the colonial period. The most direct contribution of America to speculation on prehistory was certainly fossil remains of the mastodon and mammoth. As early as 1519, Bernal Diaz del Castillo had

[101] *Ibid.*, p. 369
[102] See Martin Gardner, *Fads and Fallacies in the Name of Science*, 2nd ed. (New York, 1957), Chapter 11.

found huge bones in Tlascala which the natives believed to be the remains of giants, and judging from his description of the bones, they were undoubtedly parts of a fossil mastodon. The discovery of enormous teeth and bones along the Hudson River in 1705 excited the curiosity of New Englanders. Governor Dudley of Massachusetts wrote to Cotton Mather about them, expressing the opinion that they were the remains of an antediluvian man and that there was nothing to do but "allow Dr. Burnett and Dr. Whiston to bury him at the Deluge." Cotton Mather described the bones to Dr. John Woodward, and volunteered the suggestion that here was a proof of the giants mentioned in Genesis, Chapter 6, Verse 4.[103]

American fossil vertebrates were placed in the mainstream of European paleontological development when Charles Le Moyne, second Baron de Longueuil, discovered some "elephant" remains along the Ohio River in 1739 and deposited them in the Cabinet du Roi the following year, where they were studied by Guettard, Daubenton, Buffon, and eventually by Cuvier. The discovery of mastodon fossils at Big Bone Lick, and the famous collection made from it by Croghan in 1767, further accelerated interest in the origin and nature of these huge animals. Their affinity with elephants was established, but whether or not they were representatives of extinct species remained a lively question until the end of the century. Jefferson, who had made a tremendous effort in promoting the collection and study of these mastodon remains, refused to believe that they were extinct species, "For if one link in nature's chain might be lost, another and another might be lost, till this whole system of things should evanish piecemeal."[104]

---

[103] George Gaylord Simpson, "The Beginnings of Vertebrate Paleontology in North America," *Proceedings of the American Philosophical Society*, LXXXVI (1942), 130-188.

[104] *Ibid.*, p. 157. The statement was made in "A Memoir on the Discovery of Certain Bones of a Quadruped of the Clawed Kind in the Western Parts of Virginia," *Transactions of the American Philosophical Society*, IV (1797), 246-60. Jefferson was also interested in theories of the earth. For his criti-

Benjamin Franklin, as might have been expected, was interested in the theories of the earth. He was in correspondence with John Whitehurst, an English instrument maker and author of a highly respected work in geology, *Inquiry into the Original State and Formation of the Earth* (1778).[105] To the Abbé Soulavie, Franklin reported his own observations on strata in a letter from Passy, September 22, 1782, which was read before the American Philosophical Society in 1788 as "Conjectures concerning the formation of the earth."[106] Franklin thought that the strata of Derby was a proof of a great *bouleversement* in the surface of that Island, and that such changes would not be likely to have happened if the earth were solid to its center. With considerable ingenuity, he suggested that the internal parts were fluid and the surface of the globe was a shell floating on it, capable of being broken and disordered by movements of the fluid on which it rested. Franklin was too good a Newtonian not to realize that water would not serve as such a fluid. Using the analogy of experiments made on the compression of air, Franklin suggested that a dense internal fluid, heavier than gold, had been formed at the core through pressure as the earth was formed. The theory of Franklin was suggestive of current theories of a magma, subject to tidal waves, supporting an outer shell. However, in the cosmogonic speculation of his day, this theory of Franklin was of much less importance than his work in electricity, which had been put to service in a number of hypotheses to explain the formation of the earth.

Americans as a whole were interested in the geology of their country and the speculations that were coming from Europeans

cism of Buffon's central heat, as set forth in the *Epochs*, see TJ to James Madison, Jan. 1, 1784, *The Papers of Thomas Jefferson*, ed. Julian P. Boyd, VI, 436-8, and for remarks on Whitehurst's theory, TJ to Charles Thomson, Dec. 17, 1786, *ibid.*, X, 608-9.

[105] Franklin to Whitehurst, June 27, 1763, Franklin Papers, Yale University Library.

[106] *The Writings of Benjamin Franklin*, ed. Albert Henry Smyth (New York, 1907), VIII, 597-602.

on the formation of the earth. The state of knowledge on this subject in America is best revealed in that remarkable history of Samuel Miller, *A Brief Retrospect of the Eighteenth Century* (1803). Miller was a young Presbyterian minister when he composed his *Retrospect*, and although he was a member of the American Philosophical Society, he was completely undistinguished in the field of science. Yet, his sketch was judicious, learned, and reliable. In every respect it was the equal of European works on the subject, and in many respects superior. As might be expected, he had a religious bias, but his views were representative of the enlightened reader of his time. Under "Geology," Miller noted that the investigation of the natural history of the earth had made little progress prior to the beginning of the eighteenth century, but during the century, geology had become an object of attention and investigation. "And, although modern times have produced many visionary theories, and crude conjectures on this subject, they have also given birth to some important acquisitions, and much correct philosophy, which will be highly prized by all who study the history and structure of our globe."[107]

The theories of Burnet, Woodward, and Whiston formed Miller's point of departure in reviewing the history of geology. Hutchinson, Lazzaro de Moro, Lecat, Maillet, Buffon, Bailly, Deluc, Hutton, Delametherie, Howard, and many others were treated, and their theories classified as being for or against scriptural history and chronology. It was evident that Maillet, Buffon, and Hutton were not among his favorites. Dr. Hutton's system was "among those which are hostile to the sacred history," as well as the principles of probability.[108] Richard Kirwan was praised as the most judicious and enlightened of the cosmogonists, and, of course, his theory of the earth was drawn around Mosaic history. In summing up his review of geology, Miller stated:

Finally, the researches of modern geologists have given

107 *Brief Retrospect*, I, 156.
108 *Ibid.*, I, 174.

abundant confirmation to the sacred history, not only with respect to the general *deluge*, but also with regard to the *age* of the earth. Early in the century, and, indeed, until within a few years, several geological phenomena were considered, by super-ficial inquirers, as indicating that the creation of the globe we inhabit was an event much more remote than the sacred history represents it; and some theorists even went so far as to profess a belief that it existed from eternity. These opinions were kept in countenance only as long as geology was in its infancy. Every successive step which has been lately taken in the improvement of this science has served to show their fallacy. The investiga-tions of the latest and most accurate philosophers have afforded proof little short of demonstration, that the earth, at least in its present form, cannot have existed longer than appears from the Mosaic account; the absolute falsehood of many positive asser-tions, and specious inferences, hostile to the scripture chronol-ogy, has been evinced; and thence has arisen a new presumptive argument in support of the authenticity of that Volume, which contains the most ancient, and the most precious of all rec-ords.[109]

Americans were well informed on the geological science of Europe, and increasingly turned to the study of their own geol-ogy. There is no need here to enter upon the history of this move-ment. Variations were made by Americans upon theories held by Europeans and a wealth of new observations from America ad-vanced the subject, but theoretical guidance came from Europe. On the whole, in the early nineteenth century, the naturalists were guided by the principles of Mosaic geology, but there were exceptions, such as the stormy Thomas Cooper of South Carolina College.[110] Changes in outlook on cosmogony also paralleled those

[109] *Ibid.*, I, 188.

[110] *On the Connection between Geology and the Pentateuch; in a letter to Professor Silliman, from Thomas Cooper, M.D., to which is added the defence of Dr. Cooper before the Trustees of the South Carolina College* (Columbia, 1836). Cooper's most notorious work was *The Fabrication of the Pentateuch Proved, by the anachronisms contained in those books*, 2nd ed. (Middletown, N. J., 1840). The first edition was published anonymously in 1829. Cooper was not a geologist, but Richard Harlan was an able paleon-

in Europe, and Americans displayed a no less progressive attitude than Europeans. One of the leaders in American geology, Benjamin Silliman, worked valiantly for an extension of outlook on the age of the world during the pre-Lyellian period. His arguments for an extended "Days of Creation" interpretation and his highly esteemed reputation among European geologists, who frequently cited him as an authority, served to loosen the theological grip in America on concepts of past duration. Another well-known American in the field of reconciliation, and one whose work was cited in Europe on the same footing with J. Pye Smith and Hugh Miller, was Edward Hitchcock, President of Amherst College and Professor of Natural Theology and Geology. His geological survey of Massachusetts, commenced in 1830, with its published *Reports* between 1833 and 1841, was a landmark in American Geology. His *Elementary Geology* (1840) went through thirty editions, making his name a byword among students of the science. Through all his works, Hitchcock appealed for an acceptance of the geological time scale, but it was his *Religion of Geology and its Connected Sciences* (1851) which pinpointed his views on the relation of religion and geology.

The attempt by some scientists to separate religion and geology was reprehensible to Hitchcock, for in this science new views of the vast plans of the Deity are disclosed to us, and "no science is so prolific of direct testimony to the benevolence of the Deity as geology." Worse was the blind opposition to geology by those who were fearful that every new disclosure was going to discredit the Bible. He turned to the question of whether or not the Bible fixes the time when the universe was created out of nothing, and wrote:

---

tologist, and his views were based on fossil evidence rather than anticlericalism when he wrote in 1835: "Millions and millions of years have been consumed in establishing the present order of creation; countless myriads of animated beings had appeared and disappeared from the diversified scene, ere yet the wonder, *Man*, was accomplished." (Simpson, *op. cit.*, p. 161).

The prevalent opinion, until recently, has been, that we are there taught that the world began to exist on the first of the six days of creation, or about six thousand years ago. Geologists, however, with one voice declare that their science indicates the earth to have been of far greater antiquity. The question becomes, therefore, of deep interest, whether the common interpretation of the Mosaic record is correct.[111]

Hitchcock adopted the interpretation of Rosenmüller, one of the German Mosaic visionists, that the Scriptures speak "according to optical, and not physical truth." If the first verse is understood as the announcement in Genesis of an act of creation at some indefinite point in past duration, he believed that the difficulties in finding adequate time in the Mosaic account could be resolved, while the optical nature of the account by Moses explained why there was a lack of direct correspondence between the words of Genesis and physical facts. Furthermore, he maintained, if the high antiquity of the globe be admitted, it added to the exhibition of the power and wisdom of God, "carrying forward, with infinite skill, a vast series of operations, each successive link springing out of that before it, and becoming more and more beautiful, until the glorious universe in which we live comes forth, not only the last, but the best of all."[112]

In a lecture on "The Vast Plans of Jehovah," Hitchcock outlined what he conceived to be the steps, or epochs, in the history of man's progress in learning the nature of the Deity's plans. Man in the rudest condition of society was barely aware that there were beings superior to himself, but as he came to the realization, he attributed the superior forces to objects in nature. Later he advanced to a stage of polytheism. The next step was the revelation God made of himself to the Jews in the Old Testament, but even then the Jews thought of God in anthropomorphic terms, for God only revealed as much of himself as the rude and unculti-

[111] *The Religion of Geology and its Connected Sciences* (Boston, 1851), pp. 33-4.
[112] *Ibid.*, p. 68.

vated men of the time could understand. The revelations of Christianity brought to fulfillment the knowledge of Jehovah's moral character and moral government, as well as His spiritual nature. After advancement through revelation had reached this pinnacle, it was left to man to unfold the evidences of God's plan further through science. The next step was modern astronomy, which revealed to man the nature and extent of the universe. The telescope opened to view the magnitude of creation, while the following step, discovery of the microscopic world, unfolded the infinity of creation at the other end of the scale. Between the two ranges the spatial immensity of God's work was brought to man's understanding.

The last step in the progress of human understanding of God's creative plan was found in the development of geology, which "expands our ideas of the time in which the material universe has been in existence as much as astronomy does in regard to its extent."[113] In addition, it shows us the enormity of organic life in the past, that present life is but a link in the entire series, and that there is a continuing improvement in the nature of organic life. The great drama formed a chain of life "stretching so far into the eternity that is past and the eternity that is to come, that the extremities are lost to mortal vision." The view of duration which geology opened to man's understanding brought a new dimension to his appreciation of the scope of God's operations.

> Do any shrink back from these immense conclusions, because they so much surpass the views they have been accustomed to entertain respecting the beginning and the end of the material universe? But why should they be unwilling to have geology liberalize their minds as much in respect to duration as astronomy has done in respect to space?[114]

The common opinion has been, and indeed still is, Hitchcock wrote, that about six thousand years ago this earth, and, in fact,

113 *Ibid.*, p. 456.
114 *Ibid.*, pp. 472-3.

the whole material universe, was brought into existence in a moment of time and in a few thousand more will be swept out of existence.[115] Once the narrow shell of prejudice was broken, and he "anticipated the time as not distant, when the high antiquity of the globe will be regarded as no more opposed to the Bible than the earth's revolution round the sun and on its axis,"[116] those who had hearts warmed with true piety would grasp the noble thoughts connected with the fields opened by geology. And, as he had explained in his chapter on "The World's Supposed Eternity," geology brought the only proof we have that the world had been created. The course of the earth from a state of molten fluidity through the stages of refrigeration was a concept gained from geology, and it had done what the philosophers and theologians could not do in defending Genesis from the imputations of the eternalists. Being able to point to the epoch when entire races of animals and plants began to exist was another striking confirmation of a created earth. "Having once admitted the conclusions of geology as to the great age of the world, and a flood of light is shed upon some of the most difficult points both of natural and revealed religion," he asserted.[117] Coming from so respected a member in the ranks of devout Christians, the arguments of Hitchcock could not have failed to carry conviction to the minds of many hesitant Americans that the time had come for a revamping of their outlook on the temporal size of the universe. The assurance that geology was not hostile to religion, but instead formed one of its mainstays, made the path easier.

What was the reaction of the enlightened, but religiously conservative, American to the rising geological history? A Huxley could justifiably lose his patience with the reactionary and irrational behaviour of Victorian time-serving clerics, and "Soapy Sam" Wilberforce's welts from Huxley are not likely to evoke

[115] *Ibid.*, p. 472.
[116] *Ibid.*, p. 70.
[117] *Ibid.*, p. 481.

much sympathy, but it is possible to feel a certain amount of pathos for the decent, sincere, person who sees his whole world of values crumbling all about him, and who, try as he will to comprehend the changes, cannot grasp the new values which are infiltrating the outlook of his age. The religionist had great difficulty in setting aside Biblical "facts" as less true than physical facts. In the ground swell of shifting assumptions about the relative priority of physical to theological evidences in ideas about what was true, he could not understand why the old formulas of Mosaic history could no longer put down the speculative systems of geologists. The finest illustration of this situation which I have been able to find for the pre-Darwinian period in America is a long manuscript letter of Gardiner Spring to Benjamin Silliman, July 26, 1854.

Gardiner Spring (1785-1873) was the very embodiment of Americanism. He was descended from John Spring, who settled in Massachusetts in 1634. After graduating from Yale in 1805, Spring entered a New Haven law office, taught school, and was admitted to the bar in 1808. He had a deep religious experience and abandoned law for theology, studied at the Andover Theological Seminary, and in 1810 became pastor of the Brick Presbyterian Church on Beekman Street in New York City. The sermons of this staunch Calvinist were based on diligent study and wide reading, but he practiced the revivalist methods for gaining converts. "He held a commanding position in the life of New York and was active in all sorts of religious and charitable enterprises, local and national, especially in missionary causes."[118]

In June, 1854, the Reverend Dr. Spring participated in a celebration marking the opening of a railroad between Chicago and Rock Island. It was a gala event, and the party rode the train to its terminus on the Mississippi and there boarded the steamer *War Eagle* for more celebrations and an excursion. Also a member of the party was Benjamin Silliman, and the two were soon involved

[118] *Dictionary of American Biography.*

in discussions about geology and theology.[119] Silliman had presented his views on Mosaic geology in an appendix to Robert
Bakewell's *Introduction to Geology* (1829), entitled in later editions as "Consistency of the Discoveries of Modern Geology, with
the Sacred History of the Creation and the Deluge," and he apparently sent a copy of this and some other writings to Spring.
The following excerpts are from Spring's reply:

> It so happens that I am just now reading *Bakewell's Geology*
> to which a neat & characteristic Introduction is prefixed from
> your own pen. This, together with the more elaborate Disserta-
> tion you have just sent me, lead me to conclude that your own
> views are not to be changed, more especially by any suggestions
> of my own. I perceive the absorbing influence which the sci-
> ence of Geology exerts over your own mind; & although I can-
> not subscribe to some of your conclusions, I have no fear that
> you will be personally injured by them. I greatly rejoice that,
> instead of countervailing, they establish your own religious
> faith, hopes, & character, & trust that they may not diminish
> your religious *influence*.
>
> In three years past, I have paid some attention to the subject
> of Geology; & the more I have read, the more dissatisfied I am
> with the early date it ascribes to the material creation. Thus far,
> its researches are too limited to justify its advocates in pro-
> nouncing so definitely on so important a question. They accuse
> *us* of not being acquainted with the *facts;* while, by their own
> showing *they* are well nigh as ignorant of them as their less
> learned friends. It strikes me as somewhat marvellous that they
> should be so confident of the truth of their system, when the
> extent of their researches is so limited, that in a globe whose
> equatorial diameter is eight thousand miles, they have pene-
> trated but about three thousand feet. The deep mines in Bo-
> hemia, & the silver mines on the southern slope of the Carpathian
> mountains have scarcely penetrated the earth's crust. When
> geologists themselves make the acknowledgment, "We have
> attempted to penetrate as far as possible beneath the surface
> into the interior of the earth; but if we compare the depth to

---

[119] Fulton & Thomson, *Silliman*, p. 251.

which we have actually penetrated, with the real diameter of the earth, it will be seen that we have scarcely broken the surface, & that the scratch of a needle on the varnish of one of our terrestrial globes is proportionally much deeper than the deepest perforations which we have made into the interior of the earth;" for myself I draw the inference that a science which is thus in its infancy may not diminish my confidence in the *literal* narrative of the creation as given in the first chapter of Genesis & in the fourth commandment. The fact that Geology is so progressive a science, shows how changing it is & must be. When Geologists have penetrated deeper, they may find what they have not yet found, & have fewer scruples in endorsing the Mosaic narrative as it is generally received.

I remarked to you on board the "War Eagle," that Geologists are not agreed among themselves. If you adopt the theory of Dr. John P. Smith of a pre-Adamite earth, in which for unnumbered ages its component parts were first held in solution by fire, & then by water; & that during this period rocks were crystallized, & masses of animal & vegetable matter made their appropriate deposits in strata conformed to subsequent geological discoveries; & that when the requisite materials were thus laid up in store houses, from these God formed the world we inhabit; I can only say it is sufficiently romantic, but not sufficiently in accordance with Moses, Job, David, or Isaiah. If you adopt the theory of Professor Jameson, sustained in part by Dr. Buckland, that the *six days* are *six indefinite periods*, all sound philology is against it. If the great & unerring Teacher understood the primer of language, he intended to teach us that the world we inhabit was created in six natural days, bounded by the morning & evening light. In literal rendering "there was a morning & there was an evening; *day one.*" If you adopt the theory, that the two first verses in the book of Genesis specify a work which was not comprised in the first day, & that this chaotic period is left undefined; the difficulty lies in the fact that Geologists ascribe to this period the existence of animals & vegetables the existence of which Moses ascribes to a subsequent period. It has been well remarked, that "the collision is not between the Bible & *Nature*, but between the Bible & *natural philosophers.*" I am constrained when I advert to the history of Geology to suspend my judgement on all questions which put any other construction than that which a sound philology puts upon the Mosaic narrative.

I have no doubt you think me very ignorant, quite prejudiced, & not a little presumptuous. My object, is not discussion: I have no idea just now of putting my lance at rest in such a tournament. Nor do I utter anything new to you Sir, when I remind you that in these general views I am not alone. The Editors of the Edinburgh Philosophical Journal, Vol. 14, say, "If the geological creed of Baron Cuvier & Professor Buckland be established as true in science, then must the Book of Genesis be blotted from the records of inspiration." In a work entitled "The age of the Earth considered geologically & historically," by William Rhind of Edinburgh, I find the following observations. "To any one who has watched the progress of theoretical geology for the last few years, where opinion has so often vacillated & changed in the subject, & where so many hasty conclusions have been formed, it must be obvious that scarcely has an author his speculations half through the press, when the last part must accumulate as much on the one side as they hitherto appear to have done on the other." Elsewhere the same author says, "We hold that the idea of the Adamite strata containing organic remains, in whatever condition these strata are seen, or may be discovered, whether arranged in the order of a first creation, or seen in the condition of secondary deposits from this: is at total variance with the narrative of Moses, & was never meant to be implied in his words, or dreampt of by his predecessors, or contemporaries. . . ."

I have no doubt, my dear Sir, of the great importance of geological science. . . . I rejoice that there are those who have talent, & time & enthusiasm for those delightful researches. Yet I cannot conceive what possible advantage it has been, or can be, to the science itself, or to the temporal, or spiritual benefit of men, to give these researches even the *semblance* of hostility to the Mosaic record. If like Paul, I say it "ignorantly & in unbelief" you will excuse me for saying, that the true and proper province of this beautiful science is to describe the actual condition of this globe in which we live; to mark its *changes* & the operation of physical causes in producing them. I do not perceive that it necessarily belongs to it to inform the world when, or how it was created; *that* has been done by the Great Maker.

The Scriptures emphasize the truth, that "the world by wisdom knew not God." Half a century hence, Geologists will find this to be true. The work of creation was a great *miracle*. It is not by geology that we shall ever understand it; "by FAITH we understand that the worlds were made by the *word* of God." This prescribing and limiting of omnipotence is not suited to my taste, nor to any of my habits of thinking. I cannot endure it to have the sacred record [. . .] A single blot upon that pure page, a single suspicion is more mischievous than all the services which natural science can render, were they tenfold greater than they are.[120]

Spring goes on to deplore the trend of geology to question the Sacred writings—he does not except the work of Hugh Miller, sensible writer as he was—and expresses his alarm at the impending conflict between theology and natural science. Silliman's note and pamphlet were to him cold water on his soul. "God speaks in his works, as he speaks in his word. Churchian men devoted to the study of natural science are under obligations to *make this appear*."

The Reverend Dr. Spring spoke for a lost cause. By the 1850's theological resistance to a vast antiquity for the earth and prehistoric life was rapidly receding before the evidence of science and the pleas of the harmonists. Lyellian uniformitarianism was successfully taking the cataclysms and gaps out of the geological record and bringing the earth sciences into the corral of natural law. Out of this changed outlook, time emerged as an indispensable constant in the equation of geologic dynamics. It was the silent partner of change, or as William Whewell, author of the famous *History of the Inductive Sciences*, expressed it when speaking of epochs of geological history, ". . . Time, inexhausted and unremitting, sums the series, integrates the formula of change; and thus

[120] Simon Gratz Autograph Collection, Historical Society of Pennsylvania.

passes, with sure though noiseless progress, from one geological epoch to another."[121]

In the short span of years between the acceptance of the Cuvierian Compromise about 1820 and the acceptance of Lyellian uniformitarianism about 1840, Western man's view of the temporal world was revolutionized. Not only was his perspective of the past extended from a few thousand to many millions of years, but his views on the place of man in the history of the world and in relationship to God were beginning to be transformed. Theologians were being forced to abandon their small world of divine miracles centered about man and to seek a more spiritual view of Christianity. The breaking down of Biblical chronology and Mosaic history proved to be an important link in the chain of events which led to a reassessment of the basic truths of Christianity in the nineteenth century and to an expanded conception of the Creator. But like the fledgling bird, the theologian had to be tossed from his cozy nest of Mosaic history before he would fly out in the open universe.

[121] *Of the Plurality of Worlds*, intro. by Edward Hitchcock, 2nd ed. (Boston, 1855), p. 95.

V

THE 'ORIGIN OF SPECIES'
AND THE ANTIQUITY OF MAN

DARWINIAN TIME

After extensive surveying expeditions, which had begun in 1826, His Majesty's Ships *Adventure* and *Beagle* returned to England in 1830. The following year the *Beagle* was authorized to proceed to the coast of South America and continue the surveying work. Captain Robert Fitzroy, who was in command of the venture, thought it advisable to carry along a natural scientist, and that position was assigned to Charles Darwin. It was a memorable voyage for the young scientist and for the world of science at large. From the knowledge gained on this five-year trip, Darwin's theory of evolution was to grow.

Captain Fitzroy recorded the results of his part of the expedition in the first two volumes of a three-volume *Narrative*, published in 1839. The third volume was written by Darwin and was subsequently issued separately as his "Voyage of the Beagle." At the end of Fitzroy's part of the Narrative there was a chapter entitled "A very few remarks with reference to the Deluge," in which the commander of the expedition wrote:

> I suffered much anxiety in former years from a disposition to doubt, if not disbelieve, the inspired History written by Moses. I knew so little of that record, or of the intimate manner

265

in which the Old Testament is connected with the New, that I fancied some events there related might be mythological or fabulous, while I sincerely believed the truth of others; a wavering of opinions, which could only be productive of an unsettled, and therefore unhappy, state of mind.[1]

The cause of his uneasiness Fitzroy attributed to the reading of works written by men of Voltaire's school and those geologists who contradicted the authenticity of the Scriptures. A deeper reading of Scripture had brought to him a fuller appreciation of the Mosaic revelation, but the investigations of the voyage had furnished conclusive arguments to his mind in support of Scripture. From the fossil shells it was plain that Patagonia had once been under a deep sea, and, "if Patagonia was covered to a great depth, all the world was covered to a great depth; and from these shells alone my own mind is convinced (independent of the Scripture), that this earth has undergone an universal deluge."[2]

Captain Fitzroy was as staunch a Tory as Darwin was a Whig, and they shared the same quarters amicably by observing a truce on politics, but it is doubtful if their opinions differed greatly on the Bible when they first set sail. Darwin had decided to be a clergyman prior to embarking on the *Beagle*, "nor was this intention and my father's wish ever formally given up, but died a natural death when, on leaving Cambridge, I joined the *Beagle* as naturalist."[3] Geology had bored him to the point where he had resolved as long as he lived never "to read a book on Geology, or in any way to study the science."[4] A field trip under the inspiring direction of Professor Henslow, who was to remain one of his closest friends, awakened his interest in geology, and it was through Henslow's recommendation that Darwin was offered the

[1] *Narrative of the Surveying Voyages of His Majesty's Ships Adventure and Beagle between the years 1826 and 1836* (London, 1839), II, 657.

[2] *Ibid.*, II, 666.

[3] *The Life and Letters of Charles Darwin, including an Autobiographical Chapter*, ed. Francis Darwin (New York & London, 1925), I, 39.

[4] *Ibid.*, I, 36.

position on the *Beagle*. The Professor had a parting bit of advice for his young protégé which was to have profound results on Darwin.

Darwin related, "When starting on the voyage of the *Beagle*, the sagacious Henslow, who, like all other geologists, believed at that time in successive cataclysms, advised me to get and study the first volume of the 'Principles,' which had then just been published, but on no account to accept the views therein advocated."[5] Lyell's *Principles* were put to the test by Darwin on the geology of South America, but as early as his first geologizing at Saint Jago in the Cape de Verde archipelago, he was convinced of the infinite superiority of Lyell's views over those advocated in any other work known to him.[6] Like an intellectual yeast, the *Principles* began to leaven the mind of Darwin, a mind steeped in conventional orthodoxy. "Whilst on board the *Beagle*," Darwin wrote in his autobiography, "I was quite orthodox, and I remember being heartily laughed at by several of the officers (though themselves orthodox) for quoting the Bible as an unanswerable authority on some point of morality."[7] Milton's *Paradise Lost* was his "chief favorite" reading material, and in his excursions away from the ship during the voyage when he could take only a single volume, Darwin always chose Milton.[8] The cosmogony of Milton could not go unchallenged, however, when brought into juxtaposition with Lyell's views. The intellectual yeast worked slowly, but surely. After his return to England Darwin thought much about religion, and "had gradually come by this time, *i.e.* 1836 to 1839, to see that the Old Testament was no more to be trusted than the sacred books of the Hindoos."[9] As late as 1861 Darwin expressed surprise when Leonard Horner pointed out in his Anniversary Address to the Geological Society

[5] *Ibid.*, I, 60.
[6] *Ibid.*
[7] *Ibid.*, I, 277.
[8] *Ibid.*, I, 57.
[9] *Ibid.*, I, 277.

that the chronology in the margin of the Bible was the work of Archbishop Ussher and was in no way binding on those who believed in the inspiration of the Bible.[10]

Writing to Horner in 1844, Darwin confided, "I always feel as if my books came half out of Lyell's brain, and that I never acknowledge this sufficiently; nor do I know how I can without saying so in so many words—for I have always thought that the great merit of the *Principles* was that it altered the whole tone of one's mind, and therefore that, when seeing a thing never seen by Lyell, one yet saw it partially through his eyes."[11] There can be little doubt that it was through Lyell's *Principles* that Darwin's mind was emancipated from the shackles of Biblical chronology, and had this step not taken place, it seems unlikely that the *Origin of Species* could ever have fermented out of the *Voyage of the Beagle*, for Darwin's theory of evolution required for its foundation far more historical time than even the uniformitarian geologists were accustomed to conceiving.

Although Lyell's *Principles* swept the Deluge and Biblical chronology out of geology, limitations on the span of duration were left in the minds of geologists. They were working with positive evidence and tended to stay within the bounds of that evidence in reconstructing a geological chronology, and there was undoubtedly a certain inertia of the mind which carried forward attitudes about the broken path of the geological process. Although the principle of uniformitarianism was extended to the physical processes of earth history, separate creations, the counterpart in biological history of cataclysms in geology, remained dominant, even in the thinking of Lyell. The result was that geologists and paleontologists assumed that the fossil records were complete records of past life, and gaps in the record were taken to be breaks in the continuity of life, instead of omissions

[10] *More Letters of Charles Darwin*, eds. Francis Darwin & A. C. Seward (New York, 1903), II, 30-1.
[11] *Ibid.*, II, 117.

in the record itself. This sharply curtailed their view of the duration of life on the globe, and it was Darwin who extended Lyell's geological uniformitarianism, through a kind of biological uniformitarianism, to enlarge the history of the earth.

When Darwin put forward his theory of evolution, his proofs of it were largely deductions. Where were the transitional forms connecting the change from one species to another? In trying to anticipate objections to his theory, Darwin wrote,

> Why, then, is not every geological formation and every stratum full of such intermediate links? Geology assuredly does not reveal any such finely-graduated organic chain; and this, perhaps, is the most obvious and serious objection which can be urged against the theory. The explanation lies, as I believe, in the extreme imperfection of the geological record.[12]

By the theory of natural selection all living species were connected with the parent-species of each genus by differences not greater than we see today between varieties of the same species. These parent-species, now generally extinct, were in their turn similarly connected with more ancient species, and so on backwards to a common ancestor of each great class. "So that the number of intermediate and transitional links, between living and extinct species, must have been inconceivably great."[13] If Darwin's theory was true, these transitional forms must have lived on the earth, and he reminded his readers:

> Independently of our not finding fossil remains of such infinitely numerous connecting links, it may be objected that time cannot have sufficed for so great an amount of organic change, all changes having been effected so slowly. It is hardly possible for me even to recall to the reader, who is not a practical geologist, the facts leading the mind feebly to comprehend the lapse of time. He who can read Sir Charles Lyell's grand work on the Principles of Geology, which the future historian will recognize as having produced a revolution in natural sci-

[12] *On the Origin of Species*, 6th ed. (New York, 1873), Ch. x, pp. 264-5.
[13] *Ibid.*, p. 266.

ence, yet does not admit how vast have been the past periods of time, may at once close this volume.[14]

Darwin devoted two chapters to the geological record and its imperfection. He pointed out the rare occurrence of those conditions which would preserve a record of the life existing on the earth's surface in any epoch, for in the oscillations of the earth's crust, organic remains would only be preserved during periods of subsidence and at times when the deposits were protected from degradation. The quantity of organic remains which had perished vastly exceeded the fortuitously preserved records we now find in the strata, and the intervals of time *between* the successive layers of deposits in the enormous fossil-bearing strata in existence may have been of far greater duration than those involved in the preserved strata. This was a basic premise of the Darwinian theory of evolution.

Following out an analogy of Lyell's, Darwin described the imperfection of the geological record by saying,

> . . . I look at the geological record as a history of the world imperfectly kept, and written in a changing dialect; of this history we possess the last volume alone, relating only to two or three countries. Of this volume, only here and there a short chapter has been preserved; and of each page, only here and there a few lines. Each word of the slowly-changing language, more or less different in the successive chapters, may represent the forms of life, which are entombed in our consecutive formations, and which falsely appear to us to have been abruptly introduced.[15]

It was his own theory of evolution and the bottleneck in it of an absence of transitional forms between species, he admitted, that made him suspect how poor the record, even in the best preserved geological sections, really was.[16] Any one who rejected his view of the imperfection of the geological record will rightly reject

[14] *Ibid.*
[15] *Ibid.*, p. 289.
[16] *Ibid.*, p. 282.

his whole theory, he declared,[17] and much of the early opposition he encountered was based on disbelief in the immense intervals of time which Darwin presumed must have elapsed between the successive forming of layers of strata. The less well-informed opponents of Darwin seized upon the Achilles heel he had exposed to the public. Lord Ormathwaite, in his *Astronomy and Geology Compared* (1872), for instance, argued: "Mr. Darwin requires for the development of his theory enormous periods of time, far exceeding any of which we have the slightest knowledge; this alone places his whole system beyond the domain of fact and in the regions of mere reverie and imagination." (p. 80). But scientists in the field of geology also objected to the Darwinian premise. For example, John Phillips, president of the Geological Society of London, 1859-60, and one of England's leading geologists opposed the doctrines of the *Origin*, and "an argument which evidently had great weight with Phillips, in his rejection of the theory of natural selection, was the excessive duration that it postulated for geological time."[18]

In his Recapitulation and Conclusion, Darwin outlined some of the reasons why naturalists and geologists rejected the mutability of species concept.

> The belief that species were immutable productions was almost unavoidable as long as the history of the world was thought to be of short duration; and now that we have acquired some idea of the lapse of time, we are too apt to assume, without proof, that the geological record is so perfect that it would have afforded us plain evidence of the mutation of species, if they had undergone mutation.[19]

Darwin thought that the chief cause of unwillingness to accept the idea of transmutation was the difficulty of admitting great changes when we do not see the steps by which they were brought about. "The mind cannot possibly grasp the full meaning of the

[17] *Ibid.*, p. 313.
[18] W. J. Sollas, *The Age of the Earth* (London, 1908), p. 253.
[19] *Origin*, p. 422.

term of even ten million years; it cannot add up and perceive the full effects of many slight variations, accumulated during an almost infinite number of generations."[20] Darwin's contemporaries were as appalled by the demands upon their imagination respecting the vastness of time in this biological uniformitarianism, great changes of species through the cumulative effect of small variations along a track of unlimited time, as they had been by Lyell's geological uniformitarianism.

Geikie has summed up Darwin's need for time and the reaction to it by saying,

> Until Darwin took up the question, the necessity for vast periods of time, in order to explain the characters of the geological record, was very inadequately realized. Of course, in a general sense, the great antiquity of the crust of the earth was everywhere admitted. But no one before his day had perceived how enormous must have been the periods required for the deposition of even some thin continuous groups of strata. He supplied a criterion by which, to some degree, the relative duration of formations might perhaps be apportioned. When he declared that the intervals that elapsed between consecutive formations may sometimes have been of far longer duration than the formations themselves, contemporary geologists could only smile incredulously in their bewilderment, but in a few years Ramsay showed by a detailed examination of the distribution of fossils in sedimentary strata that Darwin's suggestion must be accepted as an axiom of geological theory.[21]

THE ORIGIN OF MAN

For many of those who could accept the time span projected by Darwin for the history of the earth and its inferior organic productions, there still remained a chronological difficulty respect-

[20] *Ibid.*

[21] Sir Archibald Geikie, *The Founders of Geology* (London, 1897), pp. 283-4.

ing the antiquity of man. On this last time barrier, evolution worked a complete dissolution of Biblical concepts, and at the same time effected a revolution in Christian concepts of man's special creation by divine fiat. As long as it could be maintained that man was not much older than the period of about six thousand years allotted by Biblical chronology there was not the slightest possibility that he could have evolved from lower orders of life, but during the post-Lyellian period evidence had been accumulating which indicated man might be older than had been traditionally thought. Darwin refrained from bringing man into his hypothesis of evolution because he knew a storm would arise from it which might hamper the acceptance of his theory. He was certain, nevertheless, that man was intimately involved in the theory, and to avoid the charge later of deception he added one prophetic statement regarding man in his *Origin*, "Light will be thrown on the origin of man and his history." [22]

Fossil remains of man had often been found in early geologic investigations, but none in very old strata. Cuvier went into the question thoroughly before pronouncing that there was no evidence of man being older than Biblical chronology allowed. When he exposed Scheuchzer's famous *homo diluvii testis*, purported remains of a pre-Deluge giant, to be nothing more than the remains of a large lizard, he brought the matter of ancient human remains into ridicule. One good example of a human fossil did show up in 1805 and created a stir among geologists. Manuel Cortes y Campomanes discovered a fossil skeleton of man, lacking only the head and a few extremites, on the north-west coast of Guadeloupe. It had been fossilized in a breccia containing remnants of species of shells and corals still living in the adjacent waters, but because of its position and the extent of its fossilization the skeleton appeared quite old. It was taken to the British Museum and described in the *Philosophical Transactions* of 1814. Many conjectures appeared about the age and origin of the

[22] See his explanation in *Life and Letters*, I, 76.

Guadeloupe Skeleton, but most authorities denied to it any appreciable antiquity. Some said it was the remains of a ship-wrecked sailor whose body had settled into a crevice later filled with petrifying materials, and Cuvier concurred in this opinion.[23]

Schlotheim in his *Treatise on Petrifactions* in 1820 told of human bones found near Koestriz in very old banks, but since the circumstances of discovery were not well authenticated, this too was dismissed as a proof of ancient remains. A few years later, the claim was made that there were fossilized footprints of a man in the secondary limestone of the Mississippi Valley near St. Louis. Actually these prints had been known earlier by the French and by Frederick Rappe, but were regarded as the sacred impress of the feet of our Saviour, and it was not until about 1822 that they came to the attention of geologists.[24] Explanations appeared, such as their being skillfully carved by Indians for some religious rite, but the implication of their antiquity continued to disturb geologists. David Dale Owen of Indiana pointed this up in 1842 by saying, "The intimate connexion of the subject with those great problems, the age of our race and the gradual peopling of our globe with animated beings, invests it with additional interest."[25] He argued against their being carved by aborigines, and concluded that although no remains of man or his works have ever been found except in the most recent deposits, the limestone in which these footprints were imbedded was of an immense antiquity. His voice was lost in the vigorous defense of the recent origin of man by supporters of Biblical chronology.

In France human bones were found in the caves which were being excavated for fossil remains, but the manner and time of their deposition was far from clear. In the late twenties MM. de Christol, Marcel de Serres, and Tournal maintained that some

[23] Georges Cuvier, *Essay on the Theory of the Earth,* 4th ed. (Edinburgh, 1822), p. 130.

[24] *American Journal of Science,* v (1822), 223-231.

[25] *Ibid.,* XLIII (1842), 14-32.

of the human bones they found in the caverns of Herault were mixed with extinct species of animal remains and must therefore be of high antiquity. The assumption that these species of animals were extinct was challenged by M. Desnoyers, and the contemporaneity of the bones was challenged by others. Lyell in his *Principles*, as late as 1853, doubted the antiquity of these cave bones or those uncovered in Liege caves by Schmerling in 1833-4. Other human remains thought to be ancient were regularly turned up. Dr. Peter Wilhelm Lund found human bones mixed with extinct mammal fossils in Brazil about 1835. Ancient fossil bones were found at Torquay in 1842, and in the delta of the Mississippi near Natchez about the same time. In 1844, the fossil man of Denise was discovered, and in 1857, the Neanderthal skull. But the age of all was subject to controversy, and until after the establishment of Darwin's theory of evolution, the evidence from fossil human remains was singularly unimpressive for an antiquity of man greater than 6,000 years.[26]

Although the actual remains of man in a fossil condition were subject to debate on the matter of antiquity, there was a growing body of circumstantial evidence in the 1850's indicating that he had lived in Quaternary times. Stone arrowheads imbedded in the bones of extinct animals, cuts in the bones made by implements, sometimes with the implements found nearby, beds of ashes over which ancient man probably cooked animals of species now extinct. Boucher de Perthes in 1847 published his *Celtic and Antediluvian Antiquities*, which was the first attempt to correlate flint weapons with prehistoric man. It contained sufficient nonsense to lay itself open to the ridicule of the orthodox, but by stirring up opponents who set out to prove him wrong, it led

[26] The last line of William Whewell's, *History of the Inductive Sciences,* 3rd ed. with additions (New York, 1897), written about 1858 states: "But no fossil human remains have been discovered in the regularly deposited layers of any of the divisions (not even the pliocene) of the tertiary series; and thus we have evidence that the placing of man on the earth was the last and peculiar act of Creation."

to new studies which confirmed his main position. Dr. Rigollot, in particular, was bent on refuting Boucher when in 1855 he found deposits at St. Acheul and was completely converted to the proposition that man existed long before Biblical chronology allowed. The work of others, Falconer, Prestwich, Lartet, and eventually Lyell, left the matter beyond doubt by 1861.

Another area of circumstantial evidence for the antiquity of man was built up through the study of peat bogs in Denmark and shell-mounds, or "kitchen-middens." Series of human implements were uncovered which revealed that man may have gone through a progressive rise from a Stone Age, through a Bronze Age, to an Iron Age. Confirmatory evidence was gathered from the Irish and Swiss lake dwellings and from the deposits in caves. This evidence was not conclusive in dating man's age, but it did indicate that he had acquired his civilization through a long upward struggle.

The works in Egyptology and Assyriology in the 1850's likewise indicated that the civilizations of the Nile and Euphrates were old, perhaps older than 4,004 B.C., and certainly older than the Deluge. An extremely careful series of borings in the Nile delta lands by Leonard Horner between 1851 and 1854 exposed burnt bricks and broken pottery at great depths. Some of it appeared to be more primitive at the lower depths, making it probable that the Egyptians, too, had had a long upward struggle in their civilization. Since that civilization was full-grown in art, engineering, writing, economics, social organization, and architecture, several thousand years before Christ, the realization appeared among a few scholars, such as Baron von Bunsen, that a considerable lapse of time was required for the prehistoric development of Egyptian culture.

The developments in the study of language also began to bear heavily on the antiquity of man about the middle of the century, and against the older orthodox view that language had been given to Adam at the time of creation in all its splendor and that at the destruction of the Tower of Babel a diversity of tongues arose. Some gains were made in the comparative study of languages during the eighteenth century, but on the whole the attempt to reduce all language, learning, and mythology to branches or offshoots of Hebrew flourished. The study of Sanskrit opened up a new field of inquiry during the last quarter of the century. Mosaic history, as long as it held sway in the minds of language specialists, effectively distorted the comparative study of Sanskrit and Egyptian, but during the early part of the nineteenth century, philologists such as Frederic Schlegel, Wilhelm von Humboldt, Jacob Grimm, and Frank Bopp reworked the genealogy of the family of languages according to the principles of philology rather than the dictates of Scripture. Hebrew was relegated into a lesser place in the household of the Semitic languages. When Greek, Latin, and Sanskrit proved to be as old as Hebrew, the genealogical approach necessitated the assumption of a parent language of even greater antiquity from which they were all derived. This in turn, by mid-century, brought pressure against the short chronology of the orthodox.

The philologists could have sidestepped their chronological difficulties by abandoning the traditional, and Biblically-inspired, idea of a unitary origin of languages, but this alternative did not exert much attraction on the philologists. In ethnology, however, the plural origin of the races of man enjoyed considerable popularity. At the inception of the pluralist doctrine of race, chronology was a factor of importance. As in the case of languages, there simply was not time enough for the differentiation of races following the dispersion of peoples at the fall of the Tower of Babel. By assuming a plural origin for the races, it was possible to avoid this chronological difficulty, though it raised others.

In the seventeenth century, Isaac la Peyrère had scandalized the orthodox with his Prae-Adamite theory, by which he claimed on grounds of internal evidence in Genesis that the line of Adam was not the first and exclusive race of men. The argument re-

tained its notoriety throughout the eighteenth century and into
the nineteenth century, but the argument had shifted out of Biblical exegesis to ethnology. Following the lead of Blumenbach,
the main line of ethnology was in defense of the unitary origin of
man. The monumental work of James Cowles Prichard, *Researches
into the Physical History of Mankind* (1813) developed the unitary doctrine and in the 1836 edition, Prichard attacked pluralists
like Virey, Desmoulin, and Bory de St. Vincent for making an
apologia for the mistreatment by whites of the native populations.
As Edward Lurie has observed, the ethnologists were increasingly
involved in social issues. This was particularly true in America
where the slavery issue was ever-present in any consideration of
race origins, and pluralism dominated ethnology in America in
the ante-bellum period, largely through the influence of Samuel
George Morton and Louis Agassiz.

Morton had attended the lectures on geology given by Jameson at the University of Edinburgh in 1820, and he continued to
pursue geology avidly after he had established himself as a physician in Philadelphia. However, about 1830 his interest shifted
to craniology and he set about collecting skulls from all over the
world in order to make a study in the comparative anatomy of
the human skull. His *Crania Americana* (1839) gained international acclaim and shifted craniology from the discredited realm
of phrenology into ethnological science. At this time Morton was
a religious conservative, and his biographer says of him:

> He seems soon to have abandoned, if he ever entertained, the
> notion that ordinary physical influences will account for exist-
> ing diversities, at least within the limits of the popular short
> chronology. There are two ways of escaping this difficulty—
> one by denying entirely the competency of physical causes to
> produce the effects alleged; and the other to grant them an in-
> definite period for their operation, as Prichard did in the end,
> with his "chiliads of years," for man's existence upon earth.
> Morton inclined to the other view, mainly in consequence of
> the historical evidence he had accumulated, showing the un-

alterable permanency of the characteristics of race, within the limits of human records.[27]

Morton's study of ancient Egyptian skulls and pictures on monuments confirmed his opinion of the permanent diversity of the races of man from the beginning, although his *Crania Ægyptiaca* (1844), in which he detailed his evidence, did not pass unchallenged by the unity school. With the publication of Prichard's 1847 edition of the *Researches*, however, the chronological question was largely dropped from the debates of the ethnologists. The mature opinion of Prichard that mankind had been in existence for "chiliads of years" was seconded by Morton, for instance, in 1850, and he conceded to his disciple Josiah Clarke Nott that we all know now that the short popular chronology is a *"broken reed."* Morton's disciples shifted their defense of pluralism more and more towards an apologia for slavery, and in this they were supported by the views of Agassiz who maintained the doctrine of pluralism primarily as a support of his anti-evolutionary belief in the special creation of species.

After 1830 the archeologists and anthropologists displaced the time scheme of Biblical chronology and its fixed date for creation with a time scheme based in the present and extending backwards as far as the monuments of history would carry the origins of man. This open-ended system, like that of the geologists, prepared the way for envisioning the working of slow changes in the transformation of culture and races, in spite of the *ex abrupto* creationist philosophy of the pluralists.

It can thus be seen that during the eighteen-fifties a cluster of disciplines carried within them the seeds of rebellion against the orthodox position that mankind was only about 6,000 years old.

---

[27] Henry S. Patterson, "Memoir of the Life and Scientific Labors of Samuel George Morton," in J. C. Nott and George R. Gliddon, *Types of Mankind* (Philadelphia, 1854), pp. xlvi-xlvii. For a general treatment of the situation in America, see Edward Lurie, "Louis Agassiz and the Races of Man," *Isis*, XLV (1954), 227-42.

Added to these evidences was the corroding effect of Biblical criticism, which was trying to remove verbal revelation from Scripture and to treat it as a literature. None of these evidences were decisive, however, especially when taken individually, and they could be refuted by doctrinaire arguments. The evidences needed the key of evolution to give them direction and consistency, and though unwelcome, Darwin provided the necessary framework around which to organize the various evidences of man's antiquity in archeology, anthropology, philology, and ethnology.

Though Darwin had refrained from bringing man into the initial theory of evolution set forth in the *Origin of Species*, he had commenced taking notes on the evolution of man almost from the time he first conceived the principle of natural selection, about 1837. The transmutation theories of Lamarck and of Chambers, author of *Vestiges of Creation*, made it all too clear that man could not be excluded from consideration in a theory of evolved species. If there had been any safeguard against subjecting man to a humble origin out of lower orders, insuring his special and divine creation, there is no reason to believe that the opposition to evolution from clerics would have been particularly strong after the *Principles* of Lyell had been accepted. It was this one facet of the question which made Lyell himself hesitate so long in giving his unqualified support to Darwin, much to the exasperation of the latter. But it was Lyell who first openly tackled the problem of the antiquity of man in a comprehensive manner and prepared the way for including man in the evolution of species. It was a task he could not avoid in the interests of science, but one which his emotional sympathies abhorred.

Writing to the Reverend W. Whewell in 1837 Lyell had explained his feeling about man in the scheme of things:

Any reader of Sedgwick's Anniversary Address to the Geological Society of 1831, would suppose that I had contended for "an indefinite succession of similar phenomena," and coupling what is said about my hypothesis of a "uniform order of physical events" with what Sedgwick afterwards says of the recent appearance of man, it might naturally be imagined that I had not made due allowance for this "deviation," as I myself styled the creation of man. I brought forward this "innovation" prominently as a new cause, "differing in kind and energy from any before in operation," and mentioned it as an unanswerable objection against anyone who was contending for *absolute uniformity*.[28]

He continued to defend the view that man was a special creation about 6,000 years ago until in the fifties doubts arose from the arguments of Darwin, Nilson, Horner, Bunsen, and his own studies of ancient implements. To George Ticknor he gave some of his views on this subject in 1860:

I have been very busy with the proofs afforded by the flint implements found in the drift of the valley of the Somme at Amiens and Abbeville, and more recently in the valley of the Seine at Paris, of the high antiquity of man. That the human race goes back to the time of the mammoth and rhinoceros (Siberian) and not a few other extinct mammalia is perfectly clear, and when the physical geography was different—I presume when England was joined to France.

This will give time for the formation of many races from one, and enable us to dispense with the separate creation of several distinct starting-points, to make up for the unorthodox conclusions about 'preadamite man,' of which I see some writers are freely talking. How are you getting on with your 'Life of Prescott'? faster I hope than I am with my new edition of my 'Geology.' I am afraid there is no chance of Baron Bunsen's recovery; but when we saw him two months ago he was full of vigour and animation. His date of 10,000 years B. C. for Noah's flood must astonish some of the orthodox in Boston. This reminds me of Max Müller's Essay on 'Comparative Mythology' in the Oxford Essays for 1856, which appears to me in the philological part very excellent. The argument for the existence of some aborigine language, whether it be called Arian or by any other name, seems conclusive, and it must go a far

[28] *Life, Letters, and Journals of Sir Charles Lyell* (London, 1881), II, 2.

way back, as they branched off into such distant and ancient nations. Bunsen's testimony that there is no tradition of the Arian deluge in Egyptian history and mythology is striking.[29]

As he began to prepare for publication the information he was gathering about the age of man, Lyell was assisted somewhat by Darwin. The author of the *Origin*, however, was critical of Lyell for his reluctance in completely accepting and strongly support- ing evolution. To Hooker Lyell confided, "I can only say that I have spoken out to the full extent of my present convictions, and even beyond my state of *feeling* as to man's unbroken descent from the brutes, and I find I am half converting not a few who were in arms against Darwin, and are even now against Huxley."[30] He added:

> However, I plead guilty to going farther in my reasoning to- wards transmutation than in my sentiments and imagination, and perhaps for that very reason I shall lead more people on to Darwin and you, than one who, being born later, like Lubbock, has comparatively little to abandon of old and long cherished ideas, which constituted the charm to me of the theoretical part of the science in my earlier days, when I believed with Pascal, in the theory, as Hallam terms it, of "the archangel ruined."[31]

Lyell's *Antiquity of Man* was published in 1863. It was one long argument, documented by evidence, for extending the birth of man backwards an indefinite distance into the past. Since man's position in the scheme of evolution had been the main drawback in his acceptance of evolution, the impatience of Darwin and Huxley with Lyell was less than fair, for he went a long way on the road to evolution in his *Antiquity* by conceding man's remote origins. The entire presentation of data in the *Antiquity* was organized around the idea that man and his civilization passed through a development from a rude stone age to the present state,

[29] *Ibid.*, II, 341-2.
[30] *Ibid.*, II, 361.
[31] *Ibid.*, II, 361-2 (Mar. 9, 1863).

a process by which he also explained the diversity of the races of mankind.

Lyell noted that in his *Principles* he had remarked that if all the leading varieties of the human family sprang originally from a single pair " a much greater lapse of time was required for the slow and gradual formation of such races as the Caucasian, Mongolian, and Negro, than was embraced in any of the popular systems of chronology."[32] He added,

> So long as physiologists continued to believe that man had not existed on the earth above six thousand years, they might, with good reason, withhold their assent from the doctrine of a unity of origin of so many distinct races; but the difficulty becomes less and less, exactly in proportion as we enlarge our ideas of the lapse of time during which different communities may have spread slowly, and become isolated, each exposed for ages to a peculiar set of conditions, whether of temperature, or food, or danger, or ways of living.[33]

With this, he entered upon a discussion of theories of transmutation, leaving by implication the working of evolution over a long period of time as the answer to the differentiation of races.

Darwin was disappointed in the *Antiquity* because he had expected Lyell to make an unequivocal declaration of faith in evolution by natural selection, but he was also slightly annoyed because when Lyell did get around to discussing evolution, he devoted so much time and attention to the theories of Lamarck. It was natural that Lyell should do this, for two reasons. As a bystander he could see more clearly than Darwin the relationship of the latter's theories to Lamarck's earlier attempts to frame a theory of the transmutation of species, and, after being the chief critic of Lamarck's ideas for twenty years, Lyell wanted to unwind from his previous position gracefully. The public was entitled to know

[32] *The Geological Evidences of the Antiquity of Man* (Philadelphia, 1863), p. 385.
[33] *Ibid.*, p. 386.

why Lyell was reversing himself on evolution, and he took the opportunity in his book on the antiquity of man to explain.

Lamarck was the first, Lyell pointed out, to include the element of time in the definition of a species. As long as the conditions surrounding a species remained the same it could go on for indefinite ages unchanged, but once the conditions changed, modifications would take place in the individuals of a species. And Lamarck had also taught that there had been a progressive advance in the organic world, but had been unable to devise a satisfactory cause of change. The best he could offer was that the conditions changed and thus altered life, or characteristics of a species changed through use and disuse. To the objections of Cuvier that in 3,000 years there had been no modification of characters, Lamarck would have replied that not enough time had been allowed, continued Lyell, who then confessed:

> Although I cited this answer of Lamarck, in my account of his theory, I did not, at the time, fully appreciate the deep conviction which it displays of the slow manner in which geological changes have taken place, and the insignificance of thirty or forty centuries in the history of a species, and that, too, at a period when very narrow views were entertained of the extent of past time by most of the ablest geologists, and when great revolutions of the earth's crust, and its inhabitants, were generally attributed to sudden and violent catastrophes.[34]

When Lyell, who had done so much to broaden man's horizon respecting the earth's duration, could not fully grasp the extent of time involved in the history of the earth, it is understandable that it eluded the age. Darwin, by his own admission, was led to it only after he had framed his theory of evolution and had to assume that the geological record was incomplete in order to sustain the theory.

Lyell was sixty-six when his *Antiquity of Man* was published. Before the year was out, the work had gone through three edi-

[34] *Ibid.*, pp. 392-3.

tions. In the following year, 1864, the grand old man of geology was created a baronet and elected president of the British Association, but honors had been coming to him for many years and for some time he had been lionized as one of the leading men of science. The world had anxiously awaited his decision on evolution. Despite his personal inclinations, he had at last spoken out for science. He knew, however, that his leadership was too mild to suit the young rebels about him, and in his address to the British Association the reluctant revolutionary struck an apologetic note. "We of the living generation, when called upon to make grants of thousands of centuries, in order to explain the events of what is called the modern period, shrink naturally at first from making what seems so lavish an expenditure of past time."[35] There was a touch of stateliness about a man who could overcome his religious feelings, reverse his previous position, and inaugurate a second revolution in prehistoric chronology, applying to the epochs affecting the chronology of man the inexorable logic he had previously laid down for earlier epochs in the *Principles:*

> When speculations on the long series of events which occurred in the glacial and post-glacial periods are indulged in, the imagination is apt to take alarm at the immensity of the time required to interpret the monuments of these ages, all referable to the era of existing species. In order to abridge the number of centuries which would otherwise be indispensable, a disposition is shown by many to magnify the rate of change in pre-historic times, by investing the causes which have modified the animate and the inanimate world with extraordinary and excessive energy.[36]

The work of making known the scientific evidences for the antiquity of man quickly passed into the hands of others, and the next work of comparable influence to Lyell's *Antiquity of Man* was Sir John Lubbock's *Pre-Historic Times, as illustrated by an-*

[35] Cited in Sir John Lubbock, *Pre-Historic Times* (New York, 1872), p. 420.
[36] *Ibid.*

cient remains, and the manners and customs of modern savages
(1865), a work undoubtedly modeled upon Lyell's treatment of
the subject. It was a comprehensive survey of what was known
of prehistoric archeology and ethnology and was used as a standard textbook for many years. The author was not an original re-
searcher, but an intelligent and informed student of the subject
who did much to clarify the data, as by his invention of the
Palaeolithic and Neolithic classifications. In the same year, 1865,
that his *Pre-Historic Times* was published, Lubbock succeeded
to the baronetcy of Avebury. Banker, politician, and thoughtful
popularizer of natural history, Lubbock's voice carried weight
outside the field of science, as well as in it. He observed in his
1865 preface:

> Ethnology, in fact, is passing at present through a phase from
> which other Sciences have safely emerged; and the new views
> with reference to the Antiquity of Man, though still looked
> upon with distrust and apprehension, will, I doubt not, in a
> few years, be regarded with as little disquietude as are now
> those discoveries in astronomy and geology, which at one time
> excited even greater opposition.[37]

A succession of new journals and books began to appear on anthropology, ethnology, and archeology. Considerable caution in
handling revelation was displayed in most of them. They usually
had long dissertations devoted to the reconciling of Scripture and
the evidences of man's antiquity. In a lesser degree, the subject of
the antiquity of man went through the same vicissitudes as the
earlier subject of the antiquity of the earth, and it was one of the
minor themes in the great debate over evolution, but by now
most of the arguments of the scripturalists were pretty shopworn.
By the time Darwin brought out his *Descent of Man* (1871), he
no longer felt it necessary to even raise the question of man's antiquity, but went on to tie together the evidences that supported

[37] *Ibid.*, p. ix.

the conclusion that man was a co-descendant with other species of lowlier origins, remarking in passing:

> The high antiquity of man has recently been demonstrated by the labours of a host of eminent men, beginning with M. Boucher de Perthes; and this is the indispensable basis for understanding his origin. I shall, therefore, take this conclusion for granted, and may refer my readers to the admirable treatises of Sir Charles Lyell, Sir John Lubbock, and others.[38]

With Lyell's *Antiquity of Man* and Lubbock's *Pre-Historic Times* the last step had been taken in the overthrow of Biblical chronology as an all inclusive time span for the work of creation. The last hurdle in passing this time barrier had been made amongst scientists, and they could henceforth ignore the received systems of Ussher and Petavius. This is not to say that the received chronology was promptly abandoned—such is not the case even today, and there was a flood of works defending Moses on this point during the seventies. But the issue rapidly faded from sight in the leading scientific works. Asa Gray, after noting in 1880 how in his youth geology and modern astronomy had disquieted pious souls respecting the age of the earth, added:

> The great antiquity of the habitable world and of existing races was the next question. It gave some anxiety fifty years ago; but is now, I suppose, generally acquiesced in,—in the sense that existing species of plants and animals have been in existence for many thousands of years; and, as to their associate, man, all agree that the length of his occupation is not at all measured by the generations of the biblical chronology, and are awaiting the result of an open discussion as to whether the earliest known traces of his presence are in quaternary or in the latest tertiary deposits.[39]

Although the attention of the orthodox was diverted from Biblical chronology to evolution following the publication of Dar-

[38] *Descent of Man,* Introduction.

[39] Asa Gray, *Natural Science and Religion, Two Lectures delivered to the Theological School of Yale College* (New York, 1880), p. 7.

win's *Origin of Species* in 1859, the age of the earth remained a subject of lively debate amongst the scientists, who were now free to pursue it without consideration of Mosaic history. Astronomy and geology had been allied against Biblical chronology at the beginning of the nineteenth century, but now astrophysics contested the age of the earth given by geochronology.

Sir William Thomson, Lord Kelvin, brought the subject out into the open, attacking the doctrine of uniformity in geology for having sanctioned the geologists in borrowing too much time out of the past. In an article "On the Secular Cooling of the Earth" (1862), he reminded geologists that they had overlooked the second law of thermodynamics in arriving at the age of the earth.[40] The old doctrine of refrigeration, which had been so useful in opening up the concept of the earth's antiquity, was now, in a new form, returning to haunt the uniformitarians in geology. Using the calculations of Fourier and Bischof on the loss of energy in the earth, Kelvin estimated that the earth would not have been sufficiently cooled to support life in the ages many millions of years ago claimed by geologists. Furthermore, the early cooling would have made geological forces more intense and catastrophic than the uniformitarians would allow.

In another paper in 1862, Kelvin considered the age of the sun's heat through the application of the second law of thermodynamics.[41] The then known supplies of energy for the sun were balanced against the rate of energy loss by Kelvin, and he concluded that the sun could not be more than 500 million years old. Again, in 1865, he censured the uniformitarians for their use of unlimited drafts of time, far in excess of the age he had computed for the existence of the sun.[42] He carried his attack directly

[40] Thomson & Tait, *Treatise on Natural Philosophy* (Cambridge, 1883), II, 468-85.

[41] *Ibid.*, II, 485-94.

[42] "The Doctrine of Uniformity in Geology Briefly Refuted," in *Popular Lectures and Addresses* (London & New York, 1894), II, 6-9.

to the geologists in 1868, when he addressed the Geological Society of Glasgow.

> A great reform in geological speculation seems now to have become necessary. A very earnest effort was made by geologists, at the end of the last century, to bring geology within the region of physical science, to emancipate it from the dictation of authority and from dogmatic hypotheses. The necessity for *more time* to account for geological phenomena than was generally supposed to be necessary, became apparent to all who studied with candour and with accuracy the phenomena presented by the surface of the earth. About the end of the last century, also, physical astronomers made great steps in the theory of the motions of the heavenly bodies, and, among other remarkable propositions, the very celebrated theorem of the stability of the planetary motions was announced. That theorem was taken up somewhat rashly, and supposed to imply more than it really did with reference to the permanence of the solar system.[43]

Kelvin then accused the uniformitarians of adopting an endless cycle of time in accord with the principle of perpetual motion, and of disregarding the effects of tidal friction and the dissipation of energy.

Darwin had been disturbed by Kelvin's arguments from the time of his first paper, but it was Darwin's "Bulldog," Huxley, who launched a counterattack. Huxley denied that uniformitarianism excluded catastrophes, since these may have been a regular feature of geologic action, and he maintained that questions of origin had been ignored by geologists as irrelevant and speculative. As for evolutionists, they based their time scale on geology, and if the geologists were forced to shorten the duration of strata, it was a small matter for biologists to read the same facts from a shorter history. He was unable to refrain from pouring some of his best acid on Kelvin's vagueness and assumptions.[44]

[43] *Ibid.*, II, 10-72.
[44] "Geological Reform," (1869) in *Lay Sermons, Addresses, and Reviews* (New York, 1871), pp. 228-54.

To James Croll, who had written assurances to him, Darwin admitted, "Notwithstanding your excellent remarks on the work which can be effected within a million years, I am greatly troubled at the short duration of the world according to Sir. W. Thomson, for I require for my theoretical views a very long period *before* the Cambrian formation."[45] Kelvin's attacks forced evolutionists and geologists to think in terms of absolute time instead of vague lapses of time, but after a seesaw struggle between astrophysicists and geologists throughout the remainder of the nineteenth century, the discovery of the energy release in nuclear fission allowed the astrophysicists to revamp their calculations on the life span of the sun and earth, and today there is a measure of harmony between the two fields on the age of the earth, although precise dates have not been achieved.

CONCLUSION

The crest of the first phase of the time revolution in Western thought had been reached and passed by 1865. The enclosing dikes of Biblical chronology had been decisively burst, and henceforth no scientist had to trim his views on the duration of the world lest his religious and moral reputation be destroyed. Backwashes and bogs of prejudice remained, of course, and it took half a century more to win over the public at large, but this was no longer a matter of concern to the scientist. In the universe time was proportioned to space. Fourier could write by the third decade of the nineteenth century that duration corresponds with the dimensions of the universe and is to be measured by numbers of the same order as those which express the distances of the fixed stars.[46]

[45] Darwin, *More Letters*, II, 163-4. See also pp. 211, 212.
[46] See Alexander Bertrand, *The Revolutions of the Globe*, 5th ed. (London, 1835), p. 317.

Buffon had done what he could to proportion the duration of time to the grandeur of the works of nature, and through the steady efforts of bold thinkers following him time was brought into the operations of nature on a scale commensurate with her size. By 1858, George Poulett Scrope was writing:

> The leading idea which is present in all our researches, and which accompanies every fresh observation, the sound which to the ear of the student of Nature seems continually echoed from every part of her works, is—
> Time!—Time!—Time![47]

Again and again eternalistic systems of time were brought forward during the course of the scientific revolution, and although eternalism should be available as a scientific possibility without the prejudices of theological value-systems weighing in the balance against it, there was the danger, as we can now see, that eternalism would cut the Gordian knot in the processes of nature rather than untie it. Listen to Deluc, for instance, railing, and rightly, against Hutton:

> Among the hypotheses in opposition to this system [Deluc's], the *Huttonian theory* is the most modern of those which deserve any notice, and it contains the greatest number of real facts; but, at the same time, it not only obstructs every avenue to the investigation of any assignable *commencement* of the operations of known *physical causes* on our globe; but the impossibility of such a determination is even one of its tenets.[48]

Hutton is often hailed as marking the great shift in geology from asking "when" and "why" to "how" of the phenomena of the earth. Admittedly, this is important, but he had also answered the other questions of origins, too, by the very act of denying them. It seems to me that the constant pressure of the Christian view of historical process on views of natural process helped to

[47] *The Geology and Extinct Volcanos of Central France* (London, 1858), p. 208.
[48] Jean André Deluc, *Geological Travels* (London, 1810-11), III, 208.

preserve a genetic outlook in terms of concrete, actualistic time. It was largely a matter of conditioning and prejudice during the sixteenth, seventeenth, and eighteenth centuries, but it held the potential in readiness until the geologists discovered the real chronology of the earth in fossil strata and could substitute a scientific for a theological series of epochs and until philologists and archeologists expanded the range of their series of developments. Mosaic history, though it had ended as a crotchety scold for natural science, had had its fertile period. How much difference the Christian view of time and process may have exerted in the development of science is hard to evaluate. It appears to me as a decisive point of departure and, until the internal logic of the sciences themselves was strong enough to proceed on natural evidence, it was a continuing mould in the shaping of an historical view of natural process.

INDEX

Brongniart, A., 174
Brown, Lloyd A., 90n
Bruno, Giordano, 26, 32, 60–3, 70:
nominalism, 62; comparative
method, 62–3
Brunswick, House of, 84, 88
Buckland, William, 210–12, 215, 216,
220–2, 238, 261: supports diluvialism, 210–12; catastrophism, 210–11;
gives up diluvialism, 221
Buffon, Comte de, 7, 88, 108, 109,
114–33, 134, 135, 136, 139–43, 149,
153, 154, 156, 158, 175, 180, 182, 186,
189, 190, 193, 194, 195, 196, 224, 225,
251, 252n, 253, 291; *Theory of the
Earth*, 114; retraction for Sorbonne, 114–5; experiments on cooling bodies, 115–18; chronology of
earth's cooling, 118; *Discours sur
le style*, 119n; *Epochs*, 119–36;
unites civil with natural history,
120; nature variable in all its parts,
121; time process in nature, 121;
revolutions in nature, 121; geological time, 121; natural monuments,
122; fossils, 123; "days of creation,"
122–5; cosmic evolution, 125; progress, 125; man as Nature's agent,
125; epochs of earth's history, 126–
30; rise of civilization, 131; Flood,
131; perfectibility, 132; time dimension of history, 135–6; duration scaled to earth's monuments,
136; extends scientific revolution
to biology, 139; *Natural History*,
140–3; on method in organic nature, 140; Nature as a "web," 140;
integrating principle of nature,
141; *molécule organique*, 141–2;
moules intérieurs, 142; productiv-
ity of nature, 141–2; living forces
and nature's processes, 142;
changes in nature, 143
Bugg, George, 212, 213
Bunsen, Baron von, 276, 281, 282
Burnet, John, 38n
Burnet, Thomas, 71–84, 87, 107, 114,
123, 151n, 251, 253; *Sacred Theory*,
71–84; idea of progress, 72–3, 76;

theory of the earth, 76–81; mechanistic philosophy, 73–4, 76; Cartesianism, 73–5, 82; historicism, 75;
chronology, 76, 79; catastrophism,
77–80; chiliasm, 80–81; *Archaeol-
ogicae Philosophicae*, 83
Burtin, F. X., 190n
Burtt, E. A., 5, 156
Byron, Lord, 207–10: Cuvierian "former worlds," 207–9; emphasis on
scale of death in Cuverianism, 208

Cajori, Florian, 90n
Cambridge Platonists, 155–6
Camden, William, 49
Camerarius, Elias, 113
Campanella, T., 26
Campbell, Thomas, 228
Campomanes, M. C. y, 273
Cannon, W. B., 157n
Cardan (Cardanus), Jerome, 26, 49
Carnot, S. N. L., 186
Cassini, 91
Castillo, B. D. del, 250
Catastrophism, *see* Geology
Catherine II, 139
Central heat, *see* Earth
Cesalpino, Andrea, 49
Chain of being, *see* Nature
Chalmers, Thomas, 201–4, 205, 210,
238
Chambers, Robert, 280
Charlton, Dr., 54
Chateaubriand, Vicomte de, 187–90,
194, 223, 248
Chiliasm, 19–25, 71–2, 80–1
Christ, 15, 19, 22
Christol, M. de, 274
Chronology, *see* Genesis
Church Fathers, 14–28, 81, 203, 203n
"Circle, Breaking of the," 27, 64
Civilization, appearance of novity in,
145, 158, 162; as a creative force,
125; rise of, 131–2
Clagett, Marshall, 43n
Clairaut (Clairault), A. C., 6, 94
Clarke, Samuel, 147
Cleanthes, *see* Hume, David
Clement of Alexandria, 18